Gulf of
Thailand

Andrew Spooner & Dane Haplin

T
sta

Credits

Footprint credits
Editor: Alan Murphy
Production and layout: Jen Haddington
Maps: Kevin Feeney

Managing Director: Andy Riddle
Content Director: Patrick Dawson
Publisher: Alan Murphy
Publishing Managers: Felicity Laughton,
Jo Williams, Nicola Gibbs
Marketing and Partnerships Director:
Liz Harper
Marketing Executive: Liz Eyles
Trade Product Manager: Diane McEntee
Account Managers: Paul Bew, Tania Ross
Trade Product Co-ordinator: Kirsty Holmes
Advertising: Renu Sibal, Elizabeth Taylor

Photography credits
Front cover: Dreamstime
Back cover: Dreamstime

Printed in Great Britain by CPI Antony Rowe,
Chippenham, Wiltshire

MIX
Paper from responsible sources
FSC
www.fsc.org
FSC® C013604

Every effort has been made to ensure that
the facts in this guidebook are accurate.
However, travellers should still obtain advice
from consulates, airlines, etc about travel
and visa requirements before travelling.
The authors and publishers cannot
accept responsibility for any loss, injury or
inconvenience however caused.

Publishing information
Footprint *Focus Gulf of Thailand*
1st edition
© Footprint Handbooks Ltd
May 2012

ISBN: 978 1 908206 62 6
CIP DATA: A catalogue record for this book is
available from the British Library

® Footprint Handbooks and the Footprint
mark are a registered trademark of Footprint
Handbooks Ltd

Published by Footprints
6 Riverside Court
Lower Bristol Road
Bath BA2 3DZ, UK
T +44 (0)1225 469141
F +44 (0)1225 469461
footprinttravelguides.com

Distributed in the USA by Globe Pequot
Press, Guilford, Connecticut

The content of Footprint *Focus Gulf
of Thailand* has been extracted from
Footprint's *Thailand Handbook,* which was
researched and written by Andrew Spooner.

Contents

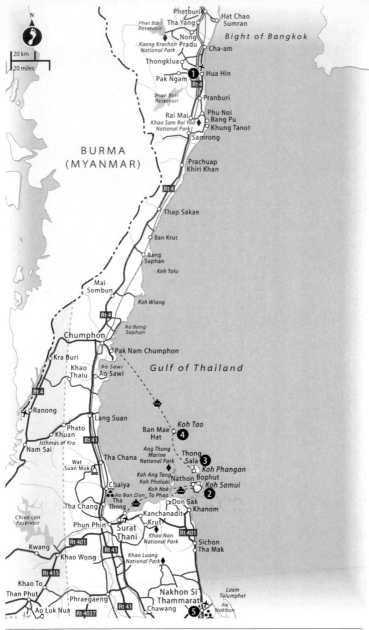

Beaches, resorts, national parks and cultured towns garland the length of the Gulf Coast, with the islands offering unbridled hedonism. Phetburi, south of Bangkok, is peppered with wats and a hilltop royal palace affording sweeping views of the plains, while Khao Sam Roi Yod National Park provides a glimpse of the rare dusky langur. Cha-am, Hua Hin and Prachuap Khiri Khan provide old-world charm, excellent spas, some outstanding resorts and fewer tourists.

The appeal of the northern Gulf Coast towns is eclipsed by the delights of Koh Samui, Koh Phangan and Koh Tao. These islands have it all: there are the pampering palaces, appealing resorts, fine dining, streets of thumping bars, action-packed beaches and quiet bays on Koh Samui; meanwhile, once a month on the smaller Koh Phangan, the world's largest outdoor party spins on the sands at Hat Rin when 10,000 people flock to dance and drink in the glow of the full moon. Around the rest of the island, particularly the east coast, the perfect getaways are waiting in cove after cove with sapphire seas tainted only by a glint of granite.

Further north at Koh Tao, the underwater world is an attraction with so many shallow reefs offshore. Around the island remote bays are guarded by huge granite boulder formations and surrounded by perfect tropical seas. At night Hat Sai Ri is enlivened by funky bars and beachfront dining.

The thriving town of Nakhon Si Thammarat, unmuddied by full-scale tourism, offers an opportunity to see the unusual art of shadow puppetry and savour confectioners' delicate pastries.

Planning your trip

Getting to Gulf of Thailand

The majority of visitors arrive in Thailand through Bangkok's **Suvarnabhumi International Airport**, which opened in 2006 but has been plagued with problems. The city's old airport, Don Muang, has been re-opened to help cope with the overflow. Phuket in the south also has an international airport. More than 35 airlines and charter companies fly to Bangkok. **THAI** is the national carrier. Fares inflate by up to 50% during high season.

Once you've flown into Bangkok (or Phuket) you'll need to either take an internal flight south, or travel overland by train or bus to the Gulf of Thailand, from where you can catch ferries to the islands, or trains and buses on elsewhere. Alternatively you can fly directly into Koh Samui's airport; if this is your destination of choice, flying is the easiest and quickest option. It is relatively expensive but hassle free. The **airport** ① *T077-428500, www.samuiairportonline.com*, in the northeast, is privately owned by **Bangkok Airways**, www.bangkokair.com. There are multiple daily connections with Bangkok, as well as flights from Phuket and Pattaya, and international connections with Singapore and Hong Kong. There is also a domestic airport at Surat Thani, which has flights from Bangkok Don Muang with **Nok Air** (www.nokair.com) and from Bangkok Suvarnabhumi with **Air Asia** (www.airasia.com), and an airport north of Nakkon Si Thammarat, which also has daily flights from Bangkok.

There are regular **trains** from Bangkok's **Hualamphong Station** ① *T1690, T02-220 4444, the advance booking office is open daily 0700-0400*, to Phetburi, Hua Hin, Chumphon, Surat Thani (although the train station is 14 km away from town in Phun Phin) and Nakkon Si Thammarat. There are then regular onward connections from and between all these stations. Regular **buses** also run from Bangkok to Phetburi, Hua Hin, Chumphon, Surat Thani and Nakkon Si Thammarat.

If you wish to explore the islands of Koh Samui, Koh Phangan and Ko Tao (and aren't flying into Koh Samui) you'll need to travel to either Chumphon or Surat Thani and then catch a **ferry** from there. There are regular connections from both towns (both express and overnight options) and you can travel between the islands with ease. See also page 9.

See the 'Arriving in' and Transport sections throughout this book for further details (including times and prices) on all the options outlined above. Also, see below for more general transport information.

Transport in Gulf of Thailand

Air

The budget airline boom has finally arrived in Thailand with carriers now offering cheap flights all over the country. As routes can change at very short notice, we would recommend travellers check the different airlines' websites to see what is available; nearly all major towns and cities and tourist destinations are served. **Air Asia** (www.airasia. com), **Bangkok Airways**, and **Nok Air** (www.nokair.com) are currently the major players in this market offering dirt cheap flights – but only if you book online and in advance. **Thai Airways** (THAI) is the national flag carrier and is also by far the largest domestic

Don't miss ...

airline. Although it has had a relatively turbulent few years and standards have declined since the halcyon days of the late 1980s, it is still okay.

THAI flies to several destinations in Thailand. Its head office is found at 89 Vibhavadi Rangsit Road, Jompol, Jatujak, Bangkok 10900, T02-2451000, www.thaiair.com. It is better to book flights through a local office or travel agent displaying the **THAI** logo. Often THAI domestic fares are cheaper when booked with a credit card over the phone than via their website.

Bangkok Airways head office is at 99 Mu 14, Vibhavadirangsit Rd, Chom Phon, Chatuchak, Bangkok 10900, T02-265 5678 (ext 1771 for reservations centre), www.bangkokair.com.

Road

Buses Private and state-run buses leave Bangkok for every town in Thailand; it is an extensive network and a cheap way to travel. The government bus company is called **Bor Kor Sor**, and every town in Thailand will have a **BKS** terminal. There are small stop-in-every-town local buses plus the faster long-distance buses (*rot duan* – express; or *rot air* – air-conditioned). **Air-conditioned buses** come in two grades: *chan nung* (first class, blue colour) and *chan song* (second class, orange colour). *Chan song* have more seats but less elbow and leg room, and will not offer hostess, food and drink services, or a toilet. *Chan nung* buses will have all of these as well as a maximum of 42 seats (adjustable to 70° recline). For longer/overnight journeys, air-conditioned de luxe (sometimes known as *rot tour*, officially Standard 1A buses, also blue like the *chan rung*) or VIP buses, stewardess service is provided with food and drink supplied en route and more leg room plus constant Thai music or videos. There should be no more than 24 seats (adjustable to 135° recline). If you're travelling on an overnight air-conditioned bus bring a light sweater and some earplugs – both the volume of the entertainment system and cooling system are likely to be turned up full blast.

The local buses are slower and cramped but worth it for those wishing to sample local life. The seats at the very back are reserved for monks, so be ready to move if necessary.

Many tour companies operate **private tour buses** in Thailand; travel agents in Bangkok will supply information. These buses are seldom more comfortable than the state buses but are usually more expensive. Overnight trips usually involve a meal stop (included in price of ticket) and stewardess service for drinks and snacks. They often leave from outside the company office, which may not be located at the central bus station. Some may also be dangerous, particularly those offered from 'backpacker' areas like Khao San Road. Our recommendation is that travellers take buses from the main bus terminals.

Car There are two schools of thought on car hire in Thailand: one, that under no circumstances should *farangs* (foreigners) drive themselves; and second, that hiring a car is one of the best ways of seeing the country and reaching the more inaccessible sights. Increasing numbers of visitors are hiring their own cars and internationally respected car hire firms are expanding their operations (such as **Hertz** and **Avis**). Roads and service stations are generally excellent. Driving is on the left-hand side of the road.

The average cost of hiring a car from a reputable firm is ฿1000-2000 per day, ฿6000-10,000 per week, or ฿20,000-30,000 per month. Some companies automatically include insurance; for others it must be specifically requested and a surcharge is added. An international driver's licence, or a UK, US, French, German, Australian, New Zealand, Singapore or Hong Kong licence is required. The lower age limit is 20 years (higher for some firms). Addresses of car hire firms are included in the sections on the main tourist destinations. If the mere thought of competing with Thai drivers is terrifying, an option is to hire a chauffeur along with the car. For this service an extra ฿300-500 per day is usually charged, more at weekends and if an overnight stay is included. Note that local car hire firms are cheaper although the cars are likely to be less well maintained and will have tens of thousands of kilometres on the clock.

There are a few safety points that should be kept in mind: accidents in Thailand are often horrific. If involved in an accident, and they occur with great frequency, you – as a foreigner – are likely to be found the guilty party and expected to meet the costs. Ensure the cost of hire includes insurance cover. Many local residents recommend that if a foreigner is involved in an accident, they should not stop but drive on to the nearest police station – if possible, of course.

Hitchhiking Thai people rarely hitchhike and tourists who try could find themselves waiting for a long time at the roadside. It is sometimes possible to wave down vehicles at the more popular beach resorts.

Motorbike Hiring a motorbike has long been a popular way for visitors to explore the local area. Off the main roads and in quieter areas it can be an enjoyable and cheap way to see the country. Some travellers are now not just hiring motorbikes to explore a local area, but are touring the entire country by motorcycle. It is the cheapest way to be independent of public transport, but the risks rise accordingly (see below).

Rental is mostly confined to holiday resorts and prices vary from place to place; ฿150-300 per day is usual for a 100-150cc machine. Often licences do not have to be shown and insurance will not be available. Riding in shorts and flip-flops is dangerous – a foot injury is easily acquired even at low speeds and broken toes are a nightmare to heal – always wear shoes. Borrow a helmet or, if you're planning to ride a motorbike on more than one occasion, consider buying one – decent helmets can be found for ฿1500 and are better than the 'salad bowls' usually offered by hire companies.

In most areas of Thailand it is compulsory to wear a helmet and while this law is not always enforced there are now periodic checks everywhere – even on remote roads. Fines are usually ฿300; if you have an accident without a helmet the price could be much higher. Thousands of Thais are killed in motorcycle accidents each year and large numbers of tourists also suffer injuries (Koh Samui has been said to have the highest death rate anywhere in the world). Expect anything larger than you to ignore your presence on the road. Be extremely wary and drive defensively.

Motorbike taxi These are becoming increasingly popular, and are the cheapest, quickest and most dangerous way to get from 'A' to 'B'. They are usually used for short rides down *sois* or to better local transport points. Riders wear coloured vests (sometimes numbered) and tend to congregate at key intersections or outside shopping centres for example. Agree a price before boarding – expect to pay ฿10 upwards for a short *soi* hop.

Songthaew ('two rows') *Songthaews* are pick-up trucks fitted with two benches and can be found in many towns. They normally run fixed routes, with set fares, but can often be hired and used as a taxi service (agree a price before setting out). To let the driver know you want to stop, press the electric buzzers or tap the side of the vehicle with a coin.

Taxi Standard air-conditioned taxis are found in very few Thai towns with the majority in the capital. In Bangkok all taxis have meters. Most Bangkok taxis will also take you on long-distance journeys either for an agreed fee or with the meter running. In the south, shared long-distance taxis are common.

Tuk-tuks These come in the form of pedal or motorized machines. Fares should be negotiated and agreed before setting off. It will not take long to discover what is a reasonable price, but don't expect to pay the same as a Thai. Drivers are a useful source of local information and will know most places of interest, plus hotels and restaurants (and sometimes their prices). In Bangkok, and most other towns, these vehicles are a motorized, gas-powered scooter. Pedal-powered *saamlors* (meaning 'three wheels') were outlawed in Bangkok a few years ago and they are now gradually being replaced by the noisier motorized version throughout the country.

Boat
There are numerous boats to and from the Gulf Coast Islands of Koh Samui, Koh Phangan and Koh Tao. Principal services run from Chumphon to Koh Tao and from Surat Thani and the port of Don Sak to Koh Samui and then on to Koh Phangan. Fast ferries, slow boats and night boats run services daily.

An alternative to the usual overland tour of Thailand is to book a berth on the *Andaman Princess*. This cruise ship sails to Koh Tao and back (three days and two nights). Passengers can snorkel at Koh Tao and the level of service and safety is high. Large numbers of young, middle-class Thais make the journey and there is lots of entertainment. It costs around ฿5000 for a single berth. Contact **Siam Cruise**, 33/10-11 Sukhumvit Soi Chaiyod (Soi 11), T02-2554563, www.siamcruise.com.

Rail
The **State Railway of Thailand**, www.railway.co.th/english, is efficient, clean and comfortable. It is safer than bus travel but can take longer. The choice is **first-class air-conditioned compartments**, **second-class sleepers**, **second-class air-conditioned sit-ups** with reclining chairs and **third-class sit-ups**. Travelling third class is often cheaper than taking a bus; first and second class are more expensive than the bus but infinitely more comfortable. **Express trains** are known as *rot duan*, **special express trains** as *rot duan phiset* and **rapid trains** as *rot raew*. Express and rapid trains are faster as they make fewer stops; there is a surcharge for the service.

Reservations for sleepers should be made in advance (up to 60 days ahead) at Bangkok's **Hualamphong station** ① *T1690, T02-220 4444, the advance booking office is open daily*

0700-0400. Some travel agencies also book tickets. A queue-by-ticket arrangement works efficiently, and travellers do not have to wait long. If you change a reservation the charge is ฿10. It is advisable to book the bottom sleeper, as lights are bright on top (in second-class compartments) and the ride more uncomfortable. It still may be difficult to get a seat at certain times of year, such as during festivals (like **Songkran** in April). Personal luggage allowance is 50 kg in first class, 40 kg in second and 30 kg in third class. Children aged three to 12 years old and under 150 cm in height pay half fare; those under three years old and less than 100 cm in height travel free, but do not get a seat. It is possible to pick up timetables at Hualamphong station (from the information booth in the main concourse). There are two types: the 'condensed' timetable (by region) showing all rapid routes, and complete, separate timetables for all classes. Timetables are available from stations and some tourist offices. If travelling north or south during the day, try to get a seat on the side of the carriage out of the sun.

You can buy a 20-day **rail pass** (blue pass) which is valid on all trains, second and third class (supplementary charges are NOT included). A more expensive red pass includes supplementary charges. For further details visit the Advance Booking Office at Hualamphong station in Bangkok, T02-223 3762, T02-224 7788.

Where to stay in Gulf of Thailand

Thailand has a large selection of hotels, including some of the best in the world. Standards outside of the usual tourist areas have improved immensely over recent years and while such places might not be geared to Western tastes they offer some of the best-value accommodation in the country. Due to its popularity with backpackers, Thailand also has many small guesthouses, serving Western food and catering to the foibles of foreigners. These are concentrated in the main tourist areas.

Hotels and guesthouses

Hotels and guesthouses are listed under eight categories, according to the average price of a double/twin room for one night. It should be noted that many hotels will have a range of rooms, some with air conditioning (a/c) and attached bathroom facilities, others with just a fan and shared facilities. Prices can therefore vary a great deal. If a hotel entry lists 'some a/c', then these rooms are likely to be in the upper part of the range, perhaps even in the next range. Few hotels in Thailand provide breakfast in the price of the room. A service charge of 10% and government tax of 7% will usually be added to the bill in the more expensive hotels (categories **$$$$-$$**). Ask whether the quoted price includes tax when checking in. Prices in Bangkok are inflated.

During the off-season, hotels and guesthouses in tourist destinations may halve their room rates so it is always worthwhile bargaining or asking whether there is a special price. Given the fierce competition among hotels, it is even worth trying during the peak season. Over-building has meant that there is a glut of rooms in some towns and hotels are desperate for business.

Until 10 years ago, most guesthouses offered shared facilities with cold-water showers and squat toilets. Levels of cleanliness were also less than pristine. Nowadays, Western toilet imperialism is making inroads into Thai culture and many of the better-run guesthouses will have good, clean toilets with sit-down facilities and, sometimes, hot water. Some are even quite stylish in their bathroom facilities. Fans are the norm in most guesthouses although, again, to cash in on the buying power of backpackers with more disposable

Price codes

Where to stay

$$$$ over US$100   **$$$** US$46-100

$$ US$20-45   **$** under US$20

Prices include taxes and service charge, but not meals. They are based on a double room, except in the **$** range, where prices are almost always per person.

Restaurants

$$$ over US$12   **$$** US$6-12   **$** under US$6

Prices refer to the cost of an average main dish. They do not include drinks.

income more and more offer air-conditioned rooms as well. Check that mosquito nets are provided.

Security is a problem, particularly in beach resort areas where flimsy bungalows offer easy access to thieves. Keep valuables with the office for safekeeping (although there are regular cases of people losing valuables that have been left in 'safekeeping') or on your person when you go out. Guesthouses can be tremendous value for money. With limited overheads, family labour and using local foods they can cut their rates in a way that larger hotels with armies of staff, imported food and expensive facilities simply cannot.

Camping and national park accommodation

It is possible to camp in Thailand and **national parks** are becoming much better at providing campsites and associated facilities. Most parks will have public toilets with basic facilities. Some parks also offer bungalows; these fall into our **$$** accommodation category but because they can often accommodate large groups their per person cost is less than this. The more popular parks will often also have privately run accommodation including sophisticated resorts, sometimes within the park boundaries. For reservations at any of the national parks contact: Reservation Office ① *National Parks Division, Royal Forestry Department, 61 Phanhonyothin Rd, Ladyao, Jatujak, Bangkok, T02-56142923. The official website, www.dnp.go.th/parkreserve, is excellent for making online bookings.* Alternatively, you can phone the park offices listed in the relevant sections of this guide. **Beaches** are considered public property – anybody can camp on them for free. If you are camping, remember that while the more popular parks have tents for hire, the rest – and this means most – do not. Bring your own torch, camp stove, fuel and toilet paper.

Food and drink in Gulf of Thailand

Thai food, for long an exotic cuisine distant from the average northerner's mind and tongue, has become an international success story. The Thai government, recognizing the marketing potential of their food, has instituted a plan called 'Global Thai' to boost the profile of Thai food worldwide as a means of attracting more people to visit its country of origin. Thai food has become, in short, one of Thailand's most effective advertisements.

Thai food is an intermingling of Tai, Chinese and, to a lesser extent, Indian cuisines. This helps to explain why restaurants produce dishes that must be some of the (spicy) hottest in the world, as well as others that are rather bland. *Larb* (traditionally raw – but now more frequently cooked – chopped beef mixed with rice, herbs and spices) is a traditional 'Tai' dish; *pla priaw waan* (whole fish with soy and ginger) is Chinese in origin; while *gaeng mussaman* (beef 'Muslim' curry) was brought to Thailand by Muslim immigrants. Even satay, paraded by most restaurants as a Thai dish, was introduced from Malaysia and Indonesia (which themselves adopted it from Arab traders during the Middle Ages).

Despite these various influences, Thai cooking is distinctive. Thais have managed to combine the best of each tradition, adapting elements to fit their own preferences. Remarkably, considering how ubiquitous it is in Thai cooking, the chilli pepper is a New World fruit and was not introduced into Thailand until the late 16th century (along with the pineapple and the papaya).

A Thai meal is based around rice, and many wealthy Bangkokians own farms upcountry where they cultivate their favourite variety. When a Thai asks another Thai whether he has eaten he will ask, literally, whether he has 'eaten rice' (*kin khao*). Similarly, the accompanying dishes are referred to as food 'with the rice'. There are two main types of rice – 'sticky' or glutinous (*khao niaw*) and non-glutinous (*khao jao*). Sticky rice is usually used to make sweets (desserts) although it is the staple in the northeastern region and parts of the north. *Khao jao* is standard white rice.

In addition to rice, a meal usually consists of a soup like *tom yam kung* (prawn soup), *kaeng* (a curry) and *krueng kieng* (a number of side dishes). Thai food is spicy, and aromatic herbs and grasses (like lemongrass, coriander, tamarind and ginger) are used to give a distinctive flavour. *Nam pla* (fish sauce made from fermented fish and used as a condiment) and *nam prik* (*nam pla*, chillies, garlic, sugar, shrimps and lime juice) are two condiments that are taken with almost all meals. *Nam pla* is made from steeping fish, usually anchovies, in brine for long periods and then bottling the peatish-coloured liquor produced. Chillies deserve a special mention because most Thais like their food HOT! Some chillies are fairly mild; others – like the tiny, red *prik khii nuu* ('mouse shit pepper') – are fiendishly hot.

Isaan food – from the northeast of Thailand – is also distinctive, very similar to Lao cuisine and very popular. Most of the labourers and service staff come from Isaan, particularly in Bangkok, and you won't have to go far to find a rickety street stall selling sticky rice, aromatic *kai yang* (grilled chicken) and fiery *som tam* (papaya salad). *Pla ra* (fermented fish) is one of Isaan's most famous dishes but is usually found only in the most authentic Isaan dishes, its salty, pungent flavour being too much for effete Bangkokians.

Due to Thailand's large Chinese population (or at least Thais with Chinese roots), there are also many Chinese-style restaurants whose cuisine is variously 'Thai-ified'. Many of the snacks available on the streets show this mixture of Thai and Chinese, not to mention Arab and Malay. *Bah jang*, for example, are small pyramids of leaves stuffed with sticky rice, Chinese sausage, salted eggs, pork and dried shrimp. They were reputedly first created for the Chinese dragon boat festival but are now available 12 months a year – for around ฿20.

To sample Thai food it is best to go in a group to a restaurant and order a range of dishes. To eat alone is regarded as slightly strange. However, there are a number of 'one-dish' meals like fried rice and *phat thai* (fried noodles) and restaurants will also usually provide *raat khao* ('over rice'), which is a dish like a curry served on a bed of rice for a single person.

Strict non-fish-eating **vegetarians** and **vegans** are in for a tough time. Nearly every cooked meal you will eat in Thailand will be liberally doused in *nam pla* or cooked with shrimp paste. At more expensive and upmarket international restaurants you'll probably be able to find something suitable – in the rural areas, you'll be eating fruit, fried eggs and rice, though not all at once. There are a network of Taoist restaurants offering more strict veggie fare throughout the country – look out for yellow flags with red Chinese lettering. Also asking for 'mai sai nam pla' (no *nam pla* please)– when ordering what should be veggie food might keep the fish sauce out of harm's reach.

Restaurants

It is possible to get a tasty and nutritious meal almost anywhere – and at any time – in Thailand. Thais eat out a great deal so that most towns have a range of places. Starting at the top, in pecuniary terms at any rate, the more sophisticated restaurants are usually air-conditioned, and sometimes attached to a hotel. In places like Bangkok they may be Western in style and atmosphere. In towns less frequented by foreigners they are likely to be rather more functional – although the food will be just as good. In addition to these more upmarket restaurants are a whole range of places from **noodle shops** to **curry houses** and **seafood restaurants**. Many small restaurants have no menus. But often the speciality of the house will be clear – roasted, honeyed ducks hanging in the window, crab and fish laid out on crushed ice outside. Away from the main tourist spots, 'Western' breakfasts are commonly unavailable, so be prepared to eat Thai-style (noodle or rice soup or fried rice). Yet, the quality of much Thai food can be mixed, with many Thai restaurants and street stalls using huge amounts of sugar, MSG and oil in their cooking.

Towards the bottom of the scale are **stalls and food carts**. These tend to congregate at particular places in town – often in the evening, from dusk – although they can be found just about anywhere: outside the local provincial offices, along a cul-de-sac, or under a conveniently placed shady tree. Stall holders will tend to specialize in either noodles, rice dishes, fruit drinks, sweets and so on. Hot meals are usually prepared to order. While stall food may be cheap – a meal costs only around ฿15-20 – they are frequented by people from all walks of life. A well-heeled businessman in a suit is just as likely to be seen bent over a bowl of noodles at a rickety table on a busy street corner as a construction worker.

A popular innovation over the last 10 years or so has been the *suan a-haan* or **garden restaurant**. These are often on the edge of towns, with tables set in gardens, sometimes with bamboo furniture and ponds. Another type of restaurant worth a mention is the **Thai-style coffee shop**. These are sometimes attached to hotels in provincial towns and feature hostesses dressed in Imelda-esque or skimpy spangly costumes. The hostesses, when they are not crooning to the house band, sit with customers, laugh at their jokes and assiduously make sure that their glasses are always full.

Tourist centres also provide good European, American and Japanese food at reasonable prices. Bangkok boasts some superb restaurants. Less expensive Western **fast-food** restaurants can also be found, including **McDonald's** and **Kentucky Fried Chicken**.

The etiquette of eating

The Thai philosophy on eating is 'often', and most Thais will snack their way through the day. Eating is a relaxed, communal affair and it is not necessary to get too worked up about etiquette. Dishes are placed in the middle of the table where diners can help themselves. In a restaurant rice is usually spooned out by a waiter or waitress – and it is considered good manners to start a meal with a spoon of rice. While food is eaten with a spoon and fork, the fork is only used to manoeuvre food onto the spoon. Because most food is prepared in bite-sized pieces it is not usually necessary to use a knife. At noodle stalls chopsticks and china soup spoons are used while in the northeast most people – at least at home – use their fingers. Sticky rice is compressed into a ball using the ends of the fingers and then dipped in the other dishes. Thais will not pile their plates with food but take several small portions from the dishes arranged on a table. It is also considered good manners when invited out to leave some food on your plate, as well as on the serving dishes on the table. This demonstrates the generosity of the host.

Drink

Water in nearly every single restaurant and street stall now comes from large bottles of purified water but if you're unsure, buy your own.

Coffee is consumed throughout Thailand. In stalls and restaurants, coffee comes with a glass of Chinese tea. Soft drinks are widely available too. Many roadside stalls prepare fresh fruit juices in liquidizers while hotels produce all the usual cocktails.

Major brands of **spirits** are served in most hotels and bars, although not always off the tourist path. The most popular spirit among Thais is Mekhong – local cane whisky – which can be drunk straight or with mixers such as Coca-Cola. However, due to its hangover-inducing properties, more sophisticated Thais prefer Johnny Walker or an equivalent brand.

Beer drinking is spreading fast. The most popular local beer is Singha beer brewed by Boon Rawd. Singha, Chang and Heineken are the three most popular beers in Thailand. Leo and Cheers are agreeable budget options although they are seldom sold in restaurants. Beer is relatively expensive in Thai terms as it is heavily taxed by the government. It is a high status drink, so the burgeoning middle class, especially the young, are turning to beer in preference to traditional, local whiskies – which explains why brewers are so keen to set up shop in this traditionally non-beer drinking country. Some pubs and bars also sell beer on tap – which is known as *bier sot*, 'fresh' beer.

Thais are fast developing a penchant for **wine**. Imported wines are expensive by international standards but Thailand now has six wineries, mainly in the northeastern region around Nakhon Ratchasima. For tours around the wine regions (including to a vineyard where the workers use elephants) contact Laurence Civil (laurence@csloxinfo.com).

Essentials A-Z

Accident and emergency
Police: T191, T123. Tourist police: T1155.
Fire: T199. Ambulance: T02-2551134-6.
Tourist Assistance Centre: Rachdamnern
Nok Av, Bangkok, T02-356 0655.

Calling one of the emergency numbers
will not usually be very productive as few
operators speak English. It is better to call
the tourist police or have a hotel employee
or other English-speaking Thai telephone
for you. For more intractable problems
contact your embassy or consulate.

Customs and duty free
Customs
Non-residents can bring in unlimited
foreign and Thai currency although
amounts exceeding US$10,000 must be
declared. Maximum amount permitted to
take out of Thailand is ฿50,000 per person.

Prohibited items
All narcotics; obscene literature,
pornography; firearms (except with a
permit from the Police Department or local
registration office); and some species of
plants and animals (for more information
contact the Royal Forestry Department,
Phahonyothin Rd, Bangkok, T02-561 0777).

Duty free
500 g of cigars/cigarettes (or 200 cigarettes)
and one litre of wine or spirits.

Export restrictions
No Buddha or Bodhisattva images or
fragments should be taken out of Thailand,
except for worshipping by Buddhists,
for cultural exchanges or for research.
However, it is obvious that many people
do – you only have to look in the antique
shops to see the abundance for sale. A
licence should be obtained from the
Department of Fine Arts, Na Prathat Rd,
Bangkok, T02-224 1370, from Chiang Mai
National Museum, T02-221308, (if you're in
the north) or from the Songkhla National
Museum, Songkhla, T02-311728. 5-days'
notice is needed; take 2 passport photos
of the object and photocopies of your
passport.

VAT refunds
Most of the major department stores have
a VAT refund desk. Go to them on your day
of purchase with receipts and ask them
to complete VAT refund form, which you
then present, with purchased goods, at
appropriate desk in any international
airport in Thailand. They'll give you another
form that you exchange for cash in the
departure lounge. You'll need to spend at
least ฿4000 to qualify for a refund.

Disabled travellers
Disabled travellers will find Thailand a
challenge. The difficulties that even the able
bodied encounter in crossing roads when
pedestrian crossings are either non-existent
or ignored by most motorists are amplified
for the disabled. Cracked pavements,
high curbs and lack of ramps add to the
problems for even the most wheelchair
savvy. Buses and taxis are not designed
for disabled access either and there are
relatively few hotels and restaurants that
are wheelchair-friendly. This is particularly
true of cheaper and older establishments.
This is not to suggest that travel in Thailand
is impossible for the disabled. On the plus
side, you will find Thais to be extremely
helpful and because taxis and tuk-tuks are
cheap it is usually not necessary to rely on
buses. The Global Access – Disabled Travel
Network website, www.globalaccess.news.
com, is useful. Another informative site,

with lots of advice on how to travel with specific disabilities, plus listings and links, belongs to the **Society for Accessible Travel and Hospitality**, www.sath.org. Another site, www.access-able.com has a specific section for travel in Thailand.

Electricity

Voltage is 220 volts (50 cycles). Most first- and tourist-class hotels have outlets for shavers and hairdryers. Adaptors are recommended, as almost all sockets are 2-pronged.

Embassies and consulates

www.thaiembassy.org is a useful resource.

Gay and lesbian travellers

On the surface, Thailand is incredibly tolerant of homosexuals and lesbians. In Bangkok and other major cities there's an openness that can make even San Francisco look tame. It is for this reason that Thailand's gay scene has flourished and, more particularly, has grown in line with international tourism. However, overt public displays of affection are still frowned upon. Attitudes in the more traditional rural areas, particularly the Muslim regions, are far more conservative than in the cities. By exercising a degree of cultural sensitivity any visit should be hassle free.

Several of the free tourist magazines distributed through hotels and restaurants in Bangkok, Pattaya, Phuket and Koh Samui provide information on the gay and lesbian scene, including bars and meeting points. The essential website before you get there is **www.utopia-asia.com** which provides good material on where to go, current events, and background information on the Thai gay scene in Bangkok and beyond. **Utopia tours** at Tarntawan Palace Hotel, 119/5-10 Suriwong Rd, T02-634 0273, www.utopia-tours.com, provides tours for gay and lesbian visitors. There's also a map of gay Bangkok. Gay clubs are listed in

Bangkok Metro magazine (www.bkkmetro. co.th) and include **DJ Station** (by far the most famous Bangkok gay club) and its sister club **Freeman Dance Arena**, 60/18-21 Silom Rd, www.dj-station.com. The main centres of activity in Bangkok are Silom Rd sois 2 and 4 and Sukhumvit Soi 23. There is also a thriving gay scene in Pattaya and, to a lesser extent, on Phuket, Koh Samui and in Chiang Mai.

See also the Thai section of **www.fridae. com**, one of Asia's most comprehensive gay sites.

Health

Hospitals/medical services are listed in the Directory sections.

Staying healthy in Thailand is straightforward. With the following advice and precautions you should keep as healthy as you do at home. Most visitors return home having experienced no problems at all beyond an upset stomach. However, in Thailand the health risks, especially in the tropical areas, are different from those encountered in Europe or the USA. It also depends on how you travel and where. The country has a mainly tropical climate; nevertheless the acquisition of true tropical disease by the visitor is probably conditioned as much by the rural nature and standard of hygiene of the surroundings than by the climate. Malaria is common in certain areas, particularly in the jungle. There is an obvious difference in health risks between the business traveller who tends to stay in international class hotels in the large cities and the backpacker trekking through the rural areas. There are no hard and fast rules to follow; you will often have to make your own judgement on the healthiness or otherwise of your surroundings. Check with your doctor on the status of Avian flu before you go. At the time of writing, Thailand was clear of bird flu.

Before you go

Ideally, you should see your GP/practice nurse or travel clinic at least 6 weeks before your departure for general advice on travel risks, malaria and recommended vaccinations. Your local pharmacist can also be a good source of readily accessible advice. Make sure you have travel insurance, get a dental check (especially if you are going to be away for more than a month), know your own blood group and if you suffer a long-term condition such as diabetes or epilepsy make sure someone knows or that you have a **Medic Alert** bracelet/necklace with this information on it.

Recommended vaccinations

No vaccinations are specifically required for Thailand unless coming from an infected area, but tuberculosis, rabies, Japanese B encephalitis and hepatitis B are commonly recommended. The final decision, however, should be based on a consultation with your GP or travel clinic. You should also confirm that your primary courses and boosters are up to date (diphtheria, tetanus, poliomyelitis, hepatitis A, typhoid).

A yellow fever certificate is required by visitors who have been in an infected area in the 10 days before arrival. Those without a vaccination certificate will be vaccinated and kept in quarantine for 6 days, or deported.

Useful websites

www.nathnac.org National Travel Health Network and Centre.
www.who.int World Health Organization.
www.fitfortravel.scot.nhs.uk Fit for Travel. This site from Scotland provides a quick A-Z of vaccine and travel health advice requirements for each country.

Books

Dawood R, editor. *Travellers' health* (3rd edition, Oxford University Press, 2002). *Expedition Medicine* (The Royal Geographic Society) Editors David Warrell and Sarah Anderson ISBN 1 86197 040-4.

Internet

Apart from a few remote islands Thailand has an excellent internet network. Tourist areas tend to be well catered for with numerous internet shops offering a connection for between ฿30-90 per hr. Some guesthouses and hotels have free wireless while the more expensive ones charge extortionate rates of up ฿1000 per day. You might also be able to pick up wireless for free from office blocks, etc. The cheapest internet options tend to be the small games rooms run primarily for Thai kids who eagerly play online games, usually ฿10-20 per hr, or by using your web-enabled mobile phone with a local simcard – see Mobiles, page 22.

Insurance

Always take out travel insurance before you set off and read the small print carefully. Check that the policy covers any activities that you may end up doing. Also check exactly what your medical cover includes, ie ambulance, helicopter rescue or emergency flights back home. And check the payment protocol; you may have to cough up first (literally) before the insurance company reimburses you. It is always best to dig out all the receipts for expensive personal effects like jewellery or cameras. Take photos of these items and note down all serial numbers. You are advised to shop around. **STA Travel** and other reputable student travel organizations offer good-value policies. Young travellers from North America can try the **International Student Insurance Service** (ISIS), which is available through **STA Travel**, T1-800-7814040, www.sta-travel.com. Other recommended travel insurance companies in North America include: **Travel Guard**, T1-800-8261300, www.noelgroup.com; **Access**

America, T1-800-2848300; **Travel Insurance Services**, T1-800-9371387; and **Travel Assistance International**, T1-800-821 2828. Older travellers should note that some companies will not cover people over 65 years old, or may charge higher premiums. The best policies for older travellers (UK) are offered by **Age Concern**, T0845-601 2234.

If diving in Thailand, it's worth noting that there are no air evacuation services, and hyperbaric services can charge as much as US$800 per hr so good dive insurance is imperative. It is inexpensive and well worth it in case of a problem, real or perceived. Many general travel insurance policies will not cover diving. Contact **DAN (the Divers' Alert Network)** for more information, www.diversalertnetwork.org; **DAN Europe**, www.daneurope.org; or **DAN South East Asia Pacific**, www.danseap.org.

Language
English is reasonably widely spoken and is taught to all school children. Off the tourist trail, making yourself understood becomes more difficult. It is handy to buy a Thai/English road atlas of the country (most petrol stations sell them) – you can then point to destinations.

The Thai language is tonal and, strictly speaking, monosyllabic. There are 5 tones: high, low, rising, falling and mid-tone. These are used to distinguish between words which would otherwise be identical. For example: *mai* (low tone, new), *mai* (rising, silk), *mai* (mid-tone, burn), *mai* (high tone, question indicator), and *mai* (falling tone, negative indicator). Not surprisingly, many visitors find it hard to hear the different tones, and it is difficult to make much progress during a short visit. The tonal nature of the language also explains why so much of Thai humour is based around homonyms – and especially when *farangs* (foreigners) say what they do not mean. Although tones make Thai a challenge

for foreign visitors, other aspects of the language are easier to grasp: there are no marked plurals in nouns, no marked tenses in verbs, no definite or indefinite articles, and no affixes or suffixes.

Visitors may well experience 2 oddities of the Thai language being reflected in the way that Thais speak English. An 'l' or 'r' at the end of a word in Thai becomes an 'n', while an 's' becomes a 't'. So some Thais refer to the 'Shell' Oil Company as 'Shen', a name like 'Les' becomes 'Let', while 'cheque bill' becomes 'cheque bin'. It is also impossible to have 2 consonants after one another in Thai. If it occurs, a Thai will automatically insert a vowel (even though it is not written). So the soft drink 'Sprite' becomes 'Sa-prite', and the English word 'start', 'sa-tart'.

Despite Thai being a difficult language to pick up, it is worth trying to learn a few words, even if your visit to Thailand is short. Thais generally feel honoured that a *farang* is bothering to learn their language, and will be patient and helpful. If they laugh at some of your pronunciations do not be put off – it is not meant to be critical.

Media
Newspapers and magazines
There are 2 major English-language dailies – the *Bangkok Post* (www.bangkokpost.net) and *The Nation* (www.nationmultimedia.com), although journalistic standards in both newspapers are very low and they have a long-standing reputation of distorting the news. There are a number of Thai-language dailies and weeklies, as well as Chinese-language newspapers. The local papers are sometimes scandalously colourful, with gruesome pictures of traffic accidents and murder victims.

International newspapers are available in Bangkok, Chiang Mai, Pattaya and on Koh Samui.

Television and radio

CNN and BBC are available in most mid- or upper-range hotels. Local cable networks will sometimes provide English language films, while a full satellite package will give you English football and various movie and other channels. Programme listings are available in *The Nation* and *Bangkok Post*.

Short wave radio frequencies are BBC, London, Southeast Asian service 3915, 6195, 9570, 9740, 11750, 11955, 15360; Singapore service 88.9MHz; East Asian service 5995, 6195, 7180, 9740, 11715, 11750, 11945, 11955, 15140, 15280, 15360, 17830, 21715. Voice of America (VoA, Washington), Southeast Asian service 1143, 1575, 7120, 9760, 9770, 15185, 15425; Indonesian service 6110, 11760, 15425. Radio Beijing, Southeast Asian service (English) 11600, 11660. Radio Japan (Tokyo), Southeast Asian service (English) 11815, 17810, 21610. For information on Asian radio and television broadcasts.

Internet

Recent events in Thailand have exposed the vested interests hiding in the background of papers such as *The Nation* and they are no longer reliable news sources. See our list of websites on page 24.

Money

Currency → €1 = ฿39.91, £1 = ฿49.90, US$1 = ฿31.38 (May 2012). For up-to-the-minute exchange rates visit www.xe.com.

The unit of Thai currency is the **baht** (฿), which is divided into 100 **satang**. Notes in circulation include ฿20 (green), ฿50 (blue), ฿100 (red), ฿500 (purple) and ฿1000 (orange and grey). Coins include 25 satang and 50 satang, and ฿1, ฿2, ฿5, and ฿10. The 2 smaller coins are disappearing from circulation and the 25 satang coin, equivalent to the princely sum of US$0.003, is rarely found. The colloquial term for 25 satang is saleng.

Exchange

It is best to change money at banks or money changers which give better rates than hotels. The exchange booths at Bangkok airport have some of the best rates available. There is no black market. First-class hotels have 24-hr money changers. Indonesian rupiah, Nepalese rupees, Burmese kyat, Vietnamese dong, Lao kip and Cambodian riels cannot be exchanged for baht at Thai banks. (Money changers will sometimes exchange kyat, dong, kip and riel and it can be a good idea to buy the currencies in Bangkok before departure for these countries as the black-market rate often applies.) There is a charge of ฿23 per cheque when changing **traveller's cheques** (passport required) so it works out cheaper to travel with large denomination traveller's cheques (or avoid them altogether).

Credit and debit cards

Plastic is increasingly used in Thailand and just about every town of any size will have a bank with an ATM. Visa and MasterCard are the most widely taken credit cards, and cash cards with the Cirrus logo can also be used to withdraw cash at many banks. Generally speaking, AMEX can be used at branches of the **Bangkok Bank**; JCB at **Siam Commercial Bank**; MasterCard at **Siam Commercial** and **Bangkok Bank**; and Visa at **Thai Farmers' Bank** and **Bangkok Bank**. Most larger hotels and more expensive restaurants take credit cards as well. Because Thailand has embraced the ATM with such exuberance, many foreign visitors no longer bother with traveller's cheques or cash and rely entirely on plastic. Even so, a small stash of US dollars cash can come in handy in a sticky situation.

Notification of credit card loss: **American Express**, SP Building, 388 Phahonyothin Rd, Bangkok 10400, T02-2735544; **Diners Club**, Dusit Thani Building, Rama IV Rd, T02-233

5644, T02-238 3660; **JCB**, T02-256 1361, T02-2561351; **Visa** and **MasterCard**, Thai Farmers Bank Building, Phahonyothin Rd, T02-251 6333, T02-273 1199.

Cost of living
One of the key pledges of the Yingluck Shinawatra government elected in 2011 was to increase the minimum wage to A300 a day (US$10). By mid-2012, despite complaints by many of the richest individuals and companies in Thailand, this was coming into force. The average salary of a civil servant is around US$250 a month. Of course, Thailand's middle classes – and especially those engaged in business in Bangkok – will earn far more than this. Thailand has appalling wealth distribution yet Thai society is remarkably cohesive. A simple but good meal out will cost ฿60; the rental of a modern house in a provincial city will cost perhaps ฿4000 a month.

Cost of travelling
Visitors staying in the best hotels and eating in hotel restaurants will probably spend at least ฿2000 per day, conceivably much much more. Tourists staying in cheaper a/c accommodation and eating in local restaurants will probably spend about ฿600-900 per day. Backpackers staying in fan-cooled guesthouses and eating cheaply, should be able to live on ฿300 per day. In Bangkok, expect to pay 20-30% more.

Opening hours
Banks: Mon-Fri 0830-1530. **Exchange:** daily 0830-2200 in Bangkok, Pattaya, Phuket and Chiang Mai. In other towns opening hours are usually shorter. **Government offices:** Mon-Fri 0830-1200, 1300-1630. **Shops:** 0830-1700, larger shops: 1000-1900 or 2100. **Tourist offices:** 0830-1630.

Safety
In general, Thailand is a safe country to visit. The vast majority of visitors to Thailand will not experience any physical threat what so ever. However, there have been some widely publicized murders of foreign tourists in recent years and the country does have a very high murder rate. It is best to avoid any situation where violence can occur – what would be a simple punch-up or pushing bout in the West can quickly escalate in Thailand to extreme violence. This is mostly due to loss of face. Getting drunk with Thais can be a risky business – Westerners visiting the country for short periods won't be versed in the intricacies of Thai social interaction and may commit unwitting and terrible faux pas. A general rule of thumb if confronted with a situation is to appear conciliatory and offer a way for the other party to back out gracefully. It should be noted that even some police officers in Thailand represent a threat – at least 3 young Western travellers have been shot and murdered by drunken Thai policemen in the last few years. Confidence tricksters, touts, all operate, particularly in more popular tourist centres. Robbery is also a threat; it ranges from pick-pocketing to the drugging (and subsequent robbing) of bus and train passengers. Watchfulness and simple common sense should be employed. Women travelling alone should be careful. Always lock hotel rooms and place valuables in a safe deposit if available (if not, take them with you).

If you do get any problems contact the tourist police rather than the ordinary police – they will speak English and are used to helping resolve any disputes, issues, etc. The country's health infrastructure, especially in provincial capitals and tourist destinations, is good.

The UK's Foreign and Commonwealth Office's 'Know Before You Go' campaign, www.fco.gov.uk/travel, offers some advice. **Foreign and Commonwealth Office** (**FCO**), T0845-850 2829, www.fco.gov.uk/travel. The UK Foreign and Commonwealth Office's travel warning section. **US State Department**, www.travel.state.

gov/travel_warnings.html. The US State Department updates travel advisories on its 'Travel Warnings and Consular Information Sheets'. It also has a hotline for American travellers, T202-647-5225.

Bribery

The way to make your way in life, for some people in Thailand, is through the strategic offering of gifts. A Chulalongkorn University report recently estimated that it 'costs' ฿10 million to become Bangkok Police Chief. Apparently this can be recouped in just 2 years of hard graft. Although bribing officials is by no means recommended, resident *farangs* report that they often resort to such gifts to avoid the time and hassle involved in filling in the forms and making the requisite visit to a police station for a minor traffic offence. As a visitor, it's best to play it straight.

Drugs and prostitution

Many prostitutes and drug dealers are in league with the police and may find it more profitable to report you than to take your custom (or they may try to do both). They receive a reward from the police, and the police in turn receive a bonus for the detective work. Note that foreigners on buses may be searched for drugs. Sentences for possession of illegal drugs vary from a fine or one year in jail for marijuana up to life imprisonment or execution for possession or smuggling of heroin. The death penalty is usually commuted.

Prisons

Thai prisons are very grim. Most foreigners are held in 2 Bangkok prisons – Khlong Prem and Bangkwang. One resident who visits overseas prisoners in jail wrote to us saying: "You cannot over-estimate the horrors! Khlong Prem has 7000 prisoners, 5 to a cell, with not enough room to stretch out, no recreation, one meal a day (an egg on Sundays) … ". One hundred prisoners in a dormitory is not uncommon, and prisoners on Death Row have waist chains and ankle fetters permanently welded on.

Tourist police

In 1982 the government set up a special arm of the police to deal with the demands of the tourist industry – the tourist police. Now, there is no important tourist destination that doesn't have a tourist police office. The Thai police have come in for a great deal of scrutiny over recent years, although most policemen are honest and only too happy to help the luckless visitor. **Tourist Police**, Bangkok, T02-2815051 or T02-2216206. Daily 0800-2400.

Traffic

Perhaps the greatest danger is from the traffic – especially if you are attempting to drive yourself. More foreign visitors are killed or injured in traffic accidents than in any other way. Thai drivers have a 'devil may care' attitude towards the highway code, and there are many horrific accidents. Be very careful when crossing the road – just because there is a pedestrian crossing, do not expect drivers to stop. Be particularly wary when driving or riding a motorcycle (see page 8).

Student travellers

Anyone in full-time education is entitled to an **International Student Identity Card** (ISIC). These are issued by student travel offices and travel agencies across the world and offer special rates on all forms of transport and other concessions and services. The ISIC head office is: **ISIC Association**, Box 9048, 1000 Copenhagen, Denmark, T45-3393 9303. Students are eligible for discounts at some museums but the use of student cards is not widespread so don't expect to save a fortune.

Tax

Airport tax is now included in the price of a ticket. For VAT refunds, see Customs and duty free, page 15.

Telephone

→ *Country code +66.*

From Bangkok there is direct dialling to most countries. To call overseas, you first need to dial the international direct dial (IDD) access code, which is 001, followed by the country code. Outside Bangkok, it's best to go to a local telephone exchange if calling internationally.

Local area codes vary according to province. Individual area codes are listed through the book; the code can be found at the front of the telephone directory.

Calls from a telephone box cost ฿1. All telephone numbers marked in the text with a prefix 'B' are Bangkok numbers.

Directory enquiries

For domestic long-distance calls including Malaysia and Vientiane (Laos): T101 (free), Greater Bangkok BMA T183, international calls T02-2350030-5, although hotel operators will invariably help make the call if asked.

Mobiles

Quite simply the cheapest and most convenient form of telephony in Thailand is the mobile/cell phone. Mobiles are common and increasingly popular – reflecting the difficulties of getting a landline as well as a desire to be contactable at all times and places. Coverage is good except in some border areas.

Sim cards and top-up vouchers for all major networks are available from every single 7-11 store in the country. You will need a sim-free, unlocked phone but you can pick up basic, second-hand phones for ฿600 from most local markets. Unfortunately for smart-phone users, most of Thailand has yet to acquire 3G, although cheap GPRS packages are available from all providers and coverage is pretty good.

AIS and *Happy D Prompt* sim cards and top ups are available throughout the country and cost ฿200 with domestic call charges from ฿3 per min and international calls from ฿8 per min. This is a very good deal and much cheaper than either phone boxes or hotels.

Internet

GPRS data deals are also incredible cheap – the AIS network offers 100 hrs of mobile internet connection for ฿300 per month. Speeds are slow though the network is perfectly adequate for text emails, basic web-browsing and social sites such as Facebook.

Time

GMT plus 7 hrs.

Tipping

Tipping is generally unnecessary. However, a 10% service charge is now expected on room, food and drinks bills in the smarter hotels as well as for any personal service. Increasingly, the more expensive restaurants add a 10% service charge; others expect a small tip.

Tour operators
UK

Asean Explorer, PO Box 82, 37 High St, Alderney, GY9 3DG, T01481-823417, www.asean-explorer.com. Holidays for adventurers and golfers in Thailand.

Buffalo Tours, the Old Church, 89b Quicks Rd, Wimbeldon, London SW19 1EX, T020-8545 2830, www.buffalotours.com. Arrange tours throughout Southeast Asia. Also has office in Bangkok, Phuket and Chiang Mai.

Exodus Travels, 9 Weir Rd, London, T020-9500039, T020-8673 0859, www.exodus.co.uk. Small group travel for walking and trekking holidays, adventure tours and more.

Magic of the Orient, 14 Frederick Pl, Bristol, BS8 1AS, T0117-3116050, www.magicofthe orient.com. Tailor-made holidays to the region. Established in 1989 the company's philosophy is to deliver first-class service from knowledgeable staff at good value.

Silk Steps, Compass House, Rowdens Rd, Wells, Somerset, BA5 1TU, T01749-685162, www.silk steps.co.uk. Tailor-made and group travel.

STA Travel, 33 Bedford St, Covent Garden, London, WC2E 9ED, T0871-468 0612, www.statravel.co.uk. Specialists in low-cost student/youth flights and tours, also good for student IDs and insurance.

Steppes Travel, 51 Castle St, Cirencester, GL7 1QD, T01285-880980, www.steppestravel.co.uk

Symbiosis Expedition Planning, Holly House, Whilton, Daventry, Northamptonshire, T0845-1232844, www.symbiosis-travel.com. Specialists in tailor-made and small group adventure holidays for those concerned about the impact of tourism on environments.

Trailfinders, 194 Kensington High St, London, W8 7RG, T020-7938 3939, www.trailfinders.co.uk.

Trans Indus, 75 St Mary's Rd and the Old Fire Station, Ealing, London, W5 5RW, T020-8566 2729, www.transindus.co.uk. Tours to Thailand and other Southeast Asian countries.

North America

Global Spectrum, 3907 Laro Court, Fairfax, VA 22031, USA, T1800-419 4446, www.globalspectrumtravel.com.

Nine Dragons Travel & Tours, 1476 Orange Grove Rd, Charleston, SC 29407, USA, T1317-281 3895, www.nine-dragons.com. Offers guided and individually customized tours.

STA Travel, 920 Westwood Blvd, Los Angeles, CA 90024, T1-310-824 1574, www.statravel.com.

Thailand

Luxury Travel Thailand, c/o East West Siam, 40/83 Intramara Soi 8, Suthisan Rd, Samseannai, Payathai, Bangkok 104000, T66-266007, www.luxurytravelvietnam.com. Asain specialist in luxury privately guided and fully bespoke holidays in Vietnam, Laos, Cambodia, Myanmar and Thailand.

Tourist information

Tourist Authority of Thailand (TAT), 1600 New Phetburi Rd, Makkasan, Ratchathewi, T02-2505500, www.tourismthailand.org; also at 4 Rachdamnern Nok Av (intersection with Chakrapatdipong Rd), Mon-Fri 0830-1630; in addition there are 2 counters at Suvarnabhumi Airport, in the Arrivals halls of Domestic and International Terminals, T02-134 0040, T02-134 0041, 0800-2400. Local offices are found in most major tourist destinations in the country. Most offices open daily 0830-1630. TAT offices are a useful source of local information, often providing maps of the town, listings of hotels/guesthouses and information on local tourist attractions. The website is a useful first stop and is generally well regarded.

Tourism authorities abroad

Australia, Suite 2002, 2nd floor, 56 Pitt St, Sydney, NSW 2000, T9247-7549, www. thailand.net.au.

France, 90 Ave des Champs Elysées, 75008 Paris, T5353-4700, tatpar@wanadoo.fr.

Germany, Bethmannstr 58, D-60311, Frankfurt/Main 1, T69-1381390, tatfra@t-online.de.

Hong Kong, 401 Fairmont House, 8 Cotton Tree Drive, Central, T2868-0732, tathkg@hk.super.net.

Italy, 4th floor, Via Barberini 68, 00187 Roma, T06-487 3479.

Japan, Yurakucho Denki Building, South Tower 2F, Room 259, 1-7-1, Yurakucho, Chiyoda-ku, Tokyo 100-0006, T03-218 0337, tattky@criss cross.com.

Malaysia, c/o Royal Thai Embassy 206 Jalan Ampang, 50450 Kuala Lumpur, T26-23480, sawatdi@po.jaring.my.

Singapore, c/o Royal Thai Embassy, 370 Orchard Rd, Singapore 238870, T2357901, tatsin@mbox5.singnet.com.sg.

UK, 1st floor, 17-19 Cockspur St, Trafalgar Sq, London SW1Y 5BL, T0870-900 2007, www.tourismthailand.co.uk.
USA, 1st floor, 611 North Larchmont Blvd, Los Angeles, CA 90004, T461-9814, tatla@ix.netcom.com.

Useful websites

www.asiancorrespondent.com Regional news website featuring guest blogs on Thai politics by writers who dig deep rather than toe the line. A better source of unbiased analysis than either the *Bangkok Post* or *The Nation*.
www.bangkokpost.com Homepage for the country's most widely read English-language daily.
www.bk.asia-city.com The online version of Bangkok's weekly freebie BK Magazine offers instant access to the hipper side of city life, from upcoming events to comment, chat and lifestyle features.
www.fco.gov.uk/travel The UK Foreign and Commonwealth Office's travel warning section.
www.paknamweb.com Umbrella website for the Paknam Network, expat Richard Barrow's assorted websites and blogs covering all facets of Thai culture.
www.thaifolk.com Good site for Thai culture, from folk songs and handicrafts through to festivals like Loi Kratong, and Thai myths and legends. Information posted in both English and Thai – although the Thai version of the site is better.
www.thai-language.com An easy-to-use Thai-English online language resource with an excellent dictionary, thousands of audio clips, lessons and a forum.
www.tourismthailand.org A useful first stop.
www.travel.state.gov/travel The US State Department updates travel advisories on its Travel Warnings & Consular Information Sheets.

Visas and immigration

For the latest information on visas and tourist visa exemptions, see the consular information section of the **Thai Ministry of Foreign Affairs** website, www.mfa.go.th. Having relocated from its central location on Soi Suan Plu, the immigration department that deals with tourists is now on the outskirts: Immigration Bureau, Government Complex Chaeng Wattana, B Building, Floor 2 (South Zone), Chaengwattana Rd Soi 7, Laksi, Bangkok 10210, T02-141 9889, www.immigration.co.th. Mon-Fri 0830-1200, 1300-1630, closed Sat, Sun, official hols.

For tourists from 41 countries (basically all Western countries, plus some Arabic and other Asian states – see www.mfa.go.th), Thai immigration authorities will issue a 30-day visa-exemption entry permit if you arrive by plane. If you enter at a land crossing from any neighbouring country, the permit is for 15 days.

Visas on arrival

Tourists from 28 countries (most of them developing countries) can apply for a 15-day visa on arrival at immigration checkpoints. Applicants must have an outbound (return) ticket and possess funds to meet living expenses of ฿10,000 per person or ฿20,000 per family. The application fee is ฿1000 and must be accompanied by a passport photo.

Tourist visas

These are valid for 60 days from date of entry and must be obtained from a Thai embassy before arrival in Thailand.

Visa extensions

These are obtainable from the Immigration Bureau (see above) for ฿1900. Applicants must bring 2 photocopies of their passport ID page and the page on which their tourist visa is stamped, together with a passport photograph. It is also advisable to dress neatly. Visas are issued by all Thai embassies and consulates. The length of time a visa is extended varies according to the office and the official.

Weights and measures

Thailand uses the metric system, although there are some traditional measures still in use, in particular the *rai*, which equals 0.16 ha. There are 4 *ngaan* in a *rai*. Other local measures include the krasorp (sack) which equals 25 kg and the *tang* which is 10-11 kg. However, for most purchases (for example fruit) the kg is the norm. Both kg and km are often referred to as lo – as in ki-lo.

Contents

Footprint features

Gulf of Thailand

Phetburi to Chumphon

The historic town of Phetburi (or Phetchaburi), with perhaps the best-preserved Ayutthayan wats in Thailand, is 160 km south of Bangkok and can be visited as a day trip from the capital. It is a historic provincial capital on the banks of the Phetburi River and is one of the oldest cities in Thailand and, because it was never sacked by the Burmese, is unusually intact.

Another 70 km south is Hua Hin, one of Thailand's premier beach resorts and the destination of choice for generations of Thai royalty. These days Hua Hin has been overshadowed – at least in terms of numbers – by Phuket and Pattaya. Yet this resort town manages to maintain some character with a waterfront of old wooden fishing houses.

Close by is Cha-am, a smaller seaside resort mostly frequented by blue-collar Thais looking for some good grilled pork, sun and sea. If you want to get into some wilder surroundings head for the Khao Sam Roi Yod National Park with its rare dusky langurs. Further south is the pleasant resort of Prachuap Khiri Khan, with the stunning beach of Ao Manao, and the long, less-developed coast down to Chumphon. Chumpon offers some local attractions such as trekking, kayaking, kitesurfing and diving but is mainly the launch pad to the island of Koh Tao.

Phetburi and around → *For listings, see pages 38-49.*

Arriving in Phetburi

The train station is about 1.5 km northeast of the town centre. Trains take 90 minutes from Hua Hin and two hours from Bangkok. The main bus terminal is about 1.5 km west of town, although air-conditioned buses stop near the town centre. Buses take about two hours from Bangkok, and there are connections south to Cha-am, Hua Hin (one hour) and onward. Songthaews meet the buses and take passengers into the town centre. The town itself is small enough to explore on foot. ▸▸ *See also Transport, page 47.*

Background

Initially, Phetburi's wealth and influence was based upon the coastal salt pans found in the vicinity of the town, and which Thai chronicles record as being exploited as early as the 12th century. By the 16th century, Phetburi was supplying salt to most of Siam and the Malay Peninsula. It became particularly important during the Ayutthaya period (14th century) and because the town was not sacked by the Burmese (as Ayutthaya was in 1767) its fine examples of Ayutthayan art and architecture are in good condition. Later, during the 19th century, Phetburi became a popular retreat for the Thai royal family and they built a palace here. Today, Phetburi is famous for its paid assassins who usually carry out their work from the backs of motorcycles with large-calibre pistols. Each time there is a national election, 15 to 20 politicians and their canvassers (so-called *hua khanen*) are killed. As in Chonburi, Thailand's other capital of crime, the police seem strangely unable to charge anyone.

Places in Phetburi

Phetburi has numerous wats. Those mentioned below are some of the more interesting examples. Although it is possible to walk around these wats in half a day, travelling by *saamlor* is much less exhausting. Note that often the ordination halls (bots) are locked; if the abbot can be found, he may be persuaded to open them up.

Situated in the centre of town on Damnoenkasem Road, **Wat Phra Sri Ratana Mahathat** can be seen from a distance. It is dominated by five much-restored, Khmer-style white *prangs*, probably dating from the Ayutthaya period (14th century); the largest is 42 m high. Inside the bot, richly decorated with murals, are three highly regarded Buddha images, arranged one in front of the other: **Luangpor Mahathat**, **Luangpor Ban Laem** and **Luangpor Lhao Takrao**. The principal image depicts the crowned Buddha. The complex makes an attractive cluster of buildings. Musicians and dancers are paid by those who want to give thanks for wishes granted.

Across Chomrut Bridge and east along Pongsuriya Road is **Wat Yai Suwannaram**; it's on the right-hand side, within a spacious compound and a large pond. The wat was built during the Ayutthaya period and then extensively restored during the reign of Rama V. The bot contains some particularly fine Ayutthayan murals showing celestial beings and, facing the principal Buddha image, Mara tempting the Buddha. Note the six-toed bronze Buddha image on the rear wall which is thought to be pre-Ayutthayan in date. Behind the bot is a large teak pavilion (*sala kan parian*) with three doorways at the front and two at the back. The front door panels have fine coloured-glass insets, while the mark on the right-hand panel is said to have been made by a Burmese warrior en route to attack Ayutthaya. The wat also houses an elegant, old wooden library. **Wat Boromvihan** and **Wat Trailok** are next to one another on the opposite side of the road and are being restored. They are distinctive only for their wooden dormitories (*kuti*) on stilts.

South down Phokarong Road and west a short distance along Phrasong Road, is **Wat Kamphaeng Laeng**. The five Khmer laterite *prangs* (one in very poor condition) have been dated to the 12th century and are reminiscent of those in the northeast of the country. Little of the original stucco work remains, but they are nonetheless rather pleasing. Surrounded by thick laterite walls, the wat may have originally been a Hindu temple – a statue of a Hindu goddess was found here in 1956.

West back towards the centre of town and south down Matayawong Road, are, in turn, **Wat Phra Song**, **Wat Laat** and **Wat Chi Phra Keut**, all on the left-hand side of the road. Just before reaching a bridge over Wat Ko Canal, is **Wat Ko Kaeo Sutharam**. The bot contains early 18th-century murals showing scenes from the Buddha's life and from Buddhist cosmology. The fact that the mural of the Buddha subduing Mara is on the rear wall, behind the principal Buddha image, has led to speculation that the entrance to the building was relocated at some time, possibly to gain access to a newly constructed road. The wat also houses interesting quarters for monks – long wooden buildings on stilts, similar to those at Wat Boromvihan.

At the western edge of the city is **Phra Nakhon Khiri**, popularly known as **Khao Wang** (Palace on the Mountain), built in 1858 during the reign of Rama IV. Perched on the top of

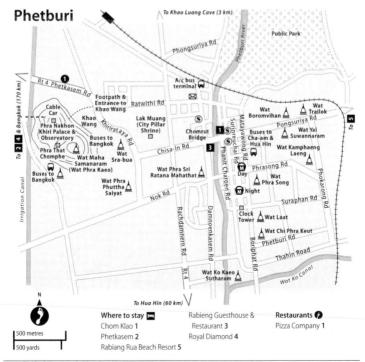

Where to stay
Chom Klao 1
Phetkasem 2
Rabiang Rua Beach Resort 5
Rabieng Guesthouse & Restaurant 3
Royal Diamond 4

Restaurants
Pizza Company 1

a 95-m hill, the palace represents an amalgam of Thai, Western and Chinese artistic styles. The hill complex is dotted with frangipani trees and there are areas of architectural interest on the three peaks. On the west rise is the **Royal Palace** ① *daily 0900-1600, ฿40*, which has recently been restored and is now a well-maintained museum. It contains an eclectic mixture of artefacts (including bed pans) collected by Ramas IV and V who regularly stayed here. The building is airy with a Mediterranean feel and has good views over the surrounding plain.

Also on this peak is the **Hor Chatchavan Viangchai**, an observatory tower which Rama IV used to further his astronomical studies. On the central rise of the hill is the **Phra That Chomphet**, a white stupa erected by Rama IV. On the east rise sits **Wat Maha Samanaram** (also known as Wat Phra Kaeo), which dates from the Ayutthayan period. Within the bot are mural paintings by Khrua In Khong, quite a well-known Thai painter. Watch out for the monkeys here; they seem innocent and friendly enough until you buy a bag of bananas or a corn on the cob. Sprawls between monkeys are quick to break out and, more often than not, the whole bag will be ripped from your hand. Just remember they are wild animals!

A **cable car** ① *Mon-Fri 0815-1700, Sat-Sun, 0815-1730, ฿30, children ฿10*, takes visitors up the west side of Khao Wang. At the foot of the cable car (more of a cable-tram) are toilets, cafés and souvenir stalls.

Wat Sra-bua, at the foot of Khao Wang, is late Ayutthayan in style. The bot exhibits some fine gables, pedestal and stucco work. Also at the foot of the hill, slightly south from Wat Sra-bua, is the poorly maintained **Wat Phra Phuttha Saiyat**. Within the corrugated-iron-roofed viharn is a notable 43-m brick and plaster reclining Buddha, which dates from the mid-18th century. The image is unusual in the moulding of the pillow and in the manner in which the arm protrudes into the body of the building.

Around Phetburi
Khao Luang Cave, 3 km north of Phetburi on Route 3173 (take a *saamlor*), contains stalactites, stupas and multitudes of second-rate Buddha images in various poses. This cave was frequently visited by Europeans who came to Phetburi in the 19th century. Mary Lovina Court (1886), an early example of the inquisitive but destructive Western tourist, wrote: "At the mouth of the cave we found some curious rocks, and succeeded in breaking off several good specimens." There is a large reclining Buddha inside the cave. Mary Court ended her sojourn telling some Buddhist visitors about "the better God than the idols by which they had knelt". On the right-hand side, at the entrance to the cave, is a monastery called **Wat Bun Thawi** with attractive carved-wooden door panels.

South from Phetburi → *For listings, see pages 38-49.*

Cha-am
Cha-am is reputed to have been a stopping place for King Naresuan's troops when they were travelling south. The name Cha-am may have derived from the Thai word *cha-an*, meaning to clean the saddle. Cha-am is a beach resort with some excellent hotels and a sizeable building programme of new hotels and condominiums for wealthy Bangkokians. The beach is a classic stretch of golden sand, filled with beach umbrellas and inner-tube renters. The northern end of the beach is much quieter, with a line of trees providing cooling shade. The town also has a good reputation for the quality of its seafood and grilled pork. It has become a popular weekend spot, so sizeable discounts are available during the week when most hotels are close to empty. At the weekend something of a transformation occurs and it buzzes with life for 48 hours before returning to its comatose

state. The **tourist office** ① *Phetkasem Rd, close to the post office, T032-471005, www.tat. or.th/central2, daily 0830-1630*, is responsible for the areas of Cha-am and Prachuap Khiri Khan, Phetburi and Hua Hin. Air-conditioned buses from Bangkok drop you right on the beach but other buses from Phetburi or Hua Hin stop on the Phetkasem Highway at its junction with Narathip Road. Motorbike taxis from here to the beach cost ฿40ish.

Between Cha-am and Hua Hin, **Maruekkhathayawan Palace** ① *daily 0800-1600, entry by donation*, was designed by an Italian and built by Rama VI in 1924; the king is reputed to have had a major influence in its design. The palace is made of teak and the name means 'place of love and hope', which is rather charming. It consists of 16 pavilions in a very peaceful setting. To get there, take a *saamlor* or catch a bus heading for Hua Hin and walk 2 km from the turn-off.

Hua Hin → *For listings, see pages 38-49.*

Thailand's first beach resort, Hua Hin, has had an almost continuous royal connection since the late 19th century. In 1868, King Mongkut journeyed to Hua Hin to observe a total eclipse of the sun. In 1910, Prince Chakrabongse, brother of Rama VI, visited Hua Hin on a hunting trip and was so enchanted by the area that he built himself a villa. Until his current bout of ill-health, the reigning monarch used to spend most of his time here too. These days, however, the olde-worlde charm that was once Hua Hin's unique selling point is all but lost – it's now a thriving resort town, packed with massage parlours, tourist shops and Western restaurants and bars. The suburbs are filled with condominiums and holiday villas, the sounds of drills and construction work are never far away, and the area is studded with high-end hotels. These luxury places are some of the best in Thailand, if not the world, and are a big draw for many visitors, especially older travellers and families.

Arriving in Hua Hin

Getting there The **train station** ① *Damnoenkasem Rd, T032-511073, T032-5111690*, is on the western edge of town, within walking distance of the centre. The journey from Bangkok takes three hours and there are onward connections to all points south. The bus terminal is quite central and provides regular connections with Bangkok and many southern towns.

Getting around Hua Hin is an increasingly compact beach resort and many of the hotels and restaurants are within walking distance of one another. There is also a good network of public transport: *songthaews* run along fixed routes, there are taxis and *saamlors*, and bicycles, motorbikes and cars are all available for hire.

Tourist information Tourist office ① *114 Phetkasem Rd, T032-532433, Mon-Fri 0830-1200, 1300-2000*. Also useful is www.huahin.go.th.

Background

The first of the royal palaces, **Saen Samran House**, was built by Prince Naris, son of Rama V. In the early 1920s, King Vajiravudh (Rama VI) – no doubt influenced by his brother Chakrabongse – began work on a teakwood palace, '**Deer Park**'. The final stamp of royal approval came in the late 1920s, when King Phrajadipok (Rama VII) built another palace, which he named **Klai Kangwon**, literally 'Far From Worries'. It was designed by one of Prince Naris' sons. The name could not have been more inappropriate: the king was staying at Klai Kangwon in 1932 when he was dislodged from the throne by a coup d'état.

Early guidebooks, nostalgic for English seaside towns, named the resort Hua Hin-on-Sea. *Hua* (head) *Hin* (rock) refers to a stone outcrop at the end of the fine white-sand beach. The resort used to promote itself as the 'Queen of Tranquillity'; until the 1980s, it was a forgotten backwater of an earlier, and less frenetic, tourist era. However, in the last few years

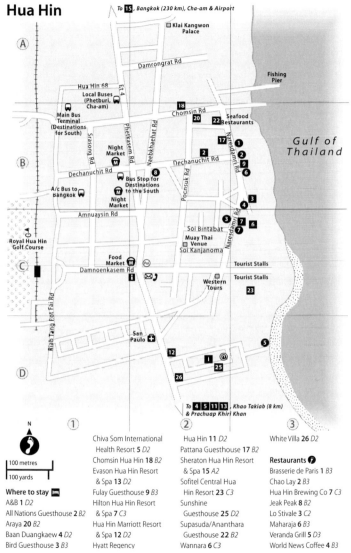

Hua Hin

To 15, Bangkok (230 km), Cha-am & Airport

Klai Kangwon Palace

Damrongrat Rd

Fishing Pier

Hua Hin 68

Local Buses (Phetburi, Cha-am)

Main Bus Terminal (Destinations for South)

Chomsin Rd

18

20   22

Seafood Restaurants

Gulf of Thailand

Night Market

17

Phetkasem Rd

Naebkhehat Rd

2   1
9
6

Dechanuchit Rd

Srasong Rd

Dechanuchit Rd

Bus Stop for Destinations to the South

Poonsuk Rd

8

Naresdamri Rd

A/c Bus to Bangkok

Night Market

4   3

Amnuaysin Rd

3   7   6

Royal Hua Hin Golf Course

Soi Bintabat

7

Muay Thai Venue

Soi Kanjanoma

Food Market

Damnoenkasem Rd

Naresdamri Rd

Tourist Stalls

1

Western Tours

Tourist Stalls

23

Riab Tang Rot Fai Rd

San Paulo

12

26

1   @

25

5

To 4 5 11 13, Khao Takiab (8 km) & Prachuap Khiri Khan

N

100 metres
100 yards

1

the constant influx of tourists has livened up the atmosphere considerably; with massage parlours, tourist shops and numerous Western restaurants and bars lining the streets, it's hard to get a moment's peace. And just when you think the town is as chock-a-block as possible, the sound of drills and construction work reminds you otherwise. Condominiums are springing up all along the coast to cater for wealthy holidaymakers from Bangkok; high-rise buildings scar the horizon and vehicles clog the streets. New golf courses are being constructed to serve Thailand's growing army of golfers – as well as avid Japanese players – and the olde-worlde charm that was once Hua Hin's great selling point has been lost.

Places in Hua Hin

As Hua Hin is billed as a beach resort people come here expecting a beautiful tropical beach but that isn't quite the case. Many of the nicest stretches of sand are in front of hotels – the **Hilton**, **Marriott** and **Sofitel** in particular.

The famous **Railway Hotel** was built in 1923 by a Thai prince, Purachatra, who headed the State Railways of Thailand. It became Thailand's premier seaside hotel, but by the 1960s had fallen into rather glorious disrepair. It experienced a short burst of stardom when the building played the role of the **Phnom Penh Hotel** in the film the *Killing Fields*, but it still seemed destined to rot into oblivion. Saved by privatization, it was renovated and substantially expanded in 1986 and is now an excellent five-star hotel. Unfortunately, it has been renamed, and goes under the unromantic name of the **Sofitel Central Hua Hin Resort** (see Where to stay, page 40). At the other end of Damnoenkasem Road from the hotel is the railway station itself. The station has a rather quaint Royal Waiting Room on the platform.

Away from the shore, there's a popular night market and myriad attractions only a short drive away to explore, including golf courses, temples and wineries. The biggest tourist-lure in town right now is the hokey (but admittedly very photogenic) faux-wooden shophouse village, **Plearn Wan** ① *Phetkasem Rd (between Soi 38 and 40), T032-520-311, www.plearnwan.com*. Over on Soi Moobaan Huana, there's now a slick modern arts complex, the Vic Hua Hin, www.vichuahin.com. Founded by Miss Patravadi Mejudho, the Thai actress and arts impresario behind Bangkok's Patravadi Theatre, it hosts art classes and weekend shops as well as weekly performances of often quite avant garde contemporary theatre. Hua Hin's staid shopping scene has also been given a bohemian shot in the arm by the Cicada Market, located on the southern outskirts (near the Hyatt Regency Hua Hin hotel). Resembling a public park, this atmospherically lit open-air night market hums with arts and crafts stalls, art galleries and live music from 1600-2300 each Friday, Saturday and Sunday.

Khao Takiab (Chopstick Hill), south of town, is a dirty, unremarkable hill with a large standing Buddha facing the sea. Nearby is **Khao Krilat**, a rock covered in assorted shrines, stupas, ponds, salas and Buddha images. To get there, take a local bus from Dechanuchit Road.

Kaeng Krachan National Park and caves

① *Park HQ, T032-619078, ฿200. Take a bus from Hua Hin to Pranburi (there are also trains to Pranburi, as well as trains and buses from Bangkok). From Pranburi it is necessary to charter a songthaew or take a motorcycle taxi to the park HQ. Be sure you are taken to Khao Sam Roi Yod National Park, and not Khao Sam Roi Yod village. For Laem Sala Beach (located within the park), there are regular songthaews from Pranburi market to Bang Pu village from 0800-1600. Or take a tour with one of the many tour operators in town.*

Khao Sam Roi Yod National Park ('Mountain of Three Hundred Peaks') occupies an area of limestone hills surrounded by saltwater flats and borders the Gulf of Thailand. It lies about 45 km south of Hua Hin, east off Route 4. Its freshwater marshes provide 11 different categories of wetland habitat – as much as the Red River Delta in Vietnam which covers an area nearly 200 times greater. The area is a haven for waterbirds and has been extensively developed (and exploited) as a centre for prawn and fish farming, limiting the marshland available to the waterbirds who breed here. The park has the advantage of being relatively small (98 sq km) with readily accessible sights: wildlife (including the rare and shy serow), forest walks and quiet beaches. The main beach is Laem Sala where a campsite, bungalows and a restaurant are located. Search the beach here for sand dollars and mother of pearl.

There are also some caves. **Phraya Nakhon**, close to Ban Bang Pu beach, has two large sinkholes where the roof collapsed a century ago, and a pavilion which was built in 1896 for the visit of King Rama V and is currently being restored. The climb to the cave takes one hour and can be slippery. If you are lucky you may spot some rare dusky langurs with their babies. **Sai Cave** contains impressive stalactites and stalagmites and a 'petrified waterfall' created from dripping water. At least 237 species of land and waterbirds have been recorded including painted storks, herons, egrets and many different waders. To visit the caves and beaches, boats can be hired from local fishermen at the park HQ

Prachuap Khiri Khan

Prachuap Khiri Khan is a small and peaceful fishing town with a long, crescent-shaped waterfront. At either end of the crescent, vegetation-draped limestone towers rear up from the sea creating beautiful symmetry and stunning views. The town is more popular with Thais than with *farangs* and has a reputation for good seafood. Buses no longer come into town, they pull over on the highway where you will need to catch a motorbike or a tuk-tuk into town. The **railway station** ① *T032-611175*, is on the west side of town.

At the northern end of town, at the end of Salashiep/Sarathip Road, is **Khao Chong Krachok**. An exhausting 15- to 20-minute climb up the 'Mountain with the Mirror' – past armies of aggressive, preening monkeys – is rewarded with fine views of the surrounding countryside and bay. At the summit there is an unremarkable shrine built in 1922 containing a footprint of the Buddha.

There is a good **night market** at the corner of Phitakchat and Kong Kiat roads and a daily market with stacks of fruit along Maitri Ngam (the road south of the post office, opposite the **Hadthong Hotel**). The daily market which runs along Salashiep/Sarathip Road has stalls of orchids, fruit and metal sculptures. South of the **Hadthong Hotel** on Susuek Road are a couple of Chinese shophouses.

Ao Manao, a gorgeous bay 5 km south of town, is one of best beaches on this stretch of coast. A gently sloping slice of sand is fringed by refreshing woodlands and framed by distant islands. At some points of the year the place can get infested with jellyfish, so bring a rash guard. Ao Manao was also the site of the Japanese invasion of the Second World War and is sited slap bang in the middle of a military base. This is no bad thing as development is strictly controlled – you'll find none of the usual trappings expected at other Thai resort towns. There is also one military-run hotel, good, cheap Thai food, toilets, deckchairs and umbrellas to hire. To get there, take a motorbike taxi or tuk-tuk (฿50-60).

Bang Saphan to Chumphon

South from Prachuap there are a number of beaches but most are infested with sandflies, difficult to reach and are set-up to cater mainly for Thai tourists. Around Bang Saphan, 60 km south of Prachuap Khiri Khan, several small beach resorts are developing. It is a pretty area and if you are heading south under your own steam then driving through this area makes for a nice diversion.

Chumphon → *For listings, see pages 38-49.*

Chumphon is considered the 'gateway to the south' and is where the southern highway divides, one route running west and then south on Route 4 to Ranong, Phuket and the Andaman Sea; the other, south on Route 41 to Surat Thani, Koh Samui, Nakhon Si Thammarat and the waters of the Gulf of Thailand.

There isn't much to see in the town itself, although there are some good beaches and islands nearby; the town is an access point for Koh Tao (see page 103). The station is at the west end of Krom Luang Chumphon Road, where the trains from Bangkok arrive.

The waters off the coast provide excellent diving opportunities. There are dive sites around the islands of **Koh Ngam Noi** (parcelled out to bird's nest concessionaires) and **Koh Ngam Yai**. Rock outcrops like **Hin Lak Ngam** and **Hin Pae**, are also becoming increasingly popular with dive companies for their coral gardens, caves and rock piles. Of particular note are the 500 varieties of rare black corals found in the vicinity of Hin Lak Ngam. The sea here is plankton-rich, which means an abundance of sea life including whaleshark, other species of shark, and sea turtles, as well as coral gardens. Visibility, though, is variable and certainly not as crystalline as on the Andaman Sea side of the isthmus. On a good day it may be more than 20 m, but at low tide less than half of this.

In his book *Surveying and exploring in Siam* (1900), James McCarthy writes of 'Champawn' marking the beginning of the Malay Peninsula. A group of French engineers had already visited the area with a view to digging a canal through the Kra Isthmus and it was clearly a little place at that time: the "harbour was full of rocks covered with oysters. The usual cocoa-nut palms and grass shanties marked the position of the village".

Around Chumphon

Pak Nam Chumphon, 11 km southeast of Chumphon on Route 4901 (take a *songthaew* from opposite the morning market on the southern side of town), lies on the coast at the mouth of the Chumphon River. It's a big fishing village with boats for hire to the nearby islands where swiftlets build their nests. The swiftlets are used to make the Chinese speciality of bird's nest soup – *yanwo*, in Chinese. Many concessionaires are accompanied by bodyguards; visitors should seek permission before venturing to the nest sites. Islands include **Koh Phrao**, **Koh Lanka Chiu** and **Koh Rang Nok**. Other activities such as diving, jungle treks and boat trips to the caves can be organized through a guesthouse or travel agent.

Much of the coastline and islands off Chumphon form part of the **Chumphon Marine National Park** (Mu Ko Chumphon). The **park headquarters** ① *T077-558144*, is 8 km from Hat Si Ree and can provide details of bungalows and campsites. The park contains mangrove forest, limestone mountain forest as well as marine life offshore.

Hat Thung Wua Laen, 18 km north of Chumphon, is a beautiful beach: a broad, curving bay and a long stretch of white sand, which slopes gently towards the sea, though this also means it's a long walk out to the water at low tide. The beach is also filled with sandflies, which makes sunbathing almost impossible. From November to January, when the winds are high and the sea is unsuitable for bathing, this beach turns into something of a mecca for kitesurfers – some claim that you can find the best kitesurfing conditions in Southeast Asia here. There are also a number of hotels and bungalows operating here but the beach is still mercifully free of tourist paraphernalia and, even when most accommodation is fully occupied, the area is large enough to maintain a sense of peace and seclusion. In March the waters become inundated with plankton, which locals harvest using nets. It is considered a delicacy and is known as 'kuey'. To get to the beach, take a songthaew (฿20) from the market in Chumphon; you can also charter a tuk-tuk (฿250).

Another beach, Hat Sai Ri, is 3 km south of Hat Pharadon and close to Koh Thong Luang. There is good snorkelling in the area. There is also a shrine to His Royal Highness Prince Chumphon, the self styled father of the Royal Thai Navy. To get to Hat Sai Ri take a songthaew (฿20) from opposite the New Infinity Travel Agency in Chumpon, or from the post office.

At Amphoe Lang Suan, 62 km south of Chumphon, there are two beautiful caves: Tham Khao Ngoen and Tham Khao Kriep. There are 370 steps leading to the latter, which is studded with stalagmites and stalactites. The district is also locally renowned for the quality of its fruit. You can take a bus there from the bus station in Chumphon.

Phetburi to Chumphon listings

For hotel and restaurant price codes and other relevant information, see pages 10-14.

🛌 Where to stay

Phetburi and around *p29, map p30*
Phetburi has limited accommodation with most visitors passing through as daytrippers.

$$$$-$$$ Rabiang Rua Beach Resort, 80/1-5 Moo 1 Anamai Rd, Chao Samran Beach, T032-44136, www.rabiangrua.com. On the beach, with great views and within easy reach of Phetburi, this is the first really comfortable, intimate and de luxe place to stay. Rooms are in 'boats' (rice-barge style) set around a small pool. Popular with Thai families. Bedrooms are strong on wood features, but light and airy nonetheless. Furnishings are refreshingly simple and although it's an odd-looking place to stay, it is fun and the staff are friendly. Bungalows also available.

$$$-$$ Phetkasem, 86/1 Phetkasem Rd, T032-425581. Best-value place to stay in this category. 30 clean rooms, some with a/c. Friendly management. There is no restaurant but it is located very close to some of the best eats in Phetburi (see Restaurants, below, page 43). Motorcycle rent ฿250 and Thai massage ฿350.

$$$-$$ Royal Diamond Hotel, 555 Phetka-sem Rd, T032-411061, www.royaldiamond hotel.com. Luxurious hotel compared to most others in Phetburi. The 58 rooms have a/c and are adequately furnished. The restaurant does a range of international food. There's a beer garden and pleasant, peaceful atmosphere. Internet access.

$ Chom Klao, 1 Tewet Rd, on the east bank of the river diagonally opposite the **Rabieng Guesthouse**, with duck-blue shutters, T032-425398. Clean, quiet and fair-sized rooms, though they are bare and unattractive. The rooms with views over the river are by far the best and have balcony areas. More expensive rooms have shower rooms attached, ones without have basins. Friendly, helpful and informative management.

$ Rabieng Guesthouse, Damnoenkasem Rd, T032-425707. Wood-panelled rooms with tiled floors on the ground floor. Pokier rooms upstairs but all are clean. A good night's sleep is impossible, though, if your room faces the noisy bridge. Open-air seating area upstairs and cleanish communal facilities. Appealing restaurant overlooking the river serving a very wide range of dishes (see Restaurants, page 43). Motorbikes can be rented out for ฿250 per day, bicycles for ฿120. Laundry service. Trekking and rafting tours in the national parks are available. Good English is spoken.

Cha-am *p31*
Mid-week tends to be quieter and cheaper.
$$$$-$$$ Bann Pantai, Ruamchit Rd, T032-433 111, www.bannpantai.com. An upmarket mini-resort complex, complete with nice pool, contemporary-Thai styled bungalows and some cheaper rooms. Everything (a/c, en suite, cable TV) you'd expect from a place in this price range. During low-season, mid-week prices can be negotiated down.

$$$$-$$$ Long Beach Cha-am Hotel, 225/75 Ruamchit Rd, T032-472444, www.longbeach-chaam.com. Huge concrete multi-storey pile set back from the main beach road. The views are fantastic and most rooms have sea-facing balconies, with the fresh breezes negating the need for a/c, which they all have as well. Friendly place, though ultimately a little dull.

$$$$-$$ Methavalai, 220 Ruamchit Rd, T032-433250, www.methavalai.com. A/c bungalows – some with several bedrooms, so they're ideal for families – and a small area of private beach, pool, good seafood and Thai restaurant.

$$$-$$ Dee-Lek, 225/30-33, Ruamchit Rd, T032-470548. Friendly little guesthouse on the main beach road. The pricier rooms have nice balconies overlooking the beach and all have hot water, TV and a/c. Everything is clean and tidy, if a little dull. Also serve decent food (see Restaurants, below, page 43). Recommended.

$$$-$$ Jitravee, 241/20 Ruamchit Rd, T032-471382. More expensive rooms have a/c, TV, fridge, room service and bathroom. Cheaper rooms have clean, shared bathrooms. Some English spoken, friendly.

$$$-$$ Viwathana, 263/21 Ruamchit Rd, T032-471289. One of the longer-established options, with some simple fan-cooled wooden bungalows, as well as a new brick-built block. All are set in a garden of sorts. The more expensive bungalows have 2 or 3 rooms and a/c. Good value for families.

$$ Pratarnchoke House, 240/3 Ruamchit Rd, T032-471215. Range of rooms available here from simple fan-cooled through to more luxurious a/c rooms with bathrooms. Some English spoken.

Hua Hin and around *p32, map p33*
Many hotels reduce prices in the low season. Rack rates are extortionate. For better deals check the internet or tour operators. Prices quoted here are for high season.

$$$$ Baan Duangkaew Resort, 83/158 Soi Moobaannongkae, T032-515 307, www.baanduangkaewhuahin.com. A sun-dappled mini-jungle with 2 small swimming pools shelters this handful of cute teak bungalows, all with a/c, hot showers, cable TV, fridge, king-size bed and wide wooden balcony. The downside? It's a little hard to find, tucked down a lane on the road from Hua Hin towards Khao Takiab beach, and mosquitoes seem to like it here

as much as we do, so come armed. Book ahead at weekends. Recommended.

$$$$ Chiva Som International Health Resort, 73/4 Phetkasem Rd, T032-536536, www.chivasom.com. This is a luxury health resort (Chiva-Som means Haven of Life) set in 3 ha of lush grounds that ooze calm and peace. It has a large spa building with a spacious gym, Roman bath, enormous jacuzzi, circular steam room and dance studio. There is also an outdoor freshwater pool close to the sea. With health consultants, hydrotherapy and lots of herbal tea and healthy food, this is the place to come to lose weight or firm up those buttocks without feeling that life is too miserable. There are numerous treatment and accommodation packages on offer.

$$$$ Evason Hua Hin Resort and Spa, 9 Paknampran Beach, Prachuap Khiri Khan, T032-618200, www.six-senses.com. About 20 km south of Hua Hin (not far from Pranburi) is this stylish resort, set in spacious grounds with a beautiful pool. It is hard to beat for anyone wanting to 'get away from it all'. The owners have created a unique environment, with light and airy rooms, furnished with contemporary, locally produced furniture. Some of the more expensive villas have private plunge pools. The groundbreaking Earth Spa, located in conical naturally cooled mud huts, provides the last word in pampering, as well as health programmes for the more committed. There are plenty of other (complimentary) facilities, including watersports (sailing, kayaking), tennis courts, a gym and archery. The kids' club has a separate pool and playground, plus daily activities. Low-season prices are good value. Recommended.

$$$$ Hilton Hua Hin Resort and Spa, 33 Naresdamri Rd, T032-512879, www.hilton.com. This rather unappealing white tower block dominates the town centre. However, it is a very pleasant and comfortable hotel offering a luscious spa, lovely pool, restaurants and a nice stretch of beach. The 296 rooms are attractively decorated, although the bathrooms lack grandeur in comparison. Views from the rooms are superb. Staff are helpful and friendly.

$$$$ Hua Hin Marriott Resort and Spa, 107/1 Phetkasem Rd, T032-511881, www. marriotthotels.com. A large resort with a very attractive lobby and top facilities in the 216 rooms. The Mandara Spa architecture and ambience is beautiful, blending Thai and Balinese style elements. There's a white, clean and pleasant beach in front of the hotel. On-site facilities include a very busy pool, 4 restaurants, 2 bars, a kids' club, tennis courts, fitness centre and watersports. Recommended.

$$$$ Hyatt Regency Hua Hin, 99 Hua Hin-Khao Takiap Rd, T032-521234, www. huahin.regency.hyatt.com. All the facilities you'd expect from a top-class hotel, including an extensive range of watersports and a cyber-games centre. It is a lovely low-rise, luxurious resort of 204 rooms set in an expanse of well-maintained gardens.

$$$$ Sheraton Hua Hin Resort and Spa, 1573 Petchkasem Rd, T032-708000, www. sheraton.com/huahin. With its entrance set on the main road between Hua Hin and Cha-am, this is the kind of resort you're not really meant to leave. The best and most unique feature is the giant snaking swimming pool, which can be reached straight from the balcony of most ground-floor rooms. Otherwise it's a standard 5-star place with all the usual trimmings. The beachside bar is a nice spot for a drink.

$$$$ Sofitel Central Hua Hin Resort, 1 Damnoenkasem Rd, T032-512021, www. sofitel.com. Hua Hin's original premier hotel, formerly the **Railway Hotel**, is a beautiful place set in luscious gardens with some very creative topiary and pools right near the beach. It maintains excellent levels of service and enjoys a very good location. The new rooms are small, but they are well

appointed and beautifully decorated, and the bathrooms are finished with marble. In addition, the seafood restaurant, run by a French chef, is worth seeking out.

$$$$-$$$ Wannara Hotel, 174/9 Naresdamri Rd, T032-532 244, www. wannarahotel.com. Attractive mid-range option in a good location near the Sofitel and tourist sprawl. A thin, low-rise block painted in beige with a modern Thai gleam, it has spacious, spotless a/c rooms with big balconies (though the views aren't up to much). There's a decent pool, and breakfast is included. No free Wi-Fi but there is an internet area. Staff are standoffish.

$$$-$$ Araya, 15/1 Chomsin Rd, T032-531130, www.araya-residence.com. Officially this is a small apartment block that offers monthly and annual rates, however it also offers rooms by the night and, while it's not the cheapest, Araya does represent excellent value. The rooms are comfy and spacious, with enough contemporary design and art to lift them into the 'cool' category. The best (and most expensive) are the two roof-top 'villas', which come complete with huge, private roof terrace, flat-screen TV, DVD players, fridge and free Wi-Fi. All this, a great location and friendly to boot. Highly recommended.

$$$-$$ Chomsin Hua Hin Hotel, 130/4 Chomsin Rd, T032-515348, www.chomsin huahin.com. Smart, well-tended boutique joint on a nice quiet street in central Hua Hin. All rooms come with a/c, en suite and TV, some have balconies. Rooms are excellent value, plus there's a small café downstairs.

$$$-$$ Fulay Guesthouse, 110/1 Naresdamri Rd, T032-513145, www.fulay-huahin.com. A delightful little place with an old world look: teak frontage, white carved wooden railings and splashes of pastel green. Only a/c rooms have hot water; fan rooms have shared bathrooms. Good restaurant. The 'Thai House' is a cute little getaway on the top deck with ocean views.

$$$-$$ Sunshine Guesthouse, 113/30 Soi Hua Hin, Phetkasem Rd, T032-515309, sunshine guesthouse@yahoo.com. Super-friendly management at this guesthouse, which is slightly cheaper than the others. Rooms have minibars, a/c and TVs. Internet café in the lobby.

$$$-$$ Supasuda/Ananthara Guesthouse, 1/8 Chomsin Rd, T032-516650, www.spg house.com. Sweet, stylish and friendly guesthouse opposite the pier in the heart of old Hua Hin. Rooms are all a/c, with TV and en suite, some have balconies with sea views. There's a private terrace on the roof and a relaxing lounge bar on the ground floor. At present it seems to be trading under 2 names.

$$$-$$ White Villa, 125/1 Phetkasem Rd, T032-532971, wwwhuahinwhitevilla. com. Sleek, modern small hotel in a busy location. Each en suite room comes with its own balcony, a/c and cable TV. There's also a pool.

$$ All Nations Guesthouse, 10 Dechanuchit Rd, T032-512747, cybercafehuahin@hotmail.com. One of the cheapest options in Hua Hin has clean rooms with fan or a/c and private balcony. English owner serves up English breakfasts. Free pool table.

$$ Bird Guesthouse, 31/2 Naret Damri Rd, T032-511630, birdguesthousehuahin@hotmail.com. 10 rooms on a wooden platform on stilts above the beach. Atmospheric place with friendly management. There is no restaurant but you can get breakfast in the seating area with views over the sea. Rooms with a/c cost more.

$$ Pattana Guesthouse, 52 Naresdamri Rd, T032-513393, huahinpattana@hotmail. com. Attractive location down a small alley. 13 twin-bedded rooms with fans in 2 original Thai teakwood buildings set around a flower-filled compound, 50 m from the beach. Some rooms have their own bathrooms. Breakfast available.

Kaeng Krachan National Park and caves *p34*

$$ Bungalows sleeping 5-6 are available at the park HQ but you must bring all necessities with you (eg blankets, food and water) as nothing is provided.

Khao Sam Roi Yod National Park *p35*

$$ Bungalows either for hire in their entirety or per couple. Camping ground, with tents for hire, and you can also pitch your own tent. Bungalows are available at both the park HQ and at Laem Sala Beach. Remember to take mosquito repellent.

Prachuap Khiri Khan *p35*

With the influx of Thais at weekends, accommodation is hard to find. During the week, room rates can be negotiated down.

$$$-$$ Fah Chom Klun, Ao Manao beachfront, T032-661088. This military-run establishment is the only accommodation next to Ao Manao beach and is often booked out. Rooms are basic but spotlessly clean, and all are en suite; some have sea views. Recommended, though reservations are essential.

$$$-$$ Hadthong, 21 Susuek Rd, T032-601050, www.hadthong.com. The best hotel in town has comfortable rooms (but small bathrooms) overlooking the sea. The pool also enjoys views of the bay. It is good value, and its restaurant serves tasty Thai food and a reasonable breakfast.

$$$-$$ Prachuap Beach Hotel, 123 Susuek Rd, T032-601288, www. prachuapbeach.com. Decent enough hotel beside the sea. Every room is en suite, with a/c, TV and balcony. However, it should be pointed out that, despite this optimistically named hotel, there is no 'beach' in Prachuap town centre.

$$$-$$ Sun Beach Guesthouse, 60 Chaitalae Rd, T032-604770, www.sunbeach-guesthouse.com. Brand new property on the seafront with a pool. Each en suite room is comfortably fitted out and has a/c and balcony, though the 'sea view' claim is a bit tenuous. Friendly atmosphere.

$ Feang Fa, 5 Soi 4, Tam pramuk, Susek Rd, T08-7792 8395. Cute, very friendly guesthouse set in a nice wooden building in a leafy compound and run by the amenable Thai owner, Maggie. The simple fan rooms are complemented by some stylish touches. Shared bathrooms. Also rent bikes from ฿100 a day.

Bang Saphan to Chumphon *p36*
The southern end of the bay near Ban Krut village has a variety of accommodation from large wood and bamboo bungalows to colourful concrete houses reminiscent of some European seaside resorts. Many of the latter are let in a timeshare style or are owned by Bangkokians looking for a quieter (and cheaper) place to stay than Hua Hin or Cha-am. The area tends to attract families rather than individuals or couples and consequently has excellent accommodation for larger groups, such as 2- or 3-bedroom bungalow houses which can be good value. Most resorts have ample and landscaped grounds. Accommodation tends to be quite simple but is clean and comfortable. Tthere are very few restaurants at the resorts and it's quite a walk to the main restaurant area.

$$ Nipa Beach Bungalows, Hat Somboon, T032-691583. A/c, hot water, telephone and TV. Good value and comfortable.

Chumphon *p36*
$$$-$ Chumphon Gardens, 66/1 Tha Tapao Rd, T077-506888. New hotel in central location, but set back a little from the road, so quiet. The cheaper rooms are excellent value: clean, with TV, en suite. Recommended.

$$ Jansom Chumphon, 188/138 Saladaeng Rd, T077-502504, jansombeach@yahoo.com. The rooms are clean, with a/c and spacious bathrooms, but the place as a whole is quite run down, and the curtains need replacing. Restaurant serves a wide range of Thai food, including a measly breakfast. Disco attached.

$$-$ Paradorn Inn, 180/12 Soi Paradorn, Saladaeng Rd, T077-511500, www.chumphon-paradorn.com. A/c rooms with TV that are brighter, whiter and nicer than anything the competition offers. The restaurant has bamboo furniture and offers a wide range of reasonably priced food (0800-2200).

$ New Chumphon Guesthouse, 27 Soi 1, Krom Luang Rd, T032-502900. Clean, cosy rooms with wood-panelled floors upstairs and darker, cheaper rooms downstairs. Shared bathrooms. Homely atmosphere and helpful management who speak good English. Tours to caves and waterfalls also arranged. Motorbike rental ฿200.

$ New Infinity, 68/2 Tha Taphao Rd, T077-570176. Offers 6 very basic but clean rooms. 1 is larger with balcony; some smaller ones have no windows but all have fans and shared bathrooms. Friendly and helpful management. A good travel service is offered here.

Beaches
There are a number of hotels and bungalow operations at Hat Thung Wua Lean. At weekends, local Thai families descend on the beach drinking beer and partying late into the night, so it can be noisy.

$$$-$$ Chuan Phun Lodge, 54/3 Moo 8, Thungwualaen Beach, T077-560120/230. Attractive en suite rooms in this newish lodge/hotel; the ones at the front have sea-facing balconies. Good value.

$$$-$$ Chumphon Cabana Resort, 69 Moo 8, T077-560245-7, www.cabana.co.th. This place has some nicely decorated a/c bungalows set in attractive gardens and 2 hotel blocks, all with a/c and hot water. The newer buildings have been designed on energy-saving principles in keeping with the owner's environmental concerns. The resort has all the usual facilities, including a pool, good watersports (including a PADI dive centre), a very peaceful location and a great view of the beach from the restaurant and some of the bungalows.

$$$-$$ Clean Wave, 54 Moo 8, Thungwualaen Beach, T077-560151. Some rooms with a/c, plus cheaper fan-cooled bungalows. Set in a big, leafy compound just back from the beach; you're pretty much guaranteed peace and quiet here. Friendly and efficient.

$$$-$$ View Seafood Resort, 13/2 Moo 8 Saplee, T077-560214. Decent range of good-value, well-kept en suite bungalows, with a/c and fan, right on the seafront with unspoiled views. The attached seafood restaurant is popular, but the owners are not particularly friendly.

$$$-$ Baan Tanaya, 16 Moo 8, T08-9592 7382. A/c, en suite rooms, each with a small balcony, open directly onto a nice stretch of the beach. Run by a friendly family who speak little English, but serve some pretty good Thai food and have a small shop. Recommended.

$$-$ Sea Beach Resort and Bungalow, 4/2 Moo 8, Thungwualaen Beach, T077-560115. Clean, cheap bungalows, some a/c, some fan, at this friendly resort, a favourite of the kitesurfing community.

$$-$ Seaside Guesthouse, 14/9 Moo 8, Saplee, T077-560178. Decent enough little guesthouse slightly away from the beach on the road in from Chumphon town. Every room is en suite but there is no hot water. Some rooms are a/c.

🍴 Restaurants

Phetburi and around *p29, map p30*
Phetburi is well known for its desserts including *khanom mo kaeng* (a hard custard made of mung bean, egg, coconut and sugar, baked over an open fire), *khao kriap* (a pastry with sesame, coconut and sugar) and excellent *kluai khai* (sweet bananas). There are several restaurants along Phetkasem Rd selling Phetburi desserts.

$ Rabieng Restaurant Guesthouse, Damnoenkasem Rd. Open 0830-0100.

Attractively furnished riverside restaurant, serving a good range of Thai and Western food. The spicy squid salad is particularly good. Breakfasts are small and overpriced. Recommended.

Foodstalls

There is a small but excellent **night market** at the southern end of Surinreuchai Rd underneath the clock tower – you can get a range of delicious snacks here and may want to try the local *patai* (omelette/pancake fried with mussels and served with bamboo shoots).

Cha-am *p31*
There are plenty of seafood restaurants along Ruamchit Rd, mostly serving the same dishes, including chilli crab and barbecued snapper with garlic. On the road into town from the highway you'll find dozens of places selling excellent grilled pork and Isaan-style food.

$$ Dee Lek, see Where to stay, above, page 39. This is a friendly-beachside café/restaurant selling decent Thai and European food. Friendly as well.

$ Moo Hang Nai Wang, almost opposite the KS golf sign on the road in from the highway. This small shack, with Thai signage only, is arguably the best purveyor of authentic Isaan food on this stretch. Succulent grilled pork and chicken come with superlative, spicy papaya salad and filling sticky rice. It might require a bit of asking but this place is highly recommended for those wishing to be more adventurous in their culinary choices.

$ Neesky Cafe, almost on the corner of the beach road and the road linking to the highway. This small, thatched place serves Thai food, steaks and supposedly the best burger in Thailand.

Hua Hin and around *p32, map p33*
Good seafood is widely available, particularly at the northern end of Naresdamri Rd. Most of the fish comes

straight from the boats, which land their catch at the pier at the northern end of the bay. There is also a concentration of restaurants and bars geared to farang visitors along Naresdamri Rd and surrounding lanes. Try the old central market, Chat Chai, on Petchkasem Rd between Soi 70 and 72, for breakfast. The neighbouring night market is packed full of enticing Thai food, as well as seafood so fresh that they have to tie the crabs' and lobsters' pincers shut. All the top-end hotels have decent restaurants, too.

$$$ Brasserie de Paris, 3 Naresdamri Rd, T032-530637. A French restaurant with a great position on the seafront, sandwiched between the squid piers. Attentive and prompt service. The speciality Hua Hin crab is absolutely delicious.

$$$ Palm Pavillion, Sofitel Central, 1 Damnoenkasem Rd. 1900-2300. This seafood restaurant is probably the best in Hua Hin. Don't expect the usual range of Thai dishes; the chef is French.

$$$-$$ Hua Hin Brewing Co, 33 Naresdamri Rd, T032-512888. Open 0900-0200. A partly open-air chaotic seafood restaurant serving good barbecued food. Also serves 3 home brews. Under-staffed during busy periods.

$$$-$$ Lo Stivale, 132 Naresdamri Rd, T032-513800. Open 1030-2230. The best Italian restaurant in town, although its pizzas are pretty standard. The house speciality of short pasta with crab meat and tomato sauce is recommended. Terrace and indoor seating available. Good and prompt service. Popular with foreign families. Recommended.

$$ Chao Lay, 15 Naresdamri Rd, T032-513436. Daily 1000-2200. This stilted building jutting out into the sea has 2 decks and is a great place to watch the sunset. Fruits of the sea, including steamed squid, huge seabass, rock lobster and prawns, are served up with military precision and presented on blue-and-white checked tablecloths. Hugely popular with Thais.

$$ Yu Yen Balcony, 29 Naep Khekat Rd, T032-531 191. Balmy offshore breezes team up with exemplary Thai/Chinese seafood at this Hua Hin favourite – a vintage seaside house. Try the steamed seabass bathed in spicy lime sauce, or curried crab.

$$-$ Maharaja, 25 Naresdamri Rd, T032-530347. Reasonable prices at this Indian restaurant, which is all excessive a/c, peach decor, flower fabrics and fake chandeliers. Great naan bread and curries. Attentive service.

$$-$ Veranda Grill, Veranda Lodge, 113 Hua Hin 67, Phetkasem Rd, T032-533678, www.verandalodge.com. 0700-2300. Enjoy terraced dining on lapis lazuli blue tiles overlooking the beach. The basil air-dried squid is worth savouring.

$ Jeak Peak, on the corner of Naebkhaehat and Dechanuchit rds. This small shophouse is one of Hua Hin's most famous noodle shops. It has been in the same location for 63 years and has lots of old world charm. Renowned for seafood noodles and pork satay, it's often packed, but the queues are worth it. Recommended.

Cafés and bakeries
Museum and tea shop, Sofitel Central, see Where to stay, page 40. Take colonial tea here for a taste of old-world charm. Earl Grey followed by ham buns, scones, jam and cream, biscuits and peach tarts is a treat.
World News Coffee, Naresdamri Rd, next to the Hilton. Daily 800-2230. Bagels, cakes, coffee and newspapers – at a price. Internet access too.

Prachuap Khiri Khan *p35*
Prachuap is famous for its seafood and there are a number of excellent restaurants (as well as some more average ones) in the centre of town and along the seafront. If you venture to Ao Manao there are plenty of small places selling very good Thai food there as well.

$$$-$$ Laplom Seafood, north of the river. Offers an extensive range of seafood, probably the best selection in town (with a few meat dishes too), reasonably priced and friendly.

$$$-$$ Shiew Ocha II, on the seafront towards the north of the town. Good range of seafood and meat dishes.

$$-$ Aroijung Steak, on main road to Ao Manao (look for the sign). Daily 0800-2100. Serves up great steaks and tasty Thai food. Very friendly and incredibly cheap.

$$-$ Mong Lai, 2.5 km north of Laplom on the north end of the bay below the mountain. Country-style restaurant that is well known for its spicy dishes.

$$-$ Panphochana, town centre, 2 doors down from the Hadthong Hotel, T032-611195. Open 1000-2200. Welcoming, English-speaking owner offers a vast range of seafood, pork and chicken. Breakfasts also served. Interior and outdoor dining possible with great views of the bay.

$$-$ Plern Samut, seafront next to the Hadthong Hotel, T032-611115. Daily 0900-2200. The very friendly owner, Khun Narong, and his family have been running this place for over 30 years. It's one of the most famous restaurants in town and serves awesome food, including divine squid and prawn. It's in a great location, too, with outside seating looking over the bay. Highly recommended.

$ Gossip, Susuek Rd. Thu-Tue 1030-2100. Small, cute café set in an old wooden shop and run by two Thai sisters. Good for coffee, waffles and ice cream. Also serves up a few Thai dishes.

Chumphon *p36*

$$-$ Farang Bar and Travel Agency, Tha Tapao Rd, T077-501003. 0430-0100. Thai-style soups and salads, noodles, spaghetti dishes and baguettes. Porridge for breakfast too. Cocktails are served at ฿100. Drink and eat while watching a movie. The night staff here are a lot friendlier than the day staff.

$$-$ Puean Djai Restaurant, opposite the railway station. Open 1000-0200. This restaurant is in an attractive garden setting. Very tasty pizzas using cheese from an Italian cheese factory in Prachuap Khiri Khan. Pasta, crêpes and Thai cuisine also concocted.

$ Lanna Han Isaan, set near the railway tracks in a cute garden. Delicious, cheaplsaan food that is very popular with locals. The food here is very spicy so ask for *pet nit noi* (a little spicy).

$ Spaghetti House, 188/132 Saladaeng Rd, T077-507320, 0900-2200. A comfortable a/c restaurant serving tasty and filling spaghetti at reasonable prices. Also delicious smoothies and ice creams with some unusual offerings: Japanese cucumber and the famous durian ice creams. There's also a coffee house inside. Staff are really friendly. Recommended.

Foodstalls
There are 2 night markets on Krom Luang Chumphon Rd and on Tha Taphao Rd.

Around Chumphon *p36*
There are now several restaurants spread along the road at Hat Thung Wua Lean Beach, but opening times can be erratic and depend on how busy things are.

$$ Ok Mai, next to Chuan Phun Lodge. 0830-2100, although may be shut during the day if the beach is very quiet. Excellent Western-style breakfasts and awesome pancakes. One of the best places to eat on the beachfront. Recommended.

$$-$ Apple Cafe, middle of the beach. 0800-1700. One of the best and only places for coffee, tea and cake on the beach. Run by a friendly Canadian and his Thai wife.

$$-$ Sabai Sabai, far end of the beach. French-run bar-cum-restaurant that serves up really good burgers, fries and the like throughout the day. Also has a pool table and plays good sounds.

Phetburi and around *p29, map p30*
Feb Phra Nakhon Khiri Fair (movable) *son et lumière* show.

Hua Hin and around *p32, map p33*
Jun Hua Hin Jazz Festival, www.huahin jazzfestival.com. Organized by the Hilton. Stages are set up in front of the Sofitel Central and railway station.
Sep The King's Cup Elephant Polo tournament, www.thaielepolo.com. Takes place at the Som Dej Phra Suriyothai military ground, south of Hua Hin. It is organized by the Anantara Hotel and has become quite an attraction in recent years.

○ Shopping

Hua Hin and around *p32, map p33*
The most distinctive buy is a locally produced printed cotton called *pha khommaphat*. The usual tourist shops and stalls can be found lining most streets in the town.
   Night market, Dechanuchit Rd, close to the bus station. Dusk-2200. Sells a range of goods including Tibetan jewellery, paper dragons, T-shirts, cassettes, watches and silk scarves.

Books
Bookazine, 116 Naresdamri Rd, T032-532071. Open 0900-2200. English-language books, magazines and stationery.

Silk
Jim Thompson shop in the Sofitel Central or the Hilton.

◑ What to do

Hua Hin and around *p32, map p33*
There are watersports and horse riding along the beach.

Golf
There are 5 championship golf courses close to Hua Hin including the **Royal Hua Hin**, the **Springfield Royal Country Club**, the **Palm Hills Golf Resort and Country Club**, **Lake View** and **Majestic Creek Country Club**.
Royal Hua Hin Golf Course, behind the railway station, T032-512475, royal_golf@ hotmail.com. Designed in 1924 by a Scottish engineer working on the Royal Siamese Railway. It is the oldest in Thailand.

Muay Thai (Thai boxing)
Muay Thai Boxing Garden, 8/1 Th Phunsuk, T032-515269. Every Tue and Sat. They are also open for training sessions daily 0900-1800.

Kitesurfing
With year round gusts and fairly calm seas, the beach at Hua Hin is fast becoming the premium kitesurfing location in the country; a Kitesurfing World Cup was held here in 2010 and 2011. The organizer, Kiteboarding Asia (T08-1591 4593, www. kiteboardingasia.com), has branches in Hua Hin, as well as further down the Gulf coastline at Pranburi and Chumphon.

Therapies
Hua Hin is home to some of the most luxurious, famous and expensive spas on the planet.
Anantara Spa, attached to the resort of the same name. Set in a quiet area with 6 suites in individual courtyards with baths filled with frangipani. Offers spa indulgence packages, which are reduced during the low season of Apr-Oct.
Mandara Spa, at the Marriott, see Where to stay, page 40, T032-511881, ext 1810, www.mandara spa.com. Open 0800-2000. A heavenly experience. Aroma-stone therapy, Thai massage) and body scrubs.
Six Senses Earth Spa, at the Evason, see Where to stay, page 39. Awesome

treatments, everything from reiki to basic Swedish massage, are available at this award-winning spa. The **Earth Spa** is sited in environmentally friendly mud huts which are designed to stay cool without a/c. Prices are high (฿2500-6000) but this is one of the most approachable and luxurious spas in Hua Hin. Recommended. **The Spa**, at the **Hilton**, see Where to stay, page 39. Open 1000-2100. Has a large menu of different massages, facials, wraps and Thai massage.

Tour operators
Tour operators are concentrated on Damnoenkasem and Phetkasem rds.
Western Tours, 1 Damnoenkasem Rd, T032-533303, www.westerntours huahin. com. Daily tours, THAI agent, transport tickets. Its trip to Khao Sam Roi Yod (฿900) is recommended. Kayaking, elephant riding and golf tours organized.

Chumphon *p36*
Diving
Easy Divers, Ta Thapao Rd, T077-570085, www.chumphoneasydivers.net. Dives at sites around the 41 islands off Chumphon. Nereides Diving & Sailing Centre, T077-505451, nereidesthailand@yahoo.com. Located on Hat Thung Wua Laen beach, this small, French-run dive shop organize tailor-made trips to most of the nearby dive sites, as well fishing tours and boat rental.

Kitesurfing
Kite Thailand, next to Seabeach Bungalows, Chumphon, T08-1090 3730 (mob), T08-9970 1797 (mob), www.kite thailand.com. At the moment, this friendly Dutch operator is the only place offering classes in this fast-growing sport.

Tour operators
Fame Tour and Service, 118/20-21 Salad-aeng Rd, T077-571077, www.chumphon-

kohtao.com. 0430-2400. Sells various tours, including trekking to Pak Lake to see wild buffaloes, elephants and monkeys, and long-tailed boat cruises.
Farang Bar and Travel Agency, Tha Taphao Rd, T077-501003, farangbar@ yahoo.com. Friendly staff offer lots of information and sell all tickets. Free taxi to train station offered.
Kiat travel, 115 Tha Tapao Rd, T077-502127, www.chumphonguide.com.
New Infinity Travel Agency, 68/2 Tha Taphao Rd, T077-570176, T08-1687 1825 (mob), new_infinity@hotmail.com. 0600-2400. Offers all tourist services, including a guesthouse, run by the very helpful manager.
Songserm, Tha Taphao Rd, next to New Infinity Travel, T077-506205.

⊖ Transport

Phetburi and around *p29, map p30*
Bus
Regular a/c connections with **Bangkok**'s Southern bus terminal near the Thonburi train station (2 hrs); non-a/c buses from the terminal near Khao Wang (2 hrs). Also connections with **Cha-am** (1½ hrs), **Hua Hin** (2¼ hrs, ฿35) and other southern destinations, between 0600-1800. These buses leave from the centre of town. Buses from Phetburi run past the turn-off for Kaeng Krachan Dam (Route 3175). From here, there are occasional minibuses which take visitors to the dam and the national park head-quarters (another 8 km), or hitch a lift.

Train
Regular connections with **Bangkok**'s Hualamphong station (2½ hrs), trains mostly leave in the morning. There are trains to **Hua Hin**, **Surat Thani** and southern destinations.

Cha-am p31
Bus

Cha-am is 25 km north of Hua Hin. There are regular connections with **Bangkok**'s Southern bus terminal (2½ hrs), **Phetburi**, **Hua Hin** and south destinations. To get to other southern destinations catch a bus to Hua Hin and change there.

Hua Hin and around p32, map p33
Air

Various small airlines have attempted to develop a route between Hua Hin and Bangkok over the years – most have failed. It is worth checking whether flights are operating, particularly for the return flight to Bangkok, as the runway at Hua Hin can only take small low-altitude aircraft. The flight back to Bangkok up the coast and over the city is one of the best in Thailand.

Bicycle

Can be hired for ฿100 per day, on Damnoenkasem and Phetkasem rds.

Bus

There are 3 bus stations. The a/c bus station to BKK is on Srasong Rd, next to the Chatchai market, T032-511654. Regular a/c connections with **Bangkok**'s Southern bus terminal near the Thonburi train station, 3½ hrs, ฿128, every 40 mins from 0300-2100. A/c buses to the south leave from the main terminal and from opposite the Bangkok bus terminal on Srasong Rd, T08-1108 5319 (mob). Departures between 2100-2300. To **Prachuap Khiri Khan**, ฿40-50, **Chumphon**, **Surat Thani**. Local buses to **Phetburi**, and **Cha-am**, leave from Srasong Rd between streets 70 and 72 off Phetkasem Rd.

Car

It is presently a 3-hr drive to **Bangkok**, along a hazardous 2-lane highway (particularly bad over the first 80 km to Phetburi), jammed with *siplors* (10-wheel trucks).

Car hire Jeeps can be hired for ฿1000-1500 per day on Damnoenkasem and Phetkasem roads. **Avis**, www.avisthailand.com, has offices at the Hyatt, Sofitel Central and Hilton. Prices from ฿1350 per day. One-way rentals are possible.

Motorbike

Can be hired for ฿200 per day upwards, on Damnoenkasem and Phetkasem roads.

Taxis

Taxis run along prescribed routes for set fares. There's a taxi stand on Phetkasem Rd, opposite **Chatchai Hotel**. Taxis can be hired for the day for ฿2000ish plus petrol. **Baipoo Service**, Baipoo shop, Dechanuchit Rd, T08-1307 2352 (mob), baipoo_shop4@hotmail.com. Also rents motorbikes and cars. Motorcycle taxis (identified by 'taxi' sign) will take you wherever you want to go. A taxi to **Bangkok** is 3 hrs (฿1600-1800).

Train

Regular connections with **Bangkok**'s Hualamphong station, same train as to Phetburi (3½-4 hrs). Regular connections with **Phetburi** (1 hr).

Prachuap Khiri Khan p35
Bus

To **Bangkok**'s Southern bus terminal, 5 hrs; also destinations south including **Chumphon**.

Saamlor

Prachuap has its own distinctive form of tuk-tuk – motorcycles with sidecars and bench seats.

Train

Regular connections with **Bangkok**, 5 hrs, **Hua Hin** and destinations south.

Chumphon p36
Boat

Lomprayah's high-speed catamarans, www.lomprayah.com, use the Thung Makham

Noi Pier and offer the quickest connection to Koh Tao, Koh Samui or Koh Phangnan. **Songserm**, www.songserm-expressboat. com, offers a slower (and cheaper) service that leaves from the nearest pier and carries on to **Samui** and **Phangan**. A night boat sails several times a week.

Bus
The terminal is 15 km outside of town, ฿200 per person in taxi to get there. There are regular a/c connections with **Chokeanan Tour** off Pracha Uthid Rd, T077-511480, office hours 0430-2130. To **Bangkok**, 1030, 1400, 2130, 7 hrs, ฿322; to **Phuket** ฿300, and **Ranong** at 0800, 1000 and 1200. To **Hat Yai**, 0830, 0930, 1130, 2130, ฿320. Minivans to **Surat Thani** leave from Krom Louang Rd, next to the 7-11 shop; depart when full (2½ hrs, ฿150). Minivans to **Ranong** depart every 40 mins from 0600-1700, ฿90, from in front of the closed Tha Taphao hotel.

Taxi
To **Hat Thung Wua Laen**, ฿250, one way; **Hat Sai Ree** ฿200, one way; **Thung Makam** (for the **Lomprayah** catamaran) ฿250; **Tha Yang** pier ฿50; to **Muang Mai**, the new out of town bus station, 15 km away, ฿200.

Train
Regular connections with **Bangkok**'s Hualamphong station (7½-9 hrs), and all stops south.

Surat Thani and around

The riverside town of Surat Thani is the main launch pad for transport to the gulf islands of Samui, Phangan and Tao. North of the town is the ancient settlement of Chaiya, once an important outpost of the Srivijayan Empire that was based in Sumatra. Also north is Wat Suan Mok, a Buddhist retreat, known for its meditation courses which are open to foreigners. The pig-tailed macaque has been trained to collect the millions of coconuts that grow in the region and on the islands. There's a macaque training centre outside Surat Thani that can be visited.

Surat Thani or 'City of the Good People' is a provincial capital and although the town has an interesting riverfront worth a visit and some fabulously stocked markets, its main purpose is as a transportation hub to the gulf islands or south to Krabi. About 50 km north of Surat Thani is the important historic town of Chaiya.

Arriving in Surat Thani
Getting there The airport is 20 km west of town; taxis and minibuses run to the city and also to the piers for connections to the Gulf Islands. Fares vary, but expect to pay from ฿200 per person or ฿1500 for a whole car to the pier. The train station is at Phun Phin, 14 km west of Surat Thani, T077-311213. From Bangkok's Hualamphong station there are about five trains a night, with the 1820 departure being the most highly sought after, arriving at a convenient time to catch an early morning ferry to Koh Samui. Local buses travel to town regularly, stopping at the Talat Kaset Nung (1) terminal, ฿12, from 0500-1900 (40 minutes). Buses also meet the train to transfer passengers to the ferry terminals for Koh Samui, Koh Phangan and Koh Tao.

The two central bus stations in Surat Thani are within easy walking distance of one another. Talat Kaset Nung (I) is for local buses and buses to Phun Phin, and Talat Kaset Song (II) is for longer-distance journeys. From Bangkok's Southern bus terminal, air-conditioned buses leave between 2000-2200 (12 hours). A popular option is to catch the 1800 bus from Khaosan Road (Bangkok). Passengers can then make their way to Koh Samui (see page 56).

Tourist information The tourist office, **TAT** ⓘ *5 Talat Mai Rd, T077-288817, tatsurat@tat. or.th, daily 0830-1200, 1300-1630*, is near **Wang Tai Hotel**, southwest of the town, is a good source of information for less-frequented sights in the province.

Places in Surat Thani
Boats can be hired for trips on the river (฿200 for up to six people). The better journey is upstream. There is a big **Chinese temple** and an attractive old viharn in the compound of **Wat Sai**, both on Thi Lek Road. The town brightens up considerably during the **Chak Phra Festival** in October or November.

Chaiya and around

ⓘ *Northbound trains from Surat Thani's Phun Phin station stop at Chaiya (40 mins). There are regular buses from Surat Thani to Chaiya from Talat Kaset Nung (I). Regular songthaews from close to Talat Kaset Song (II) (฿30).*

This city, lying 50 km north of Surat Thani on Route 41, was an important outpost of the Sumatra-based Srivijayan Empire and dates from the late seventh century making it one of the most ancient settlements in Thailand. Given the quantity of antiquities found in the area, some scholars have suggested that Chaiya may have been the capital of Srivijaya, rather than Palembang (Sumatra) as is usually thought. Recent excavations in Sumatra, however, seem to have confirmed Palembang as the capital. The Mahayana Buddhist empire of Srivijaya dominated Sumatra, the Malay Peninsula, and parts of Thailand and Java between the seventh and 13th centuries. It had cultural and commercial links with Dvaravati, Cambodia, north and south India and particularly Java. The syncretic art of this civilization clearly reveals these links. Many of the artefacts found in the area are now exhibited in the National Museum in Bangkok. Chaiya today is a pleasant, clean town with many old wooden houses.

About 2 km outside Chaiya, 1 km from the Chaiya railway station, stands **Wat Phra Boromthat Chaiya**, one of the most revered temples in Thailand. Within the wat compound, the central *chedi* is strongly reminiscent of the eighth-century *candis* of central Java, square in plan with four porches and rising in tiers topped with miniature *chedis*. The *chedi* is constructed of brick and vegetable mortar and is thought to be 1200 years old. Even though it was extensively restored in 1901 and again in 1930, its Srivijayan origins are still evident. A **museum** ① *Wed-Sun, 0900-1600, ฿30*, nearby, exhibits relics found in the vicinity which have not been 'acquired' by the National Museum in Bangkok. Another architectural link with Srivijaya can be seen at **Wat Kaeo**, which contains a restored sanctuary reminiscent of Cham structures of the ninth century (Hoa-lai type, South Vietnam), but again with Javanese overtones (with links to Candi Kalasan on the Prambanan Plain). Just outside Chaiya is the village of Poomriang, where visitors can watch silk being woven.

Wat Suan Mok

① *50 km north of Surat Thani on Route 41, T077-431597, www.suanmokkh.org. Take a bus from Talat Kaset Nung (l); the road passes the wat (1 hr). The town of Chaiya is closer to the monastery, so if arriving by train direct from Bangkok alight here and catch a songthaew to Wat Suan Mok.*

Wat Suan Mok, or Wat Suan Mokkhabalarama, is a popular forest wat (*wat pa*), which has become an international Buddhist retreat. Courses for Westerners are run with the aid of a number of foreign monks and novices. The monastery was founded by one of Thailand's most revered monks, the late Buddhadasa Bhikkhu, on a peaceful plot of land covering around 50 ha of fields and forest. Since he died in 1993, the monastery has been run by monks who have continued to teach his reformist philosophy of eschewing consumerism and promoting simplicity and purity. (Buddhadasa Bhikku developed and refined the study of Buddhist economics and he follows a long tradition in Thailand of scholar-monks.)

Ten-day *anapanasati* meditation courses are held here, beginning on the first day of each month. Enrolment onto the course takes place on the last day of the previous month, on a first-come first-served basis. Courses are ฿1500, which covers the cost of the meals (rice and vegetable dishes at 0800 and 1300). For those considering taking the course, bear in mind that students sleep on straw mats, are woken by animal noises at 0400, bathe in a communal pool, and are expected to help with chores around the monastery. No alcohol, drugs or tobacco are permitted and the sexes tend to be segregated. If intending to visit the monastery or enrol on a course, it is worth bringing a torch and mosquito repellent (or buy these at the shop by the entrance).

Kradaejae Monkey Training Centre

① *T08-9871 8017 (mob), call to make a reservation. The centre is south of Surat Thani on Route 401, towards Nakhon Si Thammarat, 2 km off the main road. Take a songthaew or bus from Surat Thani heading towards Nakhon Si Thammarat, on Talat Mai Rd, which becomes Route 401. The turning to the centre is on the right-hand side, just over the Thathong Bridge, past a wat and a school.*

The only monkey capable of being trained to pick coconuts is the pig-tailed macaque (*ling kung* in Thai). The female is not usually trained as it is smaller and not as strong as the male; strength is needed to break off the stem of the coconut. The training can start when the animals are eight months old. The course lasts three to five months, and when fully trained, the monkeys can pick as many as 800 coconuts in a day and will work for 12 to 15 years. "Working monkeys are very cheap – they cost no more than ฿10 a day but make millions of baht a year", according to Somphon Saekhow, founder of a coconut-collecting school.

Surat Thani and around listings

For hotel and restaurant price codes and other relevant information, see pages 10-14.

⊜ Where to stay

Surat Thani and around *p51*

$$$-$$ Southern Star, 253 Chonkasem Rd, T077-216414. The most luxurious hotel in the centre of town has 150 rooms, tastefully decorated and well equipped with satellite TV and minibar. There are 2 restaurants, but the one on the 16th floor, in spite of great views over the city, is not recommended. For those looking for nightlife, the Southern Star is also home to the largest disco in the south.

$$-$ 100 Islands Resort and Spa, 19/6 Moo 3, T077-201150-8, www.roikoh.com. An attractive resort-style hotel on the highway, diagonally opposite the Tesco Lotus and Boots, right out of town. Some of the pleasantly decorated rooms open directly onto the pool. There's a restaurant, jacuzzi, sauna and karaoke. Good value and recommended despite location.

$ Bandon, 268/2 Na Muang Rd, T077-272 167. The entrance is through a busy Chinese restaurant. Clean, tiled rooms, some with a/c and all with private shower rooms. Good value and quiet but the rooms get quite stuffy, even with the fan at full throttle.

$ Phongkaew Hotel, 126/3 Talat Mai Rd, T077-223410. Small, tidy rooms, complete with a/c, hot water, free Wi-Fi and cable TV, make this one of the best deals in town. Friendly and in a good location near the TAT office. Recommended.

$ Thai Thani, 442/306-8 Talat Mai Rd, T077-272977. Large, cleanish rooms with attached shower rooms. More expensive rooms have a/c and TV. Bleak corridors and a bit rough around the edges but conveniently positioned for an early bus.

⊘ Restaurants

Surat Thani and around *p51*

$$ Lucky, 452/84-85 Talat Mai Rd, T077-270 3267. Open 0900-2200. Lots of fried fish – snapper, mullet and butterfish – served up in the airy dining room with its faux-ranch ambience. Friendly, English-speaking staff.

$ Noodle shop, next to Phongkaew Hotel on Talat Mai Rd. One of the most popular noodle shops is run by a friendly and slightly eccentric Thai-Chinese man. The beef noodle soup is superb.

Foodstalls

Foodstalls on Ton Pho Rd, near to the intersection with Na Muang Rd, sell delicious mussel omelettes. There's a good **night market** on Na Muang Rd, and on Ton Pho Rd and vicinity. There's a plentiful supply of fruit and *khanom* stalls along the waterfront. Market next to the local bus terminal (Talat Kaset I).

⊛ Festivals

Surat Thani and around *p51*
Aug Rambutan Fair (movable).
Oct-Nov Chak Phra Festival (movable) marks the end of the 3-month Buddhist Rains Retreat and the return to earth of the Buddha. There are processions of Buddha images and boat races on the Tapi River, in longboats manned by up to 50 oarsmen. Gifts are offered to monks as this is also *krathin*, celebrated across Buddhist Thailand.

⊕ What to do

Phangan Tour 2000, 402/2 Talat Mai Rd, T077-205799. Open 0530-2200. Travel to Koh Phangan.
Phantip Travel, 293/6-8 Talat Mai Rd, T077-272230. A well-regarded and helpful

agency dealing with boats, buses, trains and planes. Recommended.
Samui Tour, 346/36 Talat Mai Rd, T077-282352. Open 0600-1700. Deals with Raja ferries to Koh Samui and Phangan and provides the bus transfer to Don Sak.

⊖ Transport

Surat Thani and around *p51*
Air
There are flights with Nok Air (www.nokair. com) to Bangkok Don Muang and with Air Asia (www.airasia.com) to Bangkok Suvarnabhumi. Air Asia currently also fly direct to Kuala Lumpur.

Boat
Most people these days arrive in Surat with through tickets and rarely stop in town.

Seatran Ferry, Bandon Rd, T077-275060/251555, www.seatranferry.com, office hours 0500-1800, there's a coffee bar, toilets and bag-guarding service at the office.

Night boats leave at around 2300 daily from the pier behind the **Seatran** office. To **Koh Tao**, 8 hrs, **Koh Samui** 6 hrs. To **Koh Phangan** 7 hrs. See also Transport for Koh Samui, page 81.

Bus
Some private companies run bus services to **Bangkok** (10 hrs, ฿285-440) and **Krabi** (3-4 hrs) There are also a variety of buses and minibuses to Trang (3 hrs), Phuket (4-6 hrs) – some of which also stop on the road outside Khao Sok – Nakhon Si Thammarat (2 hrs) and Chumphon (2 hrs).

International connections There are a/c buses from Surat Thani to **Kuala Lumpur** (Malaysia) and **Singapore**.

Songthaew
Known as 'taxis'. These are ubiquitous and cost up to ฿30 a ride.

Train
Trains out of Phun Phin are often full; advance booking can be made at **Phantip Travel**. Songserm Travel Service also arranges reservations. There are connections with **Hua Hin**, **Trang** and Bangkok.

International connections An international express train leaves Surat Thani for **Butterworth** (Malaysia) at 0131 (11 hrs) where you can make onward connections to **Kuala Lumpur** and **Singapore**.

Koh Samui

Koh Samui is the third largest of Thailand's islands, after Phuket and Koh Chang. Over the last decade tourism has exploded and now that it is accessible by air, the palm-studded tropical island is making the transition from a backpackers' haven into a sophisticated beach resort. The most recent development has also seen an identity shift from a simple party and pampering paradise to upmarket spa destination. Unlike Phuket, it still caters for the budget traveller with a variety of bungalows scattered around its shores. Its popularity is deserved, as it boasts some beautiful bays with sandy beaches hemmed by coconut palms seducing many a traveller in search of a paradise beach. But the only area of the island left relatively undeveloped is the southern tip, where the ring-road snakes inland from the coast, leaving a quiet corner away from the thud of dance music.

Koh Samui is slowly disappearing under concrete and billboards as the tourism bandwagon continues to gather speed. The two most popular beaches are still Lamai and Chaweng, both on the east side of the island. They are the longest uninterrupted beaches on the island, with good swimming and watersports and busy nightlife. Mae Nam and Bophut, on the north shore, are a little more laid-back and a number of good quality, low-cost accommodation options can still be found there, although expensive resorts rather than backpacker bolt-holes are rapidly taking over.

There are still isolated spots, mainly in the south and west. For a much quieter scene, head for the remote bungalows down the west shore, although it is best to hire a vehicle as many of them are off the main road. An advantage of staying on this side of the island is the sunsets.

Close to Koh Samui are the beautiful islands of the Ang Thong Marine National Park.

Arriving on Koh Samui

Getting there

Flying is the easiest and quickest option. It is relatively expensive but hassle free. The **airport** ① *T077-428500, www.samuiairportonline.com*, in the northeast, is privately owned by **Bangkok Airways**, www.bangkokair.com. There are multiple daily connections with Bangkok, as well as flights from Phuket and Pattaya, and international connections with Singapore and Hong Kong (see Transport, page 81). The airport has an information desk, which deals with hotel reservations (note that this is owned by Bangkok Airways and attempts are made to divert clients to Samui Palm Beach – also owned by the airline) and reconfirmation of flights. There is also a restaurant, free left luggage and through check-in for international flights for a large number of airlines, Hertz and Budget car rental, currency exchange and an ATM. Transport to town or the beach is by air-conditioned minibus to Bophut, Mae Nam, Chaweng (฿150), Choeng Mon, Lamai (฿300) and Big Buddha. Prices are inflated. There's a **limousine service** ① *T077-245598, samuiaccom@hotmail.com*, at domestic arrivals. The alternative is to flag down a bus out on the road, but it is a 1-km walk from the terminal and tricky with luggage.

Ferries to Samui depart regularly from one of Surat Thani's piers and take about two hours, costing around ฿200-250 depending on the operator. The slow overnight boat to Samui leaves from Surat Thani at 2300, arriving in Nathon at around 0500; expect to pay around ฿350. Note that the night boat is not particularly comfortable and, in rough seas, can be thoroughly unpleasant; if you have time, it is better simply to spend the night in Surat and get the regular ferry the next morning. If coming from Bangkok, it is possible to catch a boat from Chumphon to Koh Tao and from there to Koh Samui via Koh Phangan. But this is a much longer sea journey and only really makes sense if you're intending to stop off on Koh Tao. The State Railway runs a rail/bus/ferry service from Bangkok to Koh Samui (18 hours), which needs to be booked two to three days in advance. It is not necessary to buy a 'combination' ticket (available from any travel agent in Bangkok); buses from all the ferry companies meet the trains at Phun Phin to transfer passengers to the ferry terminals. ➤➤ *See Transport, page 81, for further information.*

Getting around

Koh Samui is a large island – well over 20 km both long and wide. Beaches, hotels and guesthouses can be found on most of the coastline, although the two most popular and developed beaches – Chaweng and Lamai – are both on the east coast. The main town of Nathon, where most of the ferries dock, is on the west side of the island. A ring road follows the coast along the north and east sides of the island, but runs inland cutting off the southwestern corner. Many resorts are on small tracks off this main circuit road running down to the beach. The most common form of transport, *songthaews* circulate between the island's northern and eastern beaches during daylight hours. Their final destination is usually written on the front of the vehicle and they stop anywhere when flagged down (prices start at ฿50 per person but are often inflated and some haggling may be required). Occasional nighttime *songthaews* run from 1830 and charge double. From Nathon, *songthaews* travel in a clockwise direction to Chaweng and anti-clockwise to Lamai. There are scores of places renting out motorbikes and jeeps but note that the accident rate on Koh Samui is horrendously high (see box, page 82).

Best time to visit

March to June is hot and fine with a good breeze and only the occasional thunderstorm. At this time of year good discounts are available on accommodation. June to October is also sunny and hot, with short showers. The 'worst' time of year is October to February, when the monsoon breaks and rain is more frequent. However, even during this period daily hours of sunshine average five to seven hours.

Tourist information

The **TAT office** ① *370 Moo 3, T077-420720, daily 0830-1630*, is helpful. Several tourist magazines and maps are distributed free of charge. Be aware that there are agencies advertising themselves as TAT booking offices in Bangkok. Customers book accommodation through them and then on arrival, if they don't like the sleeping choice they have no means to redress it. The official TAT is not a booking office. Companies using its acronym write it as follows: t.a.t. The official **Tourism Authority of Thailand** is just TAT.

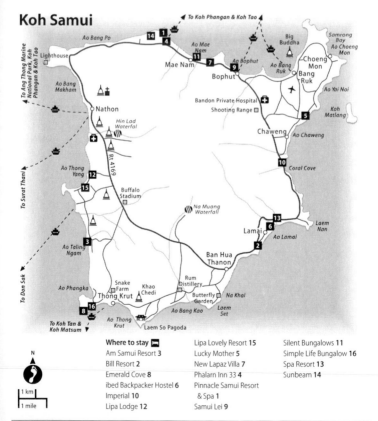

Koh Samui

Where to stay 🛏

Am Samui Resort **3**	Lipa Lovely Resort **15**
Bill Resort **2**	Lucky Mother **5**
Emerald Cove **8**	New Lapaz Villa **7**
ibed Backpacker Hostel **6**	Phalarn Inn 33 **4**
Imperial **10**	Pinnacle Samui Resort
Lipa Lodge **12**	& Spa **1**
	Samui Lei **9**

Silent Bungalows **11**
Simple Life Bungalow **16**
Spa Resort **13**
Sunbeam **14**

Background

Koh Samui is the largest in an archipelago of 80 islands, only six of which are inhabited. Many of Koh Samui's inhabitants were not Thai, but Chinese from Hainan who settled on the island between 150 and 200 years ago. Although the Chinese across Thailand have assimilated to such a degree that they are almost invisible, a number of traditional homes can still be seen.

About 60,000 people live on Koh Samui, many of whom are fishermen-turned-hoteliers. As one of Thailand's most popular tourist destinations, the number of annual visitors is many times this figure. The first foreign tourists began stepping ashore on Samui in the mid-1960s. At that time there were no hotels, electricity (except generator-supplied), telephones or surfaced roads, just an over-abundance of coconuts. This is still evident because, apart from tourism, the mainstay of the economy is coconuts; two million are exported to Bangkok each month. Monkeys are taught to scale the trees and pluck down the ripe nuts; even this traditional industry has cashed in on tourism – visitors can watch the monkeys at work. A monkey training centre has been established outside Surat Thani, see page 52.

For the moment at least, Koh Samui has largely managed to absorb a massive increase in tourist numbers without eroding the qualities that brought people to the island in the first place (although some long-term visitors would dispute that). Currently much of the island looks like a construction site as every available piece of land is built on.

Around the island → For listings, see pages 64-83.

The island's main attractions are its wonderful beaches; most people head straight to one, where they remain until they leave. However, there are motorbikes or jeeps for hire to explore inland and there are a multitude of activities on offer, see What to do, page 78. Evidence of the immigration of Hainanese can be seen reflected in the traditional architecture of the island. Houses, though they may also incorporate Indian, Thai and Khmer elements, are based on the Hainanese style. The use of fretwork to decorate balconies and windows, the tiled, pitched roofs and the decoration of the eaves make the older houses of Samui distinctive in Thai terms. Sadly, it is unlikely that many will survive the next decade or two. They are being torn down to make way for more modern structures, or renovated and extended in such a way that their origins are obscured.

Two-thirds of the island is forested and hilly with some impressive waterfalls (in the wet season). Hin Lad Waterfall and Wat are 3 km south of Nathon and can be reached from the town on foot, or by road 1 km off Route 4169. It's a 45-minute walk from the car park. Na Muang Waterfall, in the centre of the island, has a 30-m drop and a good pool for swimming. As the only waterfall on the island which is accessible by paved road it is busy at weekends and on holidays.

Nathon
Nathon is Koh Samui's capital and is where the ferry docks. It is a town geared to tourists, with travel agents, exchange booths, clothes stalls, bars and restaurants. Nathon consists of three roads running parallel to the seafront, with two main roads at either end linking them. Although it is used mainly as a transit point, it still has a friendly feel. *Songthaews* travel from Nathon to all the beaches. Motorbikes wait at the end of the pier, *songthaews* wait next to the second southernmost pier.

Ang Thong ('Golden Basin') Marine National Park

ⓘ *Daily tours leave from piers around the island. There are no public boats but you can leave the tour, stay on Koh Wua Talap and rejoin it several days later at no extra charge (make sure you tell the ferry driver which day you want to be picked up).*

The park is made up of 40 islands lying northwest of Koh Samui, featuring limestone massifs, tropical rainforests and beaches. Particular features are **Mae Koh** (a beautiful beach) and **Thale Nai** (an emerald saltwater lake), both on **Koh Mae Koh** and **Koh Sam Sao**; the latter has a coral reef and a huge rock arch as well as a hill providing good views of the surrounding islands. The area is the major spawning ground of the short-bodied mackerel, a popular edible fish in Thailand. There is also good snorkelling (the main attraction), swimming and walking. The park's headquarters are on **Koh Wua Talap**. Visibility is at its best between late March and October.

North coast

Bang Po (Ban Poh) A quiet, secluded and clean beach which is good for swimming. One of the better options for those wanting to escape the buzz of Chaweng and Lamai.

Mae Nam A clean, serene beach with lots of coconut palms and fringed with coral reefs to tempt swimmers and snorkellers. It is a popular spot and a number of new, beautifully designed resorts have opened here.

Bophut Bophut is one of the few places on the island where there are still traditional wooden Samui houses with Chinese lettering above the doors. It has grown increasingly popular in the last few years and there are now currency exchanges, bookshops, yoga schools, bars, restaurants and good watersports facilities, yet these haven't really spoilt the ambience. The beach is straight and narrow and lacks the sweeping expanse of Chaweng, or the quiet intimacy of Laem Set, yet the place maintains a refined and friendly village atmosphere with the string of restaurants making the beachfront a popular evening location. Most hotels offer fishing, snorkelling and sightseeing charters, although there are also plenty of independent outfits. As with most of the more remote beaches on Samui, the *songthaews* that are allotted for the beach run rather infrequently. It is possible to charter them and there are always motorcycle taxis around.

Big Buddha (Bang Ruk) This small bay has typically been a favourite stomping ground with expats although in recent years it has become increasingly popular with travellers. Accommodation is rather cramped and it also tends to be noisy as the bungalows are squashed between the beach and the road. However, the beach is quiet and palm-fringed and the water is always good. During the choppier weather from October to February, this sheltered cove is a popular haven with fishing boats.

The **Temple of the Big Buddha** sits on an island linked to the mainland by a short causeway, near Bophut beach. This unremarkable, rather featureless, modern seated image is 12 m high. In recent years the site has been smartened up and made into a 'proper' tourist attraction; there are now 50 or so trinket stalls at the entrance and several foodstalls.

Samrong Bay Set at the far northeastern corner of the island, this spot is also known as 'Secret Beach'. But it is not a secret any longer as there are two major resorts here. The scenery is more wild and raw.

Sea and weather conditions on Koh Samui

March-October Light winds averaging 5 knots, calm seas, the driest period but downpours can still occur. Water visibility is good. This is the period of the southwest monsoon and though generally calm, Bophut and Mae Nam can be windy, with choppy conditions offshore. Chaweng is normally calm.

October-February The northeast monsoon brings rain and stronger winds, averaging 10-15 knots but with gusts of 30 knots on some days. Sea conditions are sometimes rough and water visibility is generally poor although Koh Tao, see page 114, offers good year-round diving.

Choeng Mon At the northeast of the island is arguably the prettiest bay. The crescent of extremely fine white sand has an island at its eastern end, attached to the mainland by a sandbar, traversable at low tide. While in places it is rocky underfoot in the centre of the bay, the sand continues well out to sea. The restaurant scene is pretty lively, particularly in the centre of the beach where bamboo tables with oil lamps reach right down to the water's edge and there are a couple of beach bars at the eastern end. The beach is most popular with couples and families. There is a *songthaew* station at the far eastern side of the area, behind the beach.

South of Choeng Mon, there's good snorkelling at **Yai Noi**, north of Chaweng.

East coast
Chaweng This is the biggest beach on the island, split into three areas – north, central and Chaweng Noi. **Chaweng Noi** is to the south, round a headland, and has three of the most expensive hotels on the island. **Central Chaweng** is an attractive sweep of sand with lovely water for swimming and is lined with resorts, bungalows, restaurants and bars. The town that has grown up here is entirely geared towards tourists and in recent years it has become swamped. Along the road behind the beach there is a further proliferation of bars, clubs, tourist agencies, restaurants, fast-food chains, stalls and watersports facilities. However, the infrastructure has not kept pace with the concrete expansion; the drains stink in the searing heat and flood in the pouring rain. In comparison to the other beaches on the island, it is crowded and getting more resort-ridden by the year, but it's still Samui's most popular and by far the busiest beach. Despite the facilities and energetic activities on offer, most visitors prefer to sunbathe.

Chaweng to Lamai There is not much beach along this stretch of coast but there is some snorkelling off the rocky shore. Snorkelling is best at **Coral Cove**, between Chaweng and Lamai.

Lamai Koh Samui's 'second' beach is 5 km long and has a large assortment of accommodation. The beach is nice but rugged and not as attractive as Chaweng and the sea is rocky underfoot in many places. Cheaper accommodation can be found more readily here than on Chaweng. Just south of Lamai, there is a cultural hall and a group of phallic rock formations known as **Grandmother** and **Grandfather rocks** (*Hinyai* and *Hinta*). There's an array of tourist shops leading up to it. Companies along the main road parallel to the beach offer fishing and snorkelling trips around the islands.

Depending on who you talk to, or who you are, this is either a rather tawdry, down-market Pattaya, or an idiosyncratic, slightly hip and colourful Hua Hin. It is not particularly peaceful or picturesque. It can be fun and some people love it. The original town of Ban Lamai is quiet and separate from the tourist part, which is usually quiet during the day as most of the tourists are on the beach. The sea at Lamai can be wild and challenging during the early months of the year, and suitable only for the most competent of swimmers. Due to the tide there are not as many watersports here and the sea can appear murky, particularly at the northern end. Many hotels and restaurants are geared to the German market.

South coast

The small, often stony, beaches that line the south coast from Ban Hua Thanon west to Thong Krut are quieter and less developed with only a handful of hotels and bungalows, although construction continues at a breathless pace and the area is littered with endless 'land for sale' boards. While most tourists head for the white sands and sweeping shores elsewhere, there are some beautiful little coves peppered along this southerly stretch.

Ban Hua Thanon Ban Hua Thanon is an attractive rambling village with wooden shop-houses and *kwaytio* (noodle soup) stalls – and the only Muslim community on Koh Samui. The forebears of the inhabitants come from Pattani in Thailand's far south. With its stony beach being the biggest anchorage for fishing boats on the island, this village is quiet and rarely visited by tourists. North of the village are a couple of restaurants, well situated with cooling sea breezes, see Restaurants, page 76.

Na Khai Na Khai is a small beach with just a handful of resorts. The swimming can be rocky, but if you are looking for a quiet place to stay and don't require a classic sweep of golden sand, then this is an option.

Laem Set This is not really much of a beach compared with Chaweng and Lamai. However, it is quiet, clean and palm fringed and there is some reasonable snorkelling.
Samui Butterfly Garden ① *T077-424020, 0830-1730, ฿170*, is set on the side of the hill behind **Laem Set Inn** opposite **Central Samui Village**. It features a screened butterfly garden with a limited collection of butterflies, a display of (dead) insects, moths and butterflies, a few beehives, a hillside observatory, observation platforms for views of the coast, a glass-bottomed boat for viewing a coral reef and a restaurant.

Thong Krut Thong Krut Bay and the hamlet of Ban Thong Krut are at the southern extremity of the island. The stony beach is around a kilometre long and the swimming is average but there are excellent views from here and it is peaceful and undeveloped with just a handful of shops including a little supermarket and **The Beach**, **Java** and **Green Ta'Lay** restaurants. Boat trips to Koh Tan and Koh Matsum or to fish and snorkel can be arranged through various companies in the village.
Nearby, is the **Samui Snake Farm** ① *88/2 Moo 4, T077-423247*. Shows are held at 1100 and 1400. The commentary is hilarious. Not for the squeamish.

Koh Tan and Koh Matsum Koh Tan lies due south of Thong Krut and is about 3 km long and 2 km wide. It was first colonised by Hainanese; the Chinese cemetery on the island has graves from this time. There are three small villages and a few bungalow developments on the island which, although undeveloped, are not blessed with spotless beaches and crystal-clear waters. Still, it is quiet and just about away from it all.

Koh Matsum is a sorry sight – all the coconut trees have been stripped by beetles, leaving a desolate landscape.

West coast
Like the south coast, the western coastline south of Nathon is undeveloped with secluded coves and beautiful sunsets. Phangka, near the southwest tip of the island, has good snorkelling in the quiet waters of a small bay; Thong Yang, further north, is an isolated beach, relatively untouched by frantic development. The vehicle ferry from Don Sak, on the mainland, docks here.

Koh Samui listings

For hotel and restaurant price codes and other relevant information, see pages 10-14.

😊 Where to stay

Accommodation prices tend to soar during the peak months but are a bargain off season. Prices on Koh Samui have doubled in the past few years and it's rare to find fan bungalows under ฿400-500 in the high season. Backpacker havens are being forced out to make way for high-end establishments. High season roughly runs from Jul-Aug, Dec-Apr.

Nathon *p59, map p58*
$$-$ Jinta City Hotel, 310 Moo 3, T077-420630, www.jintasamui.com. Modern, attractive hotel on the seafront with 37 a/c and fan rooms with fridges and TVs. The more expensive modern rooms are a considerable improvement.
$$-$ Seaside Palace, 152 Moo 3 (on the seafront road), T077-421079. Offers 33 a/c, clean, adequate and well-maintained rooms with hot water.
$ Coffee Island, T077-423153. Very basic rooms above a coffeeshop right opposite the pier. A concrete slab would probably be more comfortable than one of these beds, and the rooms could be cleaner. Shared bathrooms have cold water only. Café with Wi-Fi downstairs (see Restaurants, page 72).

Ang Thong Marine National Park *p60*
Koh Wua Talap, National Park office, T077-2806025, T077-280222. Bungalows, long-houses, camping, showers and a restaurant are available along with a small visitors' centre. Accommodation sleeps up to 8 people. See the national park website, www.dnp.go.th, for details and online booking.

North coast *p60, map p58*
Bang Po (Ban Poh)
$$-$ Phalarn Inn 33, T077-247111, www.phalarninn.com. Set back some way from the beach. Concrete bungalows with big balconies, TV and a/c have a garish colour scheme. Cheaper fan rooms are available. Not the best deal considering the location but pleasant grounds, friendly staff and a good restaurant, motorbike rental, package tours and ticket reservations.
$$-$ Sunbeam, T077-420600. Secluded bungalows, quiet location, clean, friendly, private beach.

Mae Nam
$$$$ Santiburi, 12/12 Moo 1, T077-425031, www.santiburi.com. A superb and incredibly large resort of 91 beautifully furnished Thai-style villas and suites with a massive pool, watersports, sauna, tennis and squash courts, on a quiet beach. The spa (1100-2300) offers a full range of massage, reflexology and facials. There's also a **Hertz** desk. For the golf course, see What to do, page 79.
$$$$-$$ Pinnacle Samui Resort & Spa, 26/4 Moo 4, T077-427308, www.pinnaclehotels.com. The well established garden hides the 80 bungalows, creating a more intimate feel. All rooms have a good range of facilities but the interiors are a tad dated. There is a swimming pool, but pool villas are available for those who don't like to share. Suitable for families.
$$$$-$ New Lapaz Villa, Next to **Paradise Resort**, T077-425296, www.newlapaz.com. Wide range of accommodation available from basic wooden bungalows, which are typical of the budget options, except that they have hot showers. The new midrange concrete bungalows are modern with built-in wardrobes, and include nice touches such as dressing gowns and umbrellas

in the rooms. The most expensive option has a separate lounge area, a bathtub and overlooks the beach. Swimming pool and restaurant.

$$$$-$ Palm Point Village, 15 mins walk from Mae Nam village, T077-425095, www. palmpointsamui.net. This place has good-value wooden and concrete bungalows on a lovely steep-sloping beach. The more expensive rooms have a/c, hot water and balcony. Cheaper fan rooms available. Good food and motorbikes for hire.

$$$-$$ Harry's Bungalows, 26/9-5 Wat Napralan, T077-447097, www.harrys-samui. com. 50m from the beach, reached by climbing wooden steps over a wall that encloses the resort. 20 bungalows spread out amongst a huge garden. Plenty of areas to relax, including a swimming pool. Rooms are spacious, complete with a/c, cable TV, safety deposit box, however the furniture is of low quality. Free transfers from piers (airport ฿400) and Wi-Fi are a bonus.

$$$-$$ Maenam Resort, 1/3 Moo 4, T077-247 287, www.maenamresort. com. Alpinesque bungalows with little balconies, wicker furniture, wardrobes, desk and a/c in luscious gardens. Some have wonderful positions set on the gently sloping beach with shallow waters. Popular with young families. Friendly management. Recommended.

$$$-$ Home Bay Resort, 26/11 Moo 4, T077-247214. Old wooden bungalows with fan have been well manintained. The a/c rooms are cavernous and are decorated with bamboo matting. Modern bathrooms with hot water showers. Located on a tranquil stretch of beach.

$$$-$ Moonhut Bungalows, 67/2 Moo 1, T077-425247, www.moonhutsamui. com. Various types of room, from fan huts nestled in a luscious garden at the rear, to more expensive a/c bungalows with a sea view. All have been finished to a high standard and are spotlessly clean. Popular with families.

$$$-$ Shady Resort, 1/7 Moo 4, T077-425392. Offers 20 bungalows on a yellow-sand beach bordered by bowing coconut palms. Rooms are nice, white and bright with desks and fridges. A/c bungalows with gardens are the most expensive. Friendly and good value.

$$-$ Seashore 1, next to Seashore 2, T077-425280. Offers 2 options: small, cheap, cheerful and very basic wooden bungalows with fan or spacious, newer log cabin-style rooms with a/c, some of which are right on the beach. Pool table and beachfront bar.

$$-$ Silent Bungalows, on the dirt road opposite Bamboo Bar, just next to Mae Nam post office, T077-602604. There are 20 modern wooden bungalows right on the beach. Cheaper options have fan and cold water only, but the beds are new and comfy. More expensive rooms have a wooden deck around three sides with cushions overlooking the water.

$$-$ Wandee Bungalow, 151/1 Moo 1, T077-425609, wandeebungalow@hotmail. com. 3 rows of spacious, if a little Spartan, concrete bungalows parallel to the beach. Windows on 3 sides flood the rooms with natural light. Restaurant on the beach. Very peaceful.

$ Poo Bungalows, 190 Moo 1, T077-247252. Row of wooden bungalows wedged down a narrow alley behind the owner's hairdressing shop. Fan rooms are a little dark and bathrooms tired looking, but for this price are actually very good value, and even come with a TV. Discounts given for long-term stays.

$ Sea Shore 2, next to Moonhut Bungalows, T077-425192. Concrete bungalows all with fan and bathroom inside. The rooms are rather bizarrely arranged just off the beach. Friendly Thai owner. Excellent value for the location.

Bophut Village
$$$$-$$$ Eden Bungalows, 91 Moo1, T077-427645, www.edenbungalows.com.

This French-owned oasis is delightful. 15 tiled double and family fan or a/c rooms with large bathrooms and romantically dim lighting. They are cleverly arranged around a small pool, with plenty of vegetation, giving an impression of space. Fairly pricey but the ambience is worth it.

$$$$-$$$ Smile House Resort, 93 Moo 1, T077-425361, www.samuismilehouse. com. Choice of either a/c and fan bungalows in a pleasant layout. Both are kept meticulously clean and have unusual Chinese lampstands but small bathrooms. The roadside pool lacks privacy. The fan rooms are good value considering the access to the pool. Beachside restaurant over the road.

$$$$-$$$ The Waterfront, 71/2 Moo 1, T077-427165, www.thewaterfrontbophut. com. Modern and attractive bungalows set around a small pool close to the beach but still in the village itself. Renovated and expanded by its British owners in 2003, it has a cosy atmosphere and is popular with families. Rooms have kettles and DVD player. Free childminding and Wi-Fi. The low-season prices are a bargain.

$$$ The Lodge, 91/1 Moo 1, T077-425337, www.lodgesamui.com. This small, appealing hotel has 10 well-decorated a/c rooms, all of which have satellite TV, a minibar, and en suite bathroom. While there is no restaurant, there is a bar that serves basic Western food.

$$$-$$ Samui Leh (formerly **Red House**), 51/8 Moo 1, T077-245647. The new owners have decked out the 5 spacious rooms with retro furniture and a fisherman's cottage theme. Staff are not very friendly, but the place is kept meticulously clean, and there's free Wi-Fi and 2 PCs available to use in reception (which also happens to be a small clothes shop). Look for the white house with a big blue fish out the front.

$$$-$ Khun Thai Guesthouse, 88/6 Moo 6, T077-245118. Set back from the road, down a very quiet cul-de-sac, but still only a minute walk from the beach, this bright orange family home has numerous rooms on offer. A few don't have external windows, but most are bright and airy. All have hot water and TV. The ฿500 rooms are the best value.

$$-$ Oasis Bungalows, opposite **Starfish & Coffee**, see Restaurants, page 73, T077-425143. The alleyway beside the restaurant opens onto a beautiful garden with 6 bungalows ranging from concrete fan huts to larger, newer wooden bungalows. All have TV and hot water showers. Good value.

Bophut Beach

$$$$ Anantara, 99/3 Bophut Bay, T077-428300, www.anantara.com. With resorts and spas throughout Thailand, Anantara's well-designed Samui resort is chic and comfortable with a luxurious yet traditional feel. The striking lobby is dominated by a cluster of lanterns and doors imprinted with golden stencilling. This opens out onto a stunning, rectangular lotus pond. The infinity pool overlooks a well-kept section of the beach. The spa (1000-2200) is a cool oasis in the grounds.

$$$$ Paradise Beach Resort, 18/8 Moo 1, T077-247227, www.samuiparadisebeach. com. 95 bungalows on the beach and rooms in a main building. Attractive touches in rooms include brightly coloured silk cushions and drapes on the beds. There's a large secluded and nicely shaded pool, a kids' paddling pool, slides, dive shop, canoeing, windsurfing, massage and a growing number of fabulous restaurants. There's only a small beach but sunbeds are perched on a sandy terrace with great views of Koh Phangan. Popular with families.

$$$$ Zazen, west side of Bophut beach, T077-425085, www.samuizazen.com. This is a compact resort full of surprising design details like the distinctly exotic interiors and North African style beachfront façade. The small beach is framed by a headland to the west, although the sea is not at its best here. Bungalows and spa massage cabins nestle amid the vegetation. There is a beach bar and the fashionable fusion restaurant, see Restaurants, page 73.

$$$$-$$ World Resort, 175/Moo 1, T077-425355, www.samuiworldresort.com. Lots of bungalow choice here, from spacious a/c wood-panelled affairs to more modern deluxes with sea views. There are hotel rooms, too, as well as a large pool and a beach restaurant that serves Thai and Western food. Recommended.

$$$-$$ Free House, at the western end of the beach, T077-427516. Freehousesamui. com.14 smart, good-value modern bungalows. Like most places on the island they are rather squashed into limited space but the beachfront restaurant is popular.

$$$-$$ Sandy Resort and Spa, 177/1 Bophut Beach, T077-425353, www.sandy samui.com. Fan-cooled bungalows and a/c rooms in a somewhat ugly 2-storey building. There are 2 restaurants, one on the beach.

$$ Coconut Calm Beach, 180 Moo1, T077-427558, thamrug@hotmail.com. Mixture of concrete and bamboo bungalows reasonably spaced amongst coconut palms. Some effort has gone into making them presentable. Both fan and a/c available.

Big Buddha (Bang Ruk)

$$$$-$$$ Como Resort, western end of the beach, T077-425210, www.kohsamui beachresort.com. With a little pool and relaxed atmosphere, Como has 11 smart little bungalows with hot water and TVs. The friendly restaurant and quiet setting make it ideal for families.

$$$ Punnpreeda Hip Resort, 32 Moo 4, T077-246222, www.punnpreeda.com. A pebbled garden path snakes it way from the fairly bland reception area down to the beach. Apparently owned by a Thai pop star, the 25 rooms are modern, tastefully decorated and fairly spacious. Some areas are showing their age and are in need of maintenance, but it's still pretty good value.

$$$-$$ Elemental, T08-1370 3980 (mob). Boutique-style beach bar and super-chic bungalows established by a British-Canadian couple in 2006; it's since been taken over by Thai owners. The 4 stylish modern bungalows sleep up to 3, with the more expensive options offering living rooms overlooking the beach.

$$$-$$ Secret Garden, 22/1 Moo 4, T077-245255, www.secretgarden.co.th. Small family-run resort with 9 good-value concrete bungalows, some right by the beach, some slightly back from it. All have a/c, varnished teak floors, TV, fridge and hot water. There are also a few cheaper rooms in a converted building. Clean and comfortable. Friendly British owners. Recommended.

$$ Dae Tong De Samui (formerly Shambala), 23/2 Moo 4, T077-425330, www.daetongdesamui.com. 5 modern concrete bungalows set in a lush garden, all landscaped around a beach bar. All rooms have a/c, satellite TV and hot water. The beachfront bungalow is A500 extra. Repeat customers get 1 night free. Recommended.

$ Bai Di Bungalow, 28/1 Moo 4, behind Antica Locanda, T08-1894 4057 (mob). Look past the garish purple paint and these humble concrete bungalows are among the best value in the area. Each has a small kitchen with fridge and separate bathroom, as well as a small balcony and fishpond outside. Free Wi-Fi. 1-min walk to the beach.

$ Sunset Resort, 33/4 Moo 4, T077-247792, T08-9025 9778 (mob), www.sunsetresort samui,com. Log cabin-style bungalows with fan or a/c in a small garden fronting onto the beach. For this price you have to overlook the fact that the rooms are in need of some repair, however the beds are comfy.

Samrong Bay

$$$$ Arayaburi, formerly Bay View Village, 6/14 Moo 5, T077-247958, www. arayaburi.com. Offers 65 villas, with small private terraces that are fairly closely packed. Superior rooms are nice and light and there are flowers on all beds. Garden view bungalows do not get much of a view. Beachside pool, bike, motorbike and canoe hire available. It shares a private beach with the Six Senses Samui.

$$$$ Six Senses Samui, 9/10 Moo 5, T077-245678, www.sixsenses.com/sixsenses samui. Famous, ultra-chic and exclusive resort and spa with cool, calm and minimalist lines. The 66 hidden villas have rectangular private pools and luxury sun-decks. There are 2 restaurants, a gym, shop and Six Senses Spa (1000-2200), with massage rooms that overlook the sea. Recommended.

Choeng Mon

$$$$ Imperial Boat House, 83 Moo 5, T077-425041, www.imperialhotels.com. 34 converted teak rice barges make for unusual suites, 182 other rooms in 3-storey ranch-style blocks, with limited views and rather disappointing compared to the boats. Watersports are available and a boat-shaped pool adds to the theme-park feel. The garden pool is more secluded. The buffet breakfast is extensive. But it is outdated compared to its elegant neighbours.

$$$$ Sala Samui, www.salaresorts.com/samui. Immaculate luxury hotel with 69 villas that enjoy award-winning design and a fresh Mediterranean feel. The beachside pool is surrounded by decking and the hidden private villas have pools, raised platforms and outdoor bathtubs. There are also some cheaper deluxe rooms. 5-star facilities include the Mandara spa. Recommended.

$$$$ Tongsai Bay, T077-245480, www.tongsaibay.co.th. Luxury resort with 24 bungalows scattered across a hillside coconut plantation, overlooking a private bay. Watersports, tennis courts, gym and 2 pools (1 sea water) close to the sea.

3 restaurants, including beachside bar and café. Buggies are used to get around the resort but there are several flights of stairs to access some rooms.

$$$$-$$$ White House Beach Resort and Spa, centre of the beach, 59/3 Moo 5, T077-247921, www.samuithewhitehouse.com. Set in a delightful shady tropical garden, this is a small collection of large white houses with Thai details. The hotel also has a medium-sized pool in a cosy position just behind the beach and restaurants. Recommended.

$$-$ O Soleil, T077-425232, osoleil bungalow@yahoo.fr. Frenchman Jean and his wife have run this place since 1989. There's a mix of concrete bungalows of various sizes; some of the older ones are starting to show their age but it still feels homely thanks to Jean's hospitality. Also has a decent restaurant (see page 74).

East coast *p61, map p58*
Chaweng

Although Chaweng is more upmarket than Lamai, it contains a rather jarring combination of international hotels and basic bungalows. Visitors can stay in US$150 hotels then cross the road and have a full American breakfast for under US$2.

$$$$ Amari Palm Reef Samui, Northern Chaweng, T077-422 015, www.amari.com/palmreef. Spacious, well-established family-friendly resort at Chaweng's quiet north end. The highlights: 2 huge swimming pools and the breakfast buffet, which is a sumptuous affair. On-site Italian restaurant Prego is also excellent (see Restaurants). Like many resorts in the vicinity, its beachfront reception area is separated from the accommodation area by the main road; security men guide you across it safely. Comfortable but uninspiring rooms.

$$$$ Blue Lagoon, northern end, T077-422037, www.bluelagoonhotel.com. Well designed with 60 rooms in 2-storey Thai-style blocks. The resort also features an international restaurant and a large swimming pool.

$$$$ Centara Grand Beach Resort, T077-230500, www.centarahotels resorts.com. An elegant, if expensive, low-rise Greek temple comes to the Orient-style resort. Wood-panelled blocks with good facilities set in a palm grove. There's a large pool, health centre and 4 good restaurants. Popular.

$$$$ First Bungalow Beach Resort, T077-422327, www.firstbungalowsamui.com. As implied by its name, this was the first resort to appear on Chaweng beach and the a/c bungalows are spacious and nicely laid out.

$$$$ Imperial, southern end, T077-422020, www.imperialsamui.com. The first 5-star hotel on the island has rooms in a large 5-storey Tuscan-style block. The hotel also has salt and freshwater pools.

$$$$ Poppies, 119/3 Moo 2, T077-422419, www.poppiessamui.com. Beautifully designed to maximize space, these a/c Thai-style cottages have open-air bathrooms, wooden floors and detailing, and are set in a tropical garden with water running through it. There is an excellent, open-air restaurant (see Restaurants, page 75) and a small pool. The Swiss management offers outstanding service. Free Wi-Fi. Recommended.

$$$$-$$$ Al's Resort, 200 Moo 2, T077-422154, www.alsresortsamui.com. The rooms are reasonable enough but this resort operates an unfair cancellation policy; the staff can also be extremely rude and unhelpful. If you do stay here you are advised to only pay on a day-to-day basis.

$$$$-$$$ Impiana, T077-422011, www. impiana. com. A new modernized block with pool and 2 good restaurants. The downstairs Thai operation boasts a nice beach, while upstairs is **Tamarind's Restaurant** (1800-2230), which offers well-received Pacific-rim cuisine.

$$$$-$$$ Tradewinds, 17/14 Moo 3, T077-414294, www.tradewinds-samui.com. Excellent bungalows set out along an attractive swathe of the beach. As a result

of its small size, it is an intimate place and peaceful at night. There is a beachside bar and restaurant.

$$$$-$$ Samui Resotel (previously Munchies), T077-422374, www.samui resotel.com. A range of well-decorated fan rooms and luxurious suites. They are, predictably, too close to one another, but are better than most thanks to the pleasant beachside restaurant and live music.

$$$$-$$ Long Beach Lodge, 14 Chaweng Beach, Moo 2, T077-230084, www.long beachsamui.com. A large coconut-studded plot for so few bungalows. Laid back and peaceful. Bungalows are a reasonable size and a/c rooms are good value.

$$$ Chalala Samui Resort (formerly Corto Maltese), 119/3 Moo 2, T077-230041. Interestingly designed small resort next to the beach, far removed from the generic hotel room design. The bright blue huts have colourful, playfully sculpted interiors, which are very comfortable, with a/c, fridge and TV as standard. Spilt-level flooring separates the lounge from the sleeping area and bathroom. Swimming pool, jacuzzi and beachfront restaurant. Staff can be rude.

$$$-$$ The Island, northern end, T077-424202, www.theislandsamui.com. Huts on the beach with an attractive garden and run by foreigners. There's a pool and the bar is open after 2200.

$$$-$ Lucky Mother, northern end, T077-230 931, poungpakahaha@hotmail.com. Friendly and clean, with excellent food. Several different types of accommodation on offer, some private bathrooms.

$$ Beach Love, next to Impiana, T077-422531, beachlovesamui@hotmail.com. Modern building on stilts so that all 4 rooms have sea views. The rear backs on to the road. Cool urban interiors with concrete screed flooring, pale blue colour scheme and sleek white sanitary ware. TV, a/c, fridge, bay window and balcony. Very chic.

$$ Chaweng Center Hotel, 14/41 Chaweng Beach Rd, T077-413747, chawengcenter@hotmail.com. Modern hotel in the village a short walk from the beach. The rooms overlooking the road are the cheapest and have been recently refurbished with mattresses on a raised platform, modern Japanese style. All rooms have a/c, TV, fridge and hot water.

$$-$ Somwang House, 159/6 Moo 2, T077-422269, somwanghouse_hotel@ hotmail.com. A good budget option. Wooden bungalows with a/c and hot shower – proximity to the beach bars may be too noisy for some. More expensive rooms are in a bright green building further back from the beach.

$ Best Beach Bungalows, central Chaweng, look for the small yellow sign. May not be the best, but it's a decent spot if you're on a very tight budget and want to stay close to the action. Many of the old-style wooden bungalows have recently made way for a 2-storey concrete monstrosity housing a/c rooms, but some bungalows still remain and are by far the better choice, with basic bathrooms and balconies within metres of the beach. Don't leave valuables in your room.

Chaweng to Lamai

$$$$-$$$ Coral Cove Chalet, T077-448500, www.coralcovechalet.com. Charming chalets on a hillside are linked by wooden walkways. There's a small pool and steps down to small private beach that has little sand but some good snorkelling offshore. It is well run with a tropical ambience.

Lamai

$$$$-$$$ Aloha, T077-424418, www.aloha samui.com. Well-designed a/c rooms in this relaxing resort. There is a good pool and the restaurant offers a range of great seafood.

$$$$-$$ Bill Resort, T077-424403, www.billresort.com. A Lamai mainstay, this quirky and stylish retreat offers excellent standards of service and accommodation on an attractive and fairly secluded stretch of sand. The resort, with its range of well spaced, elegantly designed and well-furnished bungalows, climbs a hillside, giving it a slightly magical village feel. Pool, jacuzzi, restaurant and travel services. Recommended.

$$$$-$$ The Spa Resorts, T077-230855, www.spasamui.com. This is one of the longest-running holistic health resorts in the country. It's been upgraded, slightly, in recent years but is still excellent value. Herbal sauna, body wraps, cleansing detox programs, Reiki and raw food classes are just a few of the New Age activities and treatments offered. Avoid if you're into beer guzzling or late-night partying. Staff are welcoming and the restaurant is award-winning. The cheaper all-wood A-frame bungalows with attached bathrooms are excellent value at ฿1000. Book ahead. See also Therapies, page 80.

$$$$-$$ Sand Sea Resort & Spa, northern end of Lamai beach, T077-231127, www.samuisandsea.com. A mixture of concrete and wooden bungalows. All have tiled bathrooms and are mosquito proof. The gardens are nice and there are good views of the sea. It has a restaurant and 20-m swimming pool. During the low season room rates are cut by up to a third.

$$$ Sea Breeze, 124/446 Moo 3, T077-960601, www.samuiseabreezeplace.com. This is one of the oldest places on the island, although the basic bungalows have recently made way for a more modern concrete development with 25 rather uninspired rooms and a swimming pool. The garden restaurant serves Thai and Western food at reasonable prices and the staff are friendly.

$$ Lamai Coconut Resort, 124/4 Moo 3, T077-232169, www.lamaicoconutresort. com. With 33 immaculate bungalows close to the beach, this family-owned and run resort was established in 1985 and still has some of Lamai's best-value rooms. With shiny wooden floors, linen, fridges, elegant furniture and large windows, the bungalows feel rather luxurious despite the modest fan room rate. Recommended.

$$ Suan Thale, T077-424230. A/c and fan rooms in bungalow 'blocks' on a large plot. The rooms are reasonable with a bit more character than most.

$$-$ Amadeus Bungalows, 129 Moo 3 Maret, T077-424568. Run by a sweet old Thai family, there are a/c rooms available in a new building or cheap wooden huts on stilts up on the hill side, the sea can be seen from the balconies. The beach is a 5-min walk.

$$-$ Beer's House, 161/4 Moo 4, T077-230467, www.beerhousebungalow.com. Small wooden bungalows, some are right on the beach, others are in a garden. The cheapest options are a row of concrete rooms behind the bungalows that have a shared bathroom. Good value.

$$-$ iBed Backpacker Hostel, 124/521 Moo 3, T077-458760, www.ibedsamui. com. A very stylish addition to Samui's growing flashpacker scene. Go past the fake grass and polished concrete courtyard and up the stairs to the reception/lounge area. Each of the dorm rooms has 8 beds and is exceptionally clean. There are also double rooms available, though at ฿1100, they're a little overpriced. Free Wi-Fi. Staff are exceptionally helpful and speak good English.

$$-$ Lamai Resort, next to Sandsea Resort, T077-424124, lamairesort@hotmail. com. Simple, spacious log-style cabins with balcony affording a slither of a sea view and concrete a/c bungalows on the beach with TV and fridge.

$$-$ New Hut, next to Beer's House, T077-230437. Simple but good-quality 'A' frame bamboo huts, slap bang on the beach, with mattress on the floor, mosquito net, fan and shared bathroom. There are also bungalows with bathroom inside available. Funky restaurant. Recommended.

$ Coconut Beach Resort, 124/22 Moo 3, T077-424209. Clean, simple wooden bungalows hidden amongst coconut palms. Bathrooms have squat toilets.

South coast p62, map p58
Na Khai
$$$$-$$$ Samui Orchid Resort, 33/2 Moo 2, T077-424017, www.samui orchid.com. Rooms are cheap looking with old carpets, old-fashioned accessories and clashing colours. Beds are small. The 2 pools and beach are decent but the on-site aquarium and zoo with tigers and birds is a sorry sight and is best avoided.

Laem Set
$$$$ Kamalaya, 102/9 Moo 3, Laem Set Rd, T077-429800, www.kamalaya.com. This 'wellness sanctuary and holistic spa' is one of the latest, distinctly upmarket place to cater for Samui's spiritual tourists. Oriental and Western healing practices influence treatments. The excellent hillside spa is centred on a monk's cave and commands spectacular views. A range of exceptionally stylish rooms are available overlooking the small sandy bay. The service is unbeatable and both restaurant and poolside shalas offer detox specialities as well as indulgent delights at reasonable prices. Non-residents are welcomed. Recommended.

$$$$-$$$ Centara Villas Samui (formerly Central Samui Village), opposite the butterfly garden (see page 62), T077-424020, www.centarahotelsresorts.com. An unfortunate addition to this once-peaceful beach. The emphasis is on 'rustic' living, with 100 villas, set rather too close together in a tropical garden. 3 pools, spa, bikes for hire and beachside sports on offer. Well equipped.

Thong Krut
$$-$ Jinta Bungalow, T08-3105 9834 (mob), www.jintabeach.com. A small, friendly, family-run resort on a secluded

beach, with 5 bungalows and 7 small cottages. The white concrete bungalows look attractive from a distance, but are showing signs of decay on closer inspection. Still, at this price, it's hard to complain. Has a beachside pool and a bar with free Wi-Fi. Follow the signs to Coconut Village Resort and it's on your left.

$ Emerald Cove, 62 Moo 4 Taling Ngam, Phanga Beach, T077-334100, wesinac@ hotmail.com. Although isolated and poorly signposted, this attractive spot on the southwest corner of the island is worth seeking out. 10 en suite bungalows, with the more expensive rooms featuring a rock-lined bathroom, TV, fridge, kitchen sink and oddly dated decor. Recommended.

Koh Tan and Koh Matsum
You cannot stay on Koh Matsum. Charter a boat for ฿400.

$$-$ Coral Beach Bungalow, Koh Tan, T077-274100. Several attractive well-spaced wooden bungalows on a secluded beach varying in quality with some more substantial brick huts. There is an pretty garden and a restaurant serving Thai and Western dishes.

West coast *p63, map p58*
$$$$-$$$ Lipa Lodge, T077-485616, www.lipalodgeresort.com. These attractive white thatched bungalows with modern fittings are scattered around a lawn on a gorgeous beach. The restaurant (open 0800-2200) serves international cuisine.

$$$$-$$$ Lipa Lovely Resort (formerly Big John Resort & Seafood), 912 Moo 2, Lipanoi, T077-415537, www.thelipalovely resort.samuiwestcoast.com. Around 30 bungalows spread across 2 adjacent resorts, the garden rooms are a little over-priced and cramped. Most bungalows have a TV, DVD player, kitchen sink and fridge, and are set around a pool. The beach is not as attractive as that at **Lipa Lodge** up the coast.

$$$$-$$ Am Samui Resort (formerly the Wiesenthal Resort), 39 Moo 3 Taling Ngam, T077-235165, www.amsamuiresort.com. Standing out from its competitors to the west of the island, this quiet mid-range option is clean, excellent value, studded with palms and sits directly on an attractive beach with great views out to sea. The myriad spotless a/c bungalows, many with ocean views, have TVs and fridges. Recommended.

$$ Simple Life Bungalow, Tong Ta Node Beach, T077-334191. Offers 10 basic bungalows packed together but commanding a view of the small sweeping beach. Koh Matsum and Koh Tan can be seen from the shore. Rustic beach restaurant with bamboo furniture and simple fare. A 1-day snorkelling and fishing trip to Koh Tan is ฿850.

❻ Restaurants

Nathon *p59, map p58*
There are plenty of places to eat here, particularly good are the 'coffee shop' patisseries – there are a couple off the main road and some on the seafront. Seafood restaurants are also found on the seafront.

$$ Mai-Tai, 259/8 Moo 3, T077-236488. Open 0900-2100. German restaurant serving fantastic meats, sausages and cheeses, can also be bought by weight. The Hungarian goulash is admired by locals.

$$ Sunset, 175/3 Moo 3, T077-421244. Open 1000-2200. South end of town overlooking the sea. Great Thai food, especially the fish dishes.

$$-$ Coffee Island, opposite the pier, T077-423153. Open 0600-2400. Open-fronted café with very average coffee and a mix of Thai and Western food. A good place to wait for a ferry, but probably not worth going to otherwise. Also has cheap rooms upstairs (see Where to stay, page 64).

$ Mumthong 1, on the corner opposite the district office, one block inland from the pier, T077-420388. Open 0700-2200. Great little Thai restaurant catering to locals and foreigners. Avoid the Western food and stick to the local favourites. The roast duck is particularly good, as are the coconut shakes. Recommended.

$ Nathon Night Market, in front of the pier. Daily 1700-late. Full range of Thai street food at local prices.

$ RT Bakery. Wide range of international dishes. Great breakfasts, rolls and croissants.

$ Tang, near the market at the south end of main road. Serves up pizza, pasta, sandwiches and pastries.

North coast *p60, map p58*
Mae Nam

$$ Angela's Bakery, 64/29 Moo 1, opposite the police station on the main road, T077-427396. Open 0830-1600. Sells sandwiches, bagels, cakes and pretzels, and also has a deli offering cheeses and cold meat. Popular with foreigners.

$ Jae Mui, next to Mae Nam police station. Thu-Tue 0700-1400. The sign's in Thai and there's no English menu, but with a bit of improvisation and by pointing at some of the display pictures you can get what you want. The khao ka moo (rice with stewed pork leg) is a must.

Bophut

There are a number of restaurants that set up elaborate displays of local seafood. Naturally, the choice on offer varies from day to day. The choice has expanded astronomically over recent years, with a string of new eateries popping up, so below is just a selection.

$$$-$$ Happy Elephant, 79/1 Moo 1, on the beachfront, T077-245347. Open 1230-2200. A popular stop with travellers serving good seafood. The fish with ginger and mushroom sauce are delicious. Shark steaks and fondues also available. Staff cook on the street. Its speciality is hot stone steaks. There's a decent wine cellar.

$$$-$$ Karma Sutra, Fisherman's Village, opposite the pier, T077-425198,

www.karmasutrasamui.com. 0700-late. French owners Virginie and Laurant have injected plenty of style into this thoroughly chilled out bar/restaurant. Sample the Mediterranean plate or the Kobe beef carpaccio, but make sure you save room for dessert. Recommended.

$$$-$$ La Sirene, 65/1 Moo 1, T08-1797 3499 (mob). Open 1000-2300. A delightful little restaurant run by a friendly Frenchman. The seafood is fresh and locally caught and displayed outside the restaurant, the coffee is excellent too. French and Thai food offered. Recommended.

$$$-$$ Villa Bianca, 79/3 Moo 1, T077-245041. Open 1200-1500, 1800-2400. A good Italian-run restaurant in a romantic setting. Everything, even the ice cream, is made on the premises.

$$$-$$ Zazen Restaurant, Zazen Resort, T077-425085. A gourmet hot spot in Bophut with a Belgian chef serving up his signature 'organic and orgasmic' fusion cuisine. Candle-lit beachfront dining, excellent wine cellar.

$$ Alla Baia, 49/1 Moo 1, T077-245566. Open 1100-2300. Right on the seafront, this affordable Italian boasts impressive views of Koh Phangan in a delightful Mediterranean-style setting. Veteran chef Mario prepares his pasta and pizzas, and pulls in a good proportion of Bophut's hungry population.

$$ Restaurant Le Virage, 34/13 Moo 1, on the corner near the entrance to the Fisherman's Village, T08-7263 3497 (mob), www.restaurant-levirage-samui.com. This is something of an institution for French expats and tourists. The steaks and pizzas are excellent, but the specials board is where all the action's at. Most of the tables are on the outdoor terrace, and there's live jazz on Sun. Also has free Wi-Fi, a big screen and a pool table if you want to stay for more than just dinner.

$$ Starfish & Coffee, 51/7 Moo 1, T077-427201. Open 1100-0100. Another lovely setting for a meal or a quick drink on the outside terrace in this big airy building. Plenty of seafood and international cuisine in the maroon-themed restaurant with wrought-iron and leopard-print decor.

$$-$ The Love Kitchen, T077-430290, www.absoluteyogasamui.com. A recent addition to the healthy food scene. Delicious organic café, excellent juice bar, bakery and lounge.

$ Fisherman's Village Night Market, Fri 1700-late. The usually relaxed Fisherman's Village becomes a hive of activity with vendors selling all kinds of wonderful Thai and Western snacks. It's a little more expensive than most walking street markets, but the quality of food is unrivalled. Make sure you bring small money and a big appetite.

Big Buddha (Bang Rak)

$$$-$$ Oceans 11, Bang Rak, next to Shambala, T077-245134. Open 1400-2300. International, Thai and seafood. Great views of the sea and nearby islands from the balcony bar. Lunch, dinner and cocktails.

$$$-$ BBC (Big Buddha Café), 14/22 Moo 5, Ban Plai Laem, right next to the wat, T08-1788 9051 (mob), www.bbcrestaurant. com. 0900-2300. High-quality Thai and international food, reasonably priced in this island-style open-plan layout; an enjoyable place to sit and watch the sunset. BBC offers all-you-can eat BBQs and a full English Sun lunch.

$$ Antica Locanda, opposite Shambala, T077-245163, www.anticasamui.com. Tue-Sun 1300-2300. Italian owner, Stefano, serves up good-quality authentic Italian food, including delicious pizza and pasta dishes. Popular with the local expat community.

$ Elephant & Castle, 18 Moo 4. Open 0900-0200. Upholds the English tradition. Excellent choice of food.

Samrong Bay

$$$ Dining on the Rocks, Six Senses Samui. Eating here on a large wood platform is a fine dining experience with some of the most tantalizingly meals on the island. The 'Experiences' menu offers reduction of coconut and truffle with rosemary-roasted chicken. From the à la carte menu start with oysters in gazpacho followed by roasted duck with citrus and lavender and finish with jasmine tea chocolate pots. This is a wonderful gourmet experience with great wines on offer.

$$$-$$ O2 Beach Club, 6/14 Moo 5, T077-247958, www.o2beachclub.com/samui. Contemporary international cuisine with live entertainment nightly, set around a beachside pool. Bring your party hat.

Choeng Mon

Choeng Mon is blessed with a number of excellent eateries. This is a selection of the best.

$$$ Royal Siam Restaurant, Samui Peninsula Spa & Resort, T077-428100. Open 0630-2300. Dine in style at this superb location over-looking the infinity pool and the sea. The *gaeng poo*, blue crab curry with vermicelli, is absolutely delicious. Service is attentive but not intrusive.

$$$ Tongsai Bay, see Where to stay. This luxury hotel offers 3 restaurants, all of which are top notch. The decking – or 'Plaza' as they call it – of Chef Chom's restaurant has a marvellous view of the bay with space for 130 guests. There's a wide range of Thai dishes, all outstanding. It's less expensive than it has been, but it's still top end.

$$ Honey Seafood Restaurant, at the most easterly tip of the beach, T077-245032, www.honeyseafood.com. Great seafood. Recommended.

$$-$ Crystal, near the middle of the beach. 0830-2200. An extensive menu – almost 200 items – covering everything from burgers and BBQ to seafood and standard Thai fare. Try the seafood hot plate or the whole fried snapper (฿350).

$ O Soleil, towards the western end. 0730-2200. Open since 1988 and still good value for local specialities.

East coast *p61, map p58*

Chaweng

Chaweng offers a range of international restaurants as well as plenty of seafood. It also features many international food chains.

$$$ Betelnut Restaurant, 43/04 Moo 3, just over the road from **Central Samui Beach Resort**, T077-413370. Open 1800-2300. This small, exclusive restaurant serves fashionable Californian/Thai fusion cuisine that has locals and guests returning. Excellent food and service.

$$$ Hagi, Central Samui Beach Resort. Open 1800-2300. Japanese restaurant in sophisticated surroundings.

$$$ La Brasserie, Beachcomber Hotel, 3/5 Moo 2, T077-422041, www.beach comber-hotel.com. Open 0700-2230. Italian and Thai food. A pleasant beachfront experience, white-clothed tables are softened by night lanterns.

$$$ Poppies, see Where to stay. T077-422419, www.poppiessamui.com. An excellent Thai and international restaurant, one of the best on the beach. Live classical guitar accompaniment on Tue, Thu and Fri, and a Thai night on Sat. Booking recommended.

$$$ Prego, 155 Amari Palm Reef Resort (northern end of Chaweng Beach Rd), T077-422015, www.prego-samui.com. Upscale modern Italian. It's beside the road, not the beach, but has a sultry and atmospheric tone in the evenings, with tables arranged beneath and beside a low-lit, open-sided pavillion cooled by rotating oversize fans. Consistently good pizzas, seafood, risottos and pasta, plus an excellent wine list. Recommended.

$$$ Spice Island, part of the **Central Samui Beach Resort**. 1800-2230. Sit either in the a/c or the relaxing beachside part of the restaurant and try a wide range of excellent, sophisticated Thai dishes.

$$$ Vecchia Napoli, on the *soi* behind Starbucks, T077-231229, v.napoli@yahoo. it. 1200-2300. Beautifully decorated with a few tables spilling out from the airy interior onto the street. Friendly Italian owner who ensures his guests are happy. Always buzzing with Italians.

$$$ Zico's, 38/2 Moo 3, opposite **Central Samui Beach Resort**, T077-231560, www.zicossamui.com. 1800-2230. This 150-seater, predominantly BBQ, Brazilian restaurant is one of a wave of upmarket eateries. Contemporary Brazilian decor, roving musicians and waiters bring the action to the tables. Recommended, but be prepared to spend.

$$$-$$ The Three Monkeys, 13/11 Moo 2, Chaweng Beach Rd. 1030-0200. Great grub including chicken, salmon and beef dishes. The 'mango monkey' – marinated king prawns with a mango sauce – is filling and delicious. Canned Guinness, TV and a pool table available. Happy hour is 1430-1630 and there's free Wi-Fi.

$$ The Deck, Beach Rd. 0800-0200. Great location in the centre of the action and noise. Enjoy or tolerate the Fri night Elvis impersonator strutting his stuff in the **Quarterdeck** pub, opposite. Upstairs there's a great chilled-out drinking deck overlooking the main road with floor cushions to relax on. It serves Thai, Western and fusion dishes.

$$ Gringos Cantina, behind The Islander Restaurant, T077-413267. Authentic Tex Mex.

$$ The Islander, near SoiGreen Mango, T077-230836. Open 0800-0200. For anyone missing English dishes, this popular bar-cum-restaurant provides 'full-monty' breakfasts and roasts with all the trimmings on Sun, as well as pizzas, curry and lasagne.

$$ Mamma Roma, 155/30 Moo 2, T077-230649. Open 1100-2300. Notable for its signature pizza of tomato, cheese, ham, salami, olives and capers, which is tasty. There's also home-made pasta and seafood dishes, but these are expensive.

$$ Naam Jim Rim Talay (formerly Sandies), Silver Sand Resort, T077-422777. Daily 0800-2300. Good-quality Thai food at reasonable prices. Candle-lit tables by the beach provide a romantic setting, but the trance music blaring from next door's Monkey Bay Bar might be too much for some.

$$ Osteria, along from the **Chaweng Resort**, T077-422530. Open 0900-0100. Good pizza and pasta.

$$ Will Wait Bakery, T077-230093. Open 0700-0100. For excellent breakfast pastries or late-night snacks.

$$-$ Mitra Samui Restaurant, Pungbua Market. Has a different price for locals and foreigners, but is cheap nonetheless and is famous for offering some of the best seafood on the island. Try the whole deep-fried fish with garlic and chilli (฿300 for 800g) or the fried prawns with tamarind. Recommended.

$ Sojeng Kitchen, 155/9 Chaweng Beach, T08-1892 2841 (mob). Open 1000-2200. Opposite **My Friend Travel Agency**, offers tasty food at excellent prices.

Lamai

There are several seafood restaurants along the Lamai beach road offering a wide choice, although nowhere is particularly good and cheap. International cuisine is widely available along the road parallel to the beach in restaurants such as **Il Tempio**.

$$$ Sala Thai, T077-233180. Serves good Thai food, seafood, steaks and Italian, but it's overpriced.

$$ Will Wait Bakery, T077-424263. Delicious pastries, croissants and pizzas. A popular breakfast joint.

$$-$ The Spa, Spa Resort. An award-winning restaurant that serves a range of attractively presented vegetarian and Thai food, as well as detoxing/healthy specialities and great seafood. Well-priced menu, friendly service and a relaxed ambience. Recommended.

$ Jeerapa, 136/7 Moo 4, on Lamai Rd behind PTT petrol station, T077-963199. Open 0900-2230. Relaxed and unpretentious Thai restaurant offering cheap, quality food. Stuff-on-rice starts from ฿40. There are also some Western offerings on the menu, but these are best avoided. Good fruit shakes.

$ Scoops124/524 Unit 10 Moo 3, T08-9909 8563, www.scoopsamui.com. Roadside ice cream parlour serving smoothies, milkshakes and coffee as well as the obvious. The ice cream cakes are especially good. Free Wi-Fi.

West coast *p63, map p58*

There are 2 restaurants in Ban Hua Thanon. Try **Hua Thanan** for seafood or **Aow Thai**, T077-418348, for northeastern Thai food.

$$ Les Voiles Rouges, Thong Krut, about half way down the beach, T08-1077 6574 (mob). Open 1200-2000. French owner, Gerard, has been on Samui for 7 years, but only opened this tastefully relaxed restaurant in late 2010. It has gorgeous views over the bay towards the mainland, friendly service and well-priced food considering the quality. Longtail boats are available to charter from right in front.

$ Big John Seafood Restaurant, Lipa Lovely Resort, near the old car ferry, see Where to stay, page 72. Away from the frenetic buzzing of Chaweng and Lamai, this is a great place for food and ambience. The sunsets are arguably the best on the island and you can dine inside listening to live music and the lobsters are enormous. There's a free pickup service to and from your hotel within a 10-km range.

Bars and clubs

North coast *p60, map p58*
Bophut
Billabong Surf Club, 79/2 Moo 1, T077-430 144. A full-on Aussie sports bar with TVs and sports pictures plastering the wall and a small balcony for drinking.

Frog and Gecko, 91/2 Moo 1, T077-425248. Open 1200-0200. The first of several English pubs/sports bars on the beachfront run by Graham and Raphaela. The music and Thai food is good. They show all major sporting events on a big screen, as well as recent movies. The pool table is ฿20 a game. Pub quiz Wed nights at 2000. Popular.

The Tropicana, T077-425304. With large fish tanks built into the walls, The Tropicanaca makes a refreshing change from the popular sports bars. It's run by friendly Paul and Lek.

East coast *p61, map p58*
Chaweng

Usually revellers end up on Soi Green Mango, a U-shaped warren of mega-clubs and 'come-hither' girly-bars. The island's hedonistic nerve centre, it's also home to a handful of go-go bars.

Green Mango, at the rear of Soi Green Mango, www.thegreenmangoclub.com. Cavernous and run down, this humungous warehouse – the island's oldest mega-club – throbs nightly with 2 zones of house and hip-hop. Sunburnt farang rock up in their hundreds to sway until the lights come up (and lots of working girls tend to follow). You'll love it or hate it.

Q-BAR, T081-9562742, www.qbarsamui.com. Upscale nightclub high on the hillside north of Chaweng Lake. Best to leave the motorbike at home; the way down after a few drinks can be deadly.

The Reggae Pub, Chaweng lagoon, T077-422331, www.reggae-pub.com. This huge bar, club and live music destination a little out of town is popular as a party destination, but pick your night as sometimes it's more techno than reggae.

Sound Pub, close to **Green Mango**. Classier than the rest of the bars on this street, which are mainly girly joints. There's a DJ and tables.

Sweet Soul Café, Soi Green Mango. A smaller, more stylish alternative to Green Mango that attracts a more diverse crowd: legit locals as well as tourists.

Tropical Murphys, 14/40 Chaweng Rd, T077-413614, www.tropicalmurphys.com. Open 0900-0200. Opposite McDonald's

in Central Chaweng. An Irish pub with live music most nights and Tue night pub quizzes.

Lamai

It might be more laidback than Chaweng, but Lamai is no straight-laced early sleeper. There are lots of European-style pubs and bars, beachfront restaurants and, depressingly, girls on stools itching to spout the well-worn patter.

Shamrock Irish Pub, 124/144 Moo 3, T081-5978572, www.thesamuishamrock.com. Pretty much what you would expect. Has a good range of international beers – including Guinness and Kilkenny on tap – and authentic pub grub, and shows most major international sporting events. Live music every night from 2130.

⊕ Entertainment

East coast *p61, map p58*
Chaweng

Cabaret Moulin Rouge (formerly Christy's). If you fancy sampling some of Thailand's drag cabaret acts then this is the place to go. 3 nightly performances starting from 2000. Free entry but expensive drinks.
Star, 200/11 Chaweng Rd. A rival to **Moulin Rouge**. Puts on a pretty hilarious katoey (ladyboy) show with audience participation, a lot of feathers and make-up at 2030 and 2200 nightly. No admission charge; customers must buy drinks. Recommended.
Muay Thai (Thai boxing) Chaweng Stadium, T077-413504, free transfers. 8 fights from 2100.

Lamai

Buffalo fighting In the stadium at the north end (and several others around the island). Far tamer than it sounds, animals are rarely injured in the 'fights' and it's more a show of tradition than a fierce face-off. Ask at your hotel for date of the next event.
Muay Thai (Thai boxing) At Lamai's new stadium. Fights 2-3 times weekly during high season, ฿500.

⚙ Shopping

Nathon *p59, map p58*
Nathon is a good centre for shopping on the island. It is worth a visit to browse through the stalls and take a walk down the main road, past the fresh market on the left and on down to the 'hardware' market on the right. The stalls provide the usual T-shirts, CDs/DVDs, watches and handicrafts. The inner road – Angthong Rd – is worth walking down too.

North coast *p60, map p58*
Bophut
There are a number of shops along the main road of Bophut. There is a good German, English and French bookshop, and shops selling art, gifts, clothes and produce from around Thailand, Laos and Cambodia.

East coast *p61, map p58*
Chaweng
The main shopping centre on the island, Chaweng caters for the visiting crowds, providing necessities in the supermarkets, pharmacies and opticians, along with plenty of tourist tat and upmarket designer clothes/swimwear stores. A plethora of tailors pepper Chaweng, including **Armani International Suits**, **Joop!** and **Baron Fashion**.

There is a wide range of shops along the beach road, where most things can be bought. Many places remain open until late. There is the usual array of tourist shops selling beachwear, T-shirts, jewellery and handicrafts. A number of minimarts are scattered along the main road and the British-owned pharmacy chain, **Boots**. **Bookazine**, which sells newspapers, magazines and books, is next to Tropical Murphy's. For genuine branded surfwear, including Quiksilver and Roxy, try the shops next to McDonald's in the centre of town.

Lamai
Jewellery, beachwear and clothing boutiques are along the main road.

⚙ What to do

There are now numerous activities, including horse riding, elephant trekking, jungle canopy rides, training to be a sealion trainer, sail boat tours, snorkelling, kayaking, cooking classes, even football golf. See flyers, tour agents and adverts in the free visitors' guides.

The best time for **diving** is Apr and the best water is to be found around Koh Tao, Tan, Matsum and the Marine Park. Visibility is obviously variable, depending on the weather. Most of the schools dotted around the island organize all dive courses. PADI Open Water courses cost around ฿15,500. There is a hyperbaric chamber at Big Buddha.

Spas and **massage** places have mushroomed in the last few years. There are some gorgeous spas attached to hotels as well as day spas. Treatments vary in prices and scope.

Nathon *p59, map p58*
Spas and therapies
Samui Dharma Healing Centre, 63 Moo Tee 1, Ao Santi Beach, near Nathon, T077-234170, www.dharmahealingintl.com. Alternative health programmes to inspire and rejuvenate. 7- to 21-day fasting courses are directed according to Dharma Buddhist principles in alternative health: fasting, colonic irrigation, yoga, reflexology, iridology and many other therapies. Accommodation is available.

Tour operators
There are many travel agents cluttered along the seafront (particularly around the pier) and main roads, providing ticketing and tours.

Ang Thong Marine National Park *p60*
Tour operators
National park tax (฿200) is included in all tour prices. Operators include **Big John**, T077-42174, and **Seatran**, T077-426000.

North coast *p60, map p58*
Cookery courses
Blue Banana, 2 Moo 4, Big Buddha Beach, T077-245080. Classes with 'Toy'.

Diving
Aquademia, Bophut, T08-1091 0107 (mob), www.aquademiadive.com.

Bo Phut Diving School, next to Eden Bungalows, Bophut, T077-425496, www.bophut diving.com. Also offers snorkelling trips.

Easy Divers, Big Buddha, T077-413373, www.easydivers-thailand.com.

One Hundred Degrees East, 23/2 Moo 4 Big Buddha Beach (in front of Ocean's 11 restaurant), T077-245 936, www.100 degreeseast.com. Professional and friendly outfit.

Paradise Beach Resort, Mae Nam, www.samuiparadisebeach.com. One of many resorts offering diving.

Samui International Diving School, Big Buddha, 30/1 Moo 4, T08-9772 4002 (mob), www.dial-samui.com.

Fishing and watersports
Fishing and snorkelling are organized by most accommodation providers as well as individual tour operators scattered throughout the village of Bophut.

Golf
Minigolf International, Choeng Mon, T08-1787 9148 (mob), www.minigolf samui.com. 0900-1830. 18 tracks in Ban Plailaem, near Choeng Mon.

Santiburi Golf, Mae Nam, T077-421700, www.santiburi.com. An 18-hole course that opened in 2003. Designed by Pirapon Namatra and Edward Thiele. Green fees, ฿3350. Hotel guests enjoy a 20% discount.

Spas and therapies
Absolute Sanctuary, 88 Moo 5, Bophut, T077-601190, www.absolutesanctuary.com. A Moroccan-inspired detox and yoga resort.

Tour operators
Tours Koh Samui, 24/3 Moo 5 Choeng Mon Beach Rd, Bophut, T077-961911, T08-1396 8383 (mob), www.tourskohsamui. com. Over 10 years' experience. Snorkelling, island safaris, game fishing, kayaking and more. Also offer tailor-made tours.

East coast *p61, map p58*
Bungee jumping
Sami Bungy Jump and Entertainment Complex, Reggae Pub Rd, Chaweng, T077-414252, T08-1891 3314 (mob), www.samuibungy.com. Daily from 1000. Offers hourly jumps (50 m), huge pool and sun lounge area.

Cookery courses
Samui Institute of Thai Culinary Arts, Chaweng, T077-413172, www.sitca.net. Thai cooking and fruit- and vegetable-carving courses. All equipment is provided, and you can keep the recipes. The lunchtime cooking class costs ฿1850 per person, the evening class ฿1850 per person. Carving courses (6 hrs of lessons over 3 days) are ฿4950 per person. To get there, get dropped off at (or walk to) the **Central Samui Beach Resort** on Chaweng Beach. Walk up the side street for about 150 m across from the **Central** with **Classic Gems** jewellery store at the corner. The Institute is on the right side.

Diving
Blue Planet, near Samui International Hospital, Chaweng, and in central Lamai, T077-413106, www.blueplanetdivecentre. com. Have their own accommodation.

Calypso Diving, southern end of Chaweng beach, T077-422437, www.calypso-diving.com.

Discovery Dive Centre, Amari Palm Reef Resort, T077-413196, www.discovery divers.com.

The Dive Shop, central Chaweng Beach Rd, Chaweng, T077-230232, www.the diveshop.net.

Easy Divers, head office, Chaweng, T077-413373, www.easydivers-thailand.com.

Easy Divers, near **Lamai Resort** (north end of Lamai beach), T077-231990, www.easy divers-thailand.com. German, English and Swedish spoken.

Samui International Diving School, Chaweng Beach Rd, Chaweng, T077-413050, www.planet-scuba.net.

Mountain biking

Red Bicycle, T08-4305 2107 (mob), www.redbicycle.org. Hires bikes and offers guided trips.

Watersports

Masks and fins can be hired from most bungalows in Chaweng. For diving, see above.

Blue Stars Sea Kayaking, Chaweng Beach Rd, T077-413231, www.bluestars.info.

Coco Splash Waterpark, Lamai, T08-1082 6035, www.samuiwaterpark.com. Tue-Sun 1030-1730. Small, but inexpensive and should keep the kids entertained for a couple of hours at least.

Samui Ocean Sports, on the beach at **Chaweng Regent Hotel**, Chaweng, T08-1940 1999 (mob), www.samui.sawadee. com/oceansports. Offers a wide range of activities and lessons: kayaking, snorkelling, windsurfing, catsailing and yachting.

Tan Speed Project, in front of Banana fan. Offer banana boats, ฿400 per person per 15 mins.

Treasure Island, behind the **Islander Restaurant**, Chaweng, T077-413267. Open 1100-2400. Kayaking.

Spas and therapies

It's boom time for any kind of healing centre and Chaweng has not missed a trick here. As well as several spas within hotels, there are some independent establishments in town.

Four Seasons Tropical Spa, next to the Baan Samui Resort, close to McDonald's,

T077-414141, www.spafourseasons.com. A recommended relaxing experience.

Spa Resort, Lamai, T077-230855, www. spasamui.com, at the north end of the beach with a sister resort in the hills. See Where to stay, page 70. Offers 'exotic rejuvenation', anything from a herbal steam room to a 'liver flush fast' as well as yoga, t'ai chi and meditation. Day visitors are welcomed. A 3½-day fast costs ฿12,000.

Tamarind Springs, 205/7 Thong Takian, Lamai, T077-230571, www.tamarindsprings. com. 1000-2000. Just up the hill from Spa Samui is possibly the island's most relaxing and authentic spa in a spectacular natural setting. Treatment packages include body scrubs and a variety of massages, which include the divine combination of herbal spa and waterfall dip pool.

Tour operators

There are dozens along Chaweng Beach Rd.

Blue Stars, 83/23 Moo.2, Chaweng Lake Rd, T077-961911/413231, www.bluestars.info. Daily kayaking and snorkelling tours of the caves and hidden lagoons at Ang Thong Marine National Park. Free early morning pickup from your hotel.

Travel Solutions, Chaweng, T077-230203, www.travelsoultions.co.th. Down the side of **The Pizza Company** opposite the **Baan Samui Resort**. Highly recommended, Western-Thai run business with over 13 years' of experience in the industry. Trustworthy information and travel advice/ bookings.

South coast *p62, map p58*
Rum tasting

Magic Alambic Rum Distillery, 44/5 Moo 3 Namnuang, T08-6282 6230 (mob), www. rhumdistillerie.com. Run by French couple, Elissa and Michel, this small distillery has been turning sugar cane into magical alcoholic concoctions since 2003. They produce 4 flavours of rum – natural, lemon, orange and coconut – plus a premium blend. You can sample them for ฿50 per glass, or purchase by the bottle. Tours available.

Therapies

Kamalaya, 102/9 Moo 3, Laem Set Rd, Laem Set, T077-429800, www.kamalaya. com.

The latest addition to Samui's sophisticated holistic spa scene, **Kamalaya** offers non-residents access to its healing events as well as yoga, t'ai chi, cleanses, massage and oriental and Western healing practices at its stunning hillside spa. See also Where to stay, page 71.

Watersports

Jetskis, windsurfing and snorkelling equipment is available for hire at the southern end of the beach.

⊖ Transport

Koh Samui *p56, maps p58*
Air

Koh Samui Airport, www. samuiairportonline.com, is privately owned by **Bangkok Airways** (at the airport, T077 601300, and at southern end of Chaweng, T077-422512, www. bangkokair.com), which accounts for the inflated airport international departure tax (฿700); domestic departure tax is ฿300 and should be included in the ticket price. There are multiple daily connections to **Bangkok** with Bangkok Airways, Air Berlin, Finnair, KLM, Air France, EVA Air and Etihad, and regular flights to **Phuket**, **U-Tapao** (Pattaya), **Krabi** and **Chiang Mai** with Bangkok Airways. Etihad and Finnair also fly to Singapore, while Malaysia Airlines, Firefly and Berjaya Air fly to Kuala Lumpur.

Boat

There are numerous daily boat options. Schedules, journey times and prices change according to the season. Tickets from travel agents will cost more but include scheduling advice and transfers. See Transport sections for **Surat Thani**, **Koh Phangan** and **Koh Tao** for boat services to Samui.

Lomprayah, T077-427765, www. lomprayah.com, operates a daily catamaran service from Nathon pier to Koh Phangan (฿300), Koh Tao (฿600) and Chumpon (฿1100), and has recently started a service to Surat Thani (฿450) via Don Sak (which takes longer than the advertised 45 mins). It also sells combined bus/boat tickets to Hua Hin (฿1400) and Bangkok (฿1400). Prices include transfer to the pier.

Songserm Travel, on the seafront in Nathon, T077-420157, www.songserm-expressboat.com, office hours 0800-1800, runs express passenger boats departing daily from the southern pier in Nathon to **Surat Thani**, 0800 and 1300, 2½ hrs, ฿300, and to **Koh Phangan** 1100, 40 mins, ฿250, continuing on to **Koh Tao**, 2½ hrs, ฿400. Be aware that snacks and drinks on board are horribly overpriced, so it is best to come prepared. They can also arrange connecting train tickets from Surat Thani up to Bangkok. For the latest schedules call their helpful Bangkok office, T022-808073, daily 0900-2000.

Seatran, office on pier, T077-426000, www.seatranferry.com, daily 0500-1700, operates large, comfortable a/c boats to **Surat Thani** from the main northerly pier in Nathon hourly 0500-1800 with the bus arriving in Surat Thani 2½ hrs later, ฿240, including bus. Also has 2 daily departures, 0800 and 1330 to **Koh Phangan** (฿250), **Koh Tao** (฿550), **Chumphon** (฿900), **Hua Hin** (฿900) and **Bangkok** (฿1000). Price includes transfer from hotel to Bang Ruk pier.

Night ferries leave Nathon at 2100, arriving in **Surat Thani** at around 0300/0400, ฿350. Get to the pier early during high season as places are limited and

Road madness on Samui, Phangan and Tao

By some measures, Thailand has the world's highest death rate on the roads. Koh Samui has the highest rate in Thailand and accidents, fatal and otherwise, are certainly horrifyingly common. (The islands are full of walking wounded wearing bandages on their arms legs and faces). There are several reasons for this state of affairs:

→ narrow and impossibly steep roads
→ poorly maintained vehicles/machines
→ visitors unused to driving on the left
→ visitors unused to driving in Thailand.
→ locals driving without lights
→ visitors drink-driving or on drugs

First-time riders can be absolutely fine when bowling along most of the time, however, should something happen ahead that makes an emergency stop necessary, they simply don't have the natural reflexes to handle their bikes appropriately

This means that visitors should be careful when driving on the islands and make sure that they test their motorbike or car before completing a rental agreement. It is also advised that people do not leave their passports as collateral. Should there be an accident, it leaves the renter of the vehicle at the mercy of its owner.

For more details on driving in Thailand see page 8.

demand is high. The boats will not leave in severe weather.

The **Raja** ferry leaves from the Tong Yang pier, south of Nathon, to **Don Sak**, ฿150. To get to Tong Yang, take a *songthaew* from Nathon or the beaches.

Haad Rin Queen, T077-375113, departs from Big Buddha Pier to Hat Rin on **Koh Phangan** at 1030, 1300, 1600, 1830, 50 mins, ฿200.

Speed Boat Line has departures from Bophut to Thong Sala on **Koh Phangan** at 0430, 0900, 1200 and 1430, 20 mins, ฿400. Speed boats from **Big Buddha Pier**, next to 7/11, go to Hat Rin on **Koh Phangan** at 1030, 1300, 1600 and 1830, 50 mins, ฿150. Boats from **Petcherat Marina**, 82/1 Moo 4, Bophut, T077-425262, www.samuispeed boat.com, go to Hat Rin on **Koh Phangan**, every full moon, 1700-2400 hourly, 30 mins, ฿1000 return. Boats leave when full and return from Koh Phangan 0100-0800. Make sure the boat you board does not exceed capacity and has lifejackets. (In Jan 2005 an overloaded boat capsized with the loss of more than a dozen lives.)

Bus
There are several buses that leave Surat Thani for the overnight trip to **Bangkok**, and also to Phuket or pretty much anywhere else in the south of Thailand or in to Malaysia. Ask the tour operators or an agency on the island.

Car and motorbike hire
This is cheaper from the town of Nathon than on the beaches. Motorbikes cost ฿150-200 per day, and around ฿250 for an automatic, not including insurance, although the price is negotiable if you rent for several days. Helmets must be provided. The fine for not wearing one is ฿200-500. If you are serious about doing a fair bit of riding, it is worth bringing a good helmet from home along with you; the ones provided will often do little to protect you in the event of a bad smash.

Jeep/car hire is ฿800-1000 per day, including insurance or ฿1000-1800 if you hire from an international company such as **Budget** (see box, above, for cautions about driving).

Motorbike taxi

These are available all over the island. They wait in clusters and the drivers wear coloured cloth jackets. Be prepared to bargain hard; as a rough guide: **Nathon–Chaweng**, ฿150-180. **Bophut– Chaweng**, ฿100. **Nathon–Maenam**, ฿100.

Taxi

Expensive yellow meter taxis cruise the island all day. They are scarce after 0100 but any bar or hotel owner will know one. The taxis do not use their meters, which may be fixed anyway. The minimum fare is ฿50. Fares vary according to the time of day. On average, a fare from **Nathon** or **Bophut** to **Chaweng** is ฿500. The majority of taxis are to be found in Chaweng. A taxi can be chartered for ฿400 per hr.

Train

Travel agencies in town can provide details and tickets that combine the boat from Samui, the bus from Don Sak to the railway station and the train ticket.

❶ Directory

Koh Samui *p56, maps p58*

Medical services 24-hr emergency clinic and the **Samui International Hospital**, Chaweng, T077-422272, www.sih. co.th (also has a dental clinic). It is best to take injured people to the hospital; the ambulance service can be slow. A reasonable level of English is spoken. In **Bophut**, there is **Bandon International Hospital**, T077-245236, www.bandon hospital.com. In **Big Buddha**, Hyperbaric Services, 34/8 Moo 4, at Big Buddha, T077-427427, T08-1084 8485 (mob), www. ssnsnetwork.com. **Police** Tourist police, 3 km south of Nathon, T077-4212815, open 24 hrs, past turning to Hin Lad Waterfall. T1169 emergency, T191 police.

Koh Phangan

Koh Phangan is Southeast Asia's party island. World renowned for the Full Moon Party, it attracts thousands of young people looking for the night of their life on the sands at Hat Rin, the most developed part of the island. The pace of development on the island has been rapid. Although still unspoilt in part, in the main it is not as beautiful as parts of Koh Samui and Koh Tao, although the beaches at Hat Rin and some along the east coast are attractive and – except for Hat Rin – uncrowded. The water is good for snorkelling, particularly during the dry season when clarity is at its best. Boats leave from Thong Sala, the island's main town, for nearby Ang Thong Marine National Park (see page 60). Between May and September the tide is out all day between Mae Hat and Hat Rin. Fishing and coconut production remain mainstays of the economy, and villages still have a traditional air – although tourism is now by far the largest single industry.

Arriving on Koh Phangan

Getting there

There is no airport on the island so everyone arrives by boat. There are daily ferries from Don Sak Pier and Bandon near Surat Thani on the mainland and also from the larger, neighbouring island of Koh Samui and its northerly neighbour, Koh Tao. Minibus taxis meet the boats and take people from Thong Sala pier to Hat Rin for ฿150 and to Thong Nai Pan for ฿200. Although most boats dock at the pier at Thong Sala, there's also a ferry, the *Haad Rin Queen*, T077-375113, that goes from **Big Buddha pier** on Samui straight to Hat Rin. The quickest way to Koh Phangan is to fly from Bangkok to Koh Samui and then to catch an express boat from Samui to Koh Phangan, though this is considerably more expensive than the alternative of flying to Surat Thani and taking a boat from there. ▸▸ *See Transport, page 101, for further information.*

Getting around

Koh Phangan stretches 15 km north to south and 10 km east to west. The main settlement is Thong Sala. Thong Sala and Hat Rin are connected by a paved road. Two roads run between Thong Sala and Ao Chao Lok Lum: the west coast route and the one through the centre of the island. Around the remainder of the island there is a limited network of poor roads and tracks, and the stretch from Ban Khai to Hat Rin is steep and treacherous and inadvisable for anything but a 4WD during the rainy season. The number of accidents is huge.

There are some parts of Koh Phangan that are difficult or impossible to access by road, especially during the wet season. It is possible to travel by boat, though this convenience comes at a cost. Longtail boats are the most common way to navigate Koh Phangan's waters, and are available from all main beaches. As a general guide, they leave Hat Rin to: Thong Sala, ฿1500; Hat Thian, ฿600; Thong Nai Pan, ฿1800; Bottle Beach, ฿2000. You can also charter the boats on full day trips starting from around ฿3000, depending on which/ how many beaches you would like to visit. Be aware that these prices are for the whole boat, so the larger the group the lower the cost per person. Also note that the prices are only a guide of what is reasonable to pay – be prepared to bargain hard to get these fares. Speed boats are also available to charter, and while significantly faster, will cost about three times as much as a longtail.

Motorbikes and mountain bikes are available for hire, and the most appealing areas to ride are in the north and west of the island, which are flat. *Songthaews* run from the pier to any of the bays served by road. A trip to Hat Rin from Thong Sala is ฿80-100. The cost to the other bays depends on how many people are going with you. At Hat Rin *songthaews* wait close to the **Drop in Club Resort** between Hat Rin East and West. For a few beaches walking is the best option. See also box on road madness, page 82.

Tourist information

There is no official tourist information on the island. The **TAT** on Koh Samui, see page 58, is responsible. See www.kohphangan.com and www.phangan.info, for information.

Around the island → *For listings, see pages 90-102.*

Koh Phangan offers natural sights such as waterfalls, forests, coral and viewpoints but little of historical or cultural interest. Sometimes the best way to explore the island is on foot, following tracks that link the villages and beaches, which cannot be negotiated by *songthaew* or motorbike. It is possible to walk on a trail from Hat Rin up the east coast to Hat Thien, although other paths are swiftly swallowed up by the forest.

Although it's possible to navigate the roads by motorbike, first-timers should think seriously before heading southeast to Hat Rin, as the roads are often at a 40° gradient which makes them treacherous at best and a death trap when wet. The high number of walking wounded is testimony to the danger of these hilly roads.

Thong Sala and around
The main town of Koh Phangan is the port of Thong Sala (pronounced Tong-sala) where most boats from Koh Samui, Surat Thani and Koh Tao dock. Thong Sala has banks, ATMs,

Koh Phangan

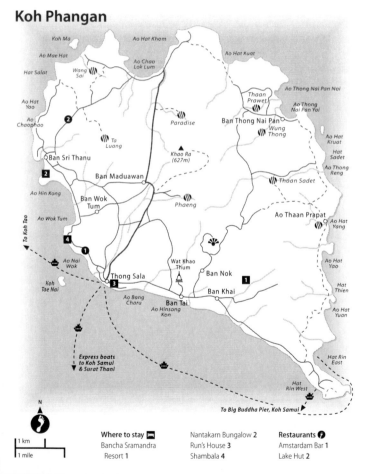

Where to stay		Restaurants
Bancha Sramandra Resort 1	Nantakarn Bungalow 2	Amsterdam Bar 1
	Run's House 3	Lake Hut 2
	Shambala 4	

telephone, internet access, travel agents, a small supermarket, dive shops, motorbike hire and a second-hand bookstore. Humming during the day with all the departures and arrivals, this can be a bit of a ghost town during the evenings, although it's a pleasant place to spend the night, with some good restaurants.

On the coast to the east of Thong Sala, outside Ban Tai, is **Wat Khao Tum** and the **Vipassana Meditation Centre** ① *all-inclusive fees are ฿4500 for 10 days, contact Wat Khao Tum, Koh Phangan, Surat Thani, for more information, or www.watkowtahm.org, where they provide a contact and booking facility*. There are views from the hilltop wat to Samui and the Ang Thong Islands. Ten-day meditation courses are held every month with 20-day courses and three-month retreats also available. All the courses are conducted in English and taught by Australian-US couple Rosemary and Steve Weissman who have been here since 1988.

The interior
Phaeng Waterfall is to be found in the interior of the island, about 4.5 km from Thong Sala and 2 km from the village of Maduawan. The walk east to Hat Sadet runs parallel to a river along which are three waterfalls and the carved initials of several Thai kings who visited here, including King Chulalongkorn (Rama V), who was so enamoured that he reportedly came here on 10 occasions between 1888 and 1909, and the present King Bhumibol (Rama IX), who came in 1962. The waterfalls can be reached on foot or on mountain bikes. Other waterfalls include **Ta Luang** and **Wang Sai** in the northwest corner, **Paradise** in the north (near the **Paradise Resort**), and **Thaan Prawet** and **Wung Thong** in the northeast corner. The highest point is **Khao Ra** (627 m). A path runs to the summit although visitors have reported that the trail is indistinct and a guide is necessary.

South coast
The stretch of beach from **Ao Bang Charu** to **Ao Hinsong Kon** is unpopular with visitors due to its proximity to Thong Sala and as a result accommodation is good value and bungalows are well spread out and quiet. The beach shelves gently and is good for children, but the water is a little murky.

The beach between **Ban Tai** and **Ban Khai** may not be as good as at Hat Rin and there is a lot of wood debris about, but this is more than made up for by cheaper accommodation and less noise. Some snorkelling and good swimming is possible and it is generally quiet, although on the monthly black moon parties the beach comes alive with techno beats. The area is also well-located for the twice-monthly half moon parties in the nearby jungle and the Wat Po herbal sauna. In July and August the tide is out all day.

Hat Rin
Hat Rin is home to the world-famous Full Moon Parties when thundering bass-lines rock the beach and the streets are awash with alcohol (see box, next page). There are also Half Moon Parties, Black Moon Parties, Pre-Full Moon Parties – in fact any excuse for a party – on the beach so it has become famous for the almighty blow outs.

Hat Rin is at the southeastern tip of Koh Phangan and has the best and most popular beach on the island with some good snorkelling. It also has the greatest concentration of bungalows which are packed close together (except on the hillsides). The 'east' beach, **Hat Rin Nok**, is more attractive and is cleaned every morning. During the day it is packed with sunbathers, coloured blow-up lilos, a small number of hawkers, volleyball nets, and the water is crammed with long-tailed boats. The 'west' beach, **Hat Rin Nai**, is smaller and almost non-existent at high tide; accommodation is slightly cheaper here. The two beaches,

Full Moon Parties

The Full Moon Parties, which have been going since 1989, are now accompanied by Half and Black Moon Parties, Saturday Night Parties and Pre-Full Moon Parties. Unfortunately, over the past few years rape and violent robbery have badly tarnished the friendly party atmosphere. Of course, many people do attend without any problems but caution is highly recommended as Thai criminal gangs now seem to be targeting party goers. There have also been several stories of post-party boats to Koh Samui being dangerously overloaded, and it is recommended that you avoid these boats completely.

On full moon night, if you are not planning to party till dawn, it is advisable to stay on Hat Rin West or elsewhere on the island, unless you feel you can sleep to the boom of the bass from the beach. Up to 10,000 people turn up on Hat Rin East every month to dance to the excellent music, watch the jugglers, fire eaters and fireworks displays and drink themselves into oblivion. Even the dogs take part as partygoers paint their pooches in psychedelic paint!

Tips for the party

→ Don't bring valuables with you; if a safety deposit box is an option at your bungalow, leave everything there. Don't leave anything of value in bungalows that are easily broken into. Reportedly it's a big night for burglars.

→ Do not eat or drink anything that is offered by strangers.

→ Wear shoes. The beach gets littered with broken glass and some people suffer serious injury from this.

→ If you lose your brain and your way (and a lot of people do) carry the business (name) card of your bungalow to show sober folk once you've left the party.

→ Don't take drugs. It's not worth the risk. At almost every party plainclothes policemen take a number of Westerners down to the jail from where they will only be released on bail if they can pay the fine. Otherwise they will be held for five to six weeks prior to trial.

Further information can be found on the following websites: www.fullmoon. phangan.info; www.halfmoonfestival. com; and www.kohphangan.com.

less than 10 minutes' walk apart, are both wonderfully quiet until about 1300, as most people are sleeping off the night's excesses. At night the noise from generators and the bars can be overpowering on Hat Rin Nok but a few minutes' walk away from the action towards Hat Rin Nai, the music, incredibly, is inaudible – this applies on full moon nights too. Theft has become a real problem in the area, use safety deposit boxes for valuables and secure bungalows with extra locks wherever possible – especially when sleeping.

East coast

These beaches and coves form **Hat Thien to Hat Sadet** are only accessible by boat. The stretch of stony coastline at Hat Thien doesn't afford much for those hoping to lie and fry, but its rocky, tree-lined character makes it an attractive and rugged area. It's not a bad option at all: there are cheap guesthouses and it's possible to walk over the headland to Hat Yuan where the beautiful and popular white-sand beach is much more palatable to sun worshippers.

Ao Thong Nai Pan Noi and **Ao Thong Nai Pan Yai** is a double bay boasting some of the most beautiful, quiet, white-sand beaches on the island, romantically hemmed in by the mountains and with among the highest recurring visitor rates. The attractive beach is topped by boulders at its northern end, hiding the enormous Santhiya resort spread up the hill beyond. Yai has more palms leaning over the beach and so is slightly more picturesque than Noi, but Noi has a wider beach and is a bit more bustling. There are several shops, ATMs and bars behind Noi beach and bikes can be rented. There's also internet, snorkel gear and kayaks for hire on the beach. It is said to have been Rama V's favourite beach on the island, and it's not hard to see why – plenty of people come here for a short holiday and end up staying for months. It remains fairly off the beaten tourist track and is more a place to relax for those whose main aim is not to party. The journey by truck from Thong Sala takes almost an hour and the road is muddy in the rainy season, but it does take you through untouched jungle and so is quite an experience. It is also possible to get a boat from Hat Rin which is much more comfortable.

North coast
About 5 km northwest of Thong Nai Pan, **Ao Hat Kuat**, more commonly known by its English translation 'Bottle Beach', is even more isolated, with a beautiful beach. Despite developing a reputation as a bit of a British ghetto and a huge new development here, it retains its escapist appeal.

Along a rutted track, **Ao Hat Khom** is another relaxed place and many stay for weeks. The bay is fringed by a reef offering some of the best snorkelling on Phangan, however, because the seabed shelves gently, swimming is sometimes only really possible at high tide and getting out to the reef can be tricky.

Ao Chao Lok Lum is a deep, sheltered bay on Koh Phangan's north coast. There is now an excellent road from Thong Sala to here and this fishing village is gradually developing into a quiet, comparatively refined resort, with the best part of the beach being to the east. In the village of Ban Chao Lok Lum there are bikes and diving equipment for rent. There's also a **7-11** shop and an ATM.

Hat Salat is one of the most peaceful parts of the island, though due to its picturesque bay it is also one of the fastest-developing spots. **Ao Mae Hat** has a super beach with a sandy bank extending outwards and along which it is possible to walk to Koh Ma when it hasn't rained for some time. There are palm trees, a few bungalows and good snorkelling.

West coast
Ao Hat Yao is an attractive curved, clean beach on the west coast with good swimming and snorkelling, 20 minutes by *songthaew* from Thong Sala. Bungalows are spread out and quiet.

To the south of Ao Hat Yao, **Ao Chaophao** is a relatively quiet and undeveloped bay with just a handful of places to stay. The perfect crescent of sand and sunsets make the bay particularly attractive. There is also good swimming because the seabed shelves steeply before reaching the reef around 100 m offshore where there is good snorkelling. At the southern end is an attractive lagoon and the coast here also has some remnant mangroves.

Ao Sri Thanu is a long but rather narrow beach, 15 minutes by *songthaew* from Thong Sala. It is a peaceful spot to spend a few days and is sparsely settled but is not very attractive. Behind the beach is a freshwater lake fringed by pine trees which is ideal for swimming.

North of Thong Sala and south of Ban Sri Thanu, the beaches at **Ao Wok Tum** are average and the swimming is poor. Accommodation is good value though.

North of Thong Sala and south of Ban Sri Thanu, the beaches between **Ao Hin Kong** and **Ao Nai Wok** aren't particularly striking and swimming is difficult as the seabed shelves so gently. However, it is quite attractive with shallow boulders near **Cookies** and it is not rocky underfoot for the first 10 m or so. Accommodation is good value.

Koh Phangan listings

For hotel and restaurant price codes and other relevant information, see pages 10-14.

🛏 Where to stay

There is just one big hotel in Thong Sala, **Phangan Centrepoint**. Hat Rin is more expensive than other beaches and some accommodation is outrageously overpriced. During the high season (Dec-Feb and Jul-Sep), prices are 50% higher than in the low season: bargain if bungalows seem empty. Over full moon most places insist on a 7-night stay at inflated prices. Don't turn up expecting to find a room in Hat Rin. At peak times around the full moon accommodation runs out and you may have to stay further afield; Thong Sala is a good option.

Thong Sala and around *p86, map p86*
$$ Phangan Centrepoint, 26/6 Moo 1, T077-377232, www.phangan.info/centrepoint. Right in the centre of town, 23 simple but spacious hotel-style a/c rooms with cable TV based around a modern shopping plaza.
$$ Phangan Chai Hotel, 45/65 Moo 1, T077-377068. All rooms are a/c, with garden or sea views, fridge, shower and Western toilet. Decor leaves something to be desired.
$$-$ Buakao Inn Guest House, 146 Thongsala, T077-377226, www.phangan.info/buakao. Comfortably furnished rooms with TV, all en suite, the cheapest is fan only, the rest are a/c. Downstairs is A's Coffee Shop, a café/bar serving decent Italian coffee, with occasional live music in the evening. Mike, the Californian owner, is friendly and helpful.
$ Run's House, Old Market Rd, next to Mr Kim's tour service, T08-1089 4337. Cheap, comfortable rooms with shared bathroom above an old wooden

shophouse, not far from the pier. Can be a bit noisy at night.

South coast *p87, map p86*
Bang Charu and Ao Hinsong Kon
$$$$-$$$ First Villa, T077-377225, www.firstvillaphangan.com. Impeccably clean a/c and fan rooms along a private beachfront and in a pleasant tropical garden. Rooms are upmarket if slightly garish, some with private jacuzzi. Free transfer to/from Thong Sala pier.
$$$-$$ Charm Beach Resort, T077-377165, www.charm-beach-resort-phangan.com. The bungalows are well laid out and the most expensive are a/c. The cheap rooms, which are bamboo and thatch huts, are particularly good value but often full. Also has a tree-house room with beach views. The restaurant serves Thai and European food. Swimming pool.
$$$-$$ Phangan Beach Resort, 112/1 Moo 1, T077-238809, www.phanganbeachresort.com. Very cosy a/c and fan bungalows. Spacious and clean with a sliding door leading to an open-air bathroom. Comfortable with nice finishes. Set in a garden that leads straight to the beach.
$ Liberty Bungalows, T077-238171, www.libertykohphangan.com. Recently merged with next door's Emerald Ocean Resort, so it now has 18 bungalows, each with bamboo furnishings and hammocks set amid bougainvillea and cactus. Rooms are clean and comfortable with attached shower rooms. The more expensive ones are on the beach. There's music and movies in the restaurant and volleyball on the beach.

Ban Tai and Ban Khai
$$$$-$$ Milky Bay Resort, Ban Tai, T077-238566, www.milkybaythailand.com. Stylishly designed resort with plush a/c rooms and bungalows on the beach and excellent facilities. Pool, bar, gym with Thai boxing, pool tables, massage shalas, herbal

steam room and Thai and Italian restaurant as well as beachfront barbecues.

$$$-$ Mac's Bay Resort, T077-238443. Basic huts and smart white concrete bungalows, lined up attractively on the beach. Slightly better than most, well run and clean. The more expensive rooms are large and have attached shower rooms and a/c. There is a restaurant with a wide menu and nightly videos plus table tennis.

$$$-$ Phangnan Rainbow, 25/3 Moo 4, T077-238236, www.rainbowbungalows. com. Very comfortable fan and a/c rooms with high-quality furnishings. The cheapest bungalows have a shared bathroom. Location and size determines the price, some have a sea view. Very friendly family fun resort. Restaurant. Make sure the taxi driver takes you to Bankai Beach and not Hat Hin, where there is another resort of the same name. Recommended.

$$-$ Bancha Sramandra Resort and Waterfall, 29/10 Moo 4, T08-7896 4309, sramanora_resort@hotmail.com. Far from the bustle of Hat Rin, these bungalows are nestled high in the hills. You'll need your own transport and a keen sense of adventure to find them; the road in is long, steep and rough, especially in the wet. Bungalows are basic, but there's a freshwater natural swimming pool with waterfall and a communal area where the owner, Buncha, will tell you all about his fascinating life. His wife, Pen, is a wonderful cook. Recommended.

$$-$ Triangle Lodge, Ban Tai, T077-377432, www.phangan.info/trianglelodge. The more expensive bungalows on the beach sport nicely carved wooden balcony decoration. The restaurant is appealing, as it has a wide and imaginative menu with tasty interpretations of Western dishes, and the staff are friendly. Bikes for rent.

$ Lee Garden Resort Ban Khai, T077-238150, lees_garden@yahoo.com. A scattering of bungalows set in a garden next to the beach with balconies and hammocks in a quiet location. There are funky tunes, a giant tree swing, good food and great views. Well run.

Hat Rin *p87, map p86*
Hat Rin Nok
Bear in mind that accommodation gets booked up around the full moon so it's worth arriving a week in advance or booking. It's also fairly standard to have minimum booking periods, so don't expect to rock up and only stay for 1 or 2 nights around full-moon period.

$$$$-$$$ Palita Lodge, 119 Moo 6, T077-375170, www.palitalodge.com. The management have moved upmarket with the construction of 10 immaculate suites with parquet floors and rain showers. There's also a range of beach and garden view rooms available, often, once the full moon has waned, for less than advertised. Breakfast is included, and there's a sparkling pool.

$$$$-$$$ Phangan Bay Shore Resort, T077-375224/375227, www.phanganbay shore. com. Nice bungalows set in rows leading down to the beach. The most expensive are well kept with a/c, fridge, TV and hot water but little furniture and cheap fluorescent lights. There are hammocks on the verandas.

$$$$-$$$ Sunrise Resort, 136 Moo 6, T077-375 145, www.sunrisephangan.com. Clean hotel rooms with small balcony, a/c, fridge and hot water. Popular with the Israeli crowd and is usually full over the full moon period. Swimming pool.

$$$$-$$$ Tommy Resort, T077-375215, www.phangantommyresort.com. All signs of Tommy's backpacker past have been removed as the resort goes upmarket, now boasting 22 pleasant traditional-style bungalows near the beach that have TV, fridges and hot water. Even the once dingy restaurant has had a facelift, and is now based on a timber deck overlooking the water.

$$$ Delight Resort, 140 Hat Rin, T077-375 527, www.delightresort.com. A street back from the beach, this place offers comfortable a/c rooms. There's a restaurant and a large clothes store next to it.

$$$-$$ Haadrin Resort, 128/9 Moo 6, T077-375258. Ranges from fan huts to a/c rooms, basic but clean. Price includes breakfast. Stones throw from the Full Moon Beach.

$$$-$$ Sea Garden Resort & Spa, 137 Moo 6, T077-375281, www.seagarden-resort.com. Bungalows and a/c rooms in a 2-storey building. Peaceful garden setting across the road from the beach. The standard bungalows are fan only, with no hot water. Nothing to tweet home about but good value for the area.

$$-$ Baan Talay, 74/1 Moo 6, T077-375083, www.phangan.info/baantalay. In the village between the sunrise and sunset beaches. Comfortable. Well-furnished rooms, either fan or a/c. Hot water showers. Good value.

$$-$ Paradise, T077-375244. The originators of the Full Moon Party, the management of this set-up run around 50 bungalows, most of which are tatty, some significantly bigger and better than others, with hot water and a/c; all have attached showers. Pleasant garden although it might be too close to the nightclubs for many. Some bungalows can accommodate 4 people in 2 double beds, which makes it the best-value option. The owners also run a restaurant, **The Rock** (see Restaurants, page 98).

$$-$ Same Same, T077-375200, www.same-same.com. A popular bar and basic guest-house which receives good reports among the backpacker scene.

$ Lazy House, on the road towards Hat Rin West, near Lazy House restaurant. The laziest thing about this place is the design and decoration; it's a hideous concrete apartment block overflowing with cramped dorm beds. For ฿400 per bed, it's not even good value.

Hat Rin Nai
The advantage of staying on Hat Rin Nai is that it is quieter and on full moon nights the party cannot be heard. It's a short stroll to the centre of Hat Rin and Hat Rin Nok beach.

$$$$-$$$ Best Western Phanganburi Resort, T077-375481, www.bestwestern phanganburi.com. A more expensive resort away from the crowds with a lovely beachfront pool and another further back. Bungalows are attractively furnished and are nicely spaced in rows leading down to the beach. Non-guests can use the resort's 2 pools for ฿100.

$$$-$$ Hillside Bungalows, a few metres along the road to Thong Sala, T077-375102. This friendly spot is run by relaxed Nepali Tacco. Almost doubles its prices at full moon. Smart rooms with fridge and hot water.

$$$-$$ Neptune's Villa, T077-375251, www.kohphganganneptune.com. There are a/c concrete bungalows and 2nd-floor rooms with great views of the sea and a fairly pleasant beach. Overpriced in peak season.

$$$-$ Blue Marine, 110/6 Hat Rin, T077-375079, www.bluemarinephangan.com. Even the fan rooms, the cheapest option, have TV, minibar and hot water. A/c available. Spacious and clean, right next to the beach. Good value.

$$$-$ Friendly Guesthouse, next to Black & White, T077-375167. Some rooms in a 2 storey Chinese looking building. Bungalows are also available. Fan and a/c, all rooms have hot water showers. The decor is a bit garish. If you check in 3 days before the full moon the price remains the same.

$$-$ Black & White, 110/2 Moo 6, T077-375187. There are over 60 rooms at this resort ranging from fan bungalows to a/c rooms in a modern building. Very close to sunset beach.

$$-$ Charung Bungalow, T077-375168, charungbungalows@hotmail.com.

Simple bungalows with attached shower room and fan. Hammocks in front of every room. The restaurant's snooker table needs serious attention.

Leela Beach

A little further out of town, on the western side of the Had Rin's peninsular, Leela beach is worth the effort to reach for its beauty and complete sense of removal from the hedonism of the party scene.

$$$$-$ Sarikantang, Hat Sikantang, towards the headland, T077-375055, www.sarikan tang.com. Gorgeous rooms with large windows at this luscious resort with a beachfront pool. The cheaper, wooden rooms are good value. It's a 10 min walk to the centre of Hat Rin.

$$-$ Lighthouse Bungalows, T077-375075, www.lighthousebungalows. com. This great place is a 20-min walk from Hat Rin on the western side of the headland. It is reached by a long romantic wooden causeway around the rocks to the bungalows of various sizes and prices. The staff are friendly and helpful and there's a sociable restaurant, which is an excellent place to make friends before the full moon madness. The sunsets are fantastic. Recommended.

East coast p88, map p86
Hat Thien to Hat Sadet

$$$$-$ The Sanctuary, Hat Yuan, T08-1271 3614 (mob), www. thesanctuarythailand.com. Renowned for its post- and pre-party 'detox and retox' programmes and unbeatably bohemian beach atmosphere. Managed by Westerners it offers everything from fasts and colonic-cleansing courses to a treat-heavy menu, cocktails and wine in the boulder-strewn café. Accommodation ranges from dorms for under ฿250 to palatial open-plan hilltop houses. The vegetarian and seafood restaurant with its home-grown produce and bakery is pricey but top quality. Self-development courses in yoga, meditation and massage run year round. Only accessible by boat or a long walk through jungle.

$$-$ Mai Pen Rai, Hat Sadet, T077-445090, www.thansadet.com. Basic fan bungalows with attached bathrooms on the beach with newer ones on the hillside. Near the biggest waterfall and although on a less than impressive beach it has a sleepy charm. Many Thai kings have visited and the present king owns the land.

$ Horizon Boxing Camp, between Ao Hat Yuan and Ao Hat Thien, T072-778570, www.horizonmuaythai.com. Basic thatched huts with outside toilets and some more expensive en suite options, overlooking the beach. The impressive boxing gym and ring sets it apart from competitors.

Ao Thong Nai Pan Yai

$$$-$ Baan Panburi Village, T077-238599, www.baanpanburivillage.com. The owners have recently picked up and moved the entire resort from Thong Nai Pan Noi, but the look and feel of the place remains the same. Higher end wooden bungalows, each with its own private terrace; more expensive huts have sea views. There is also a traditional Thai-style house for rent

$$$-$ Nice Beach Resort, T077-238547, www.nicebeachresort.net. The 27 unimaginative bungalows have seen better days.

$$-$ Su's Bakery & Bungalows, 11/2 Baan Thong Nai Pan, T077-238924, www. su-cafe-andhouseforrent.com. A range of accommodation, a min's walk from the beach, ranging from a wooden hut to a fully kitted-out house with kitchen, a/c, hot water, TV and even a washing machine, making it an excellent option for families.

$ Dolphin Bungalows, Bar & Restaurant, southern end of the beach, kimgiet@ hotmail.com. Enjoys almost legendary status amongst guests that keep returning year after year. Spectacularly and lovingly landscaped jungle-garden houses the beachfront bar and restaurant (see Restaurants, page 98) and further back, hides the wooden fan bungalows, which are all en suite with hammocks on the balcony. Everything here has been designed with genuine care for the environment. Highly recommended.

$ Pingjun, T077-445062. A friendly resort with large bungalows all of which have verandas, hammocks, fans and en suite bathrooms. Starting to show its age a little bit. Popular restaurant.

$ White Sand Resort, at the southern end of the beach, T077-445123, www.whitesand-phangan.com. This is one of the beach's best budget options. Serves some of the best Thai food on the beach, reasonably priced and the staff are friendly. Recommended.

Ao Thong Nai Pan Noi

$$$$ Panviman Resort, T077-445101, www.panviman.com. A large upmarket resort with peculiar grotto-style concrete villas and exclusive suites in the hotel set high on the cliffs commanding impressive views. Its circular formal restaurant overlooks the sea.

$$$-$ Tong Ta Pan, T077-238538, www.thongtapan.com. Large white villas set either on a picturesque rocky hillside or on the beach. The upmarket interiors are pleasantly furnished and have large tiled bathrooms with hot water. Excursions and water sports club.

$ Sandee Bungalows, T077-445089, sandee_bungalow@yahoo.com. The 1st bungalow operation to pop up on Thong Nai Pan Noi, these simple but very peaceful bungalows are about a min's walk from the beach. Great value for backpackers, though the owners are slowly heading towards a more sophisticated demographic by replacing some of the old wooden huts with newer concrete ones.

North coast *p89, map p86*
Ao Hat Kuat

Construction of a large hotel on Bottle Beach is underway.

$$-$ Bottle Beach Bungalow No 1, T077-445152, www.bottlebeach1resort.com. Polished wood bungalows under coconut palms, each set in a nice garden with little platform verandas right on the beach. The wooden ones have a Swiss feel. All have shower and fan. More expensive rooms have 4 beds.

$$-$ Haad Khuad Resort (formerly Bottle Beach Bungalow No 3), T077-445127, www.haadkhuadresort.com. A small resort with fan bungalows, some right on beach. The concrete bungalows come with pleasant roof annexes. It also has an attractive beachfront restaurant.

$ Smile, T08-1956 3133 (mob). Blue-roofed fan bungalows set amongst the boulders and reached by little stone paths; rooms with jungle views are particularly peaceful. It has an attractive restaurant with hanging shell mobiles and newspapers. There's a tree swing and sofa swings on the beach. Recommended.

Ao Hat Khom

$$-$ Coral Bay, T077-374245. Bungalows from the more basic with shared bathrooms, to posh ones with interesting bathrooms built into the rock. All have mosquito nets. The resort also rents snorkelling equipment.

$$-$ Ocean View Resort, T077-377231. Up on the headland with a great view and a range of bungalow options – the creatively designed more expensive ones with views are a particular bargain. The restaurant also has lovely sea views and serves good vegetarian food.

$ Coconut Beach, furthest end of the beach, T077-374298, www.coconutbeach-bungalows.com. At the end of a steep and treacherous dirt track. Concrete fan bungalows on the cliff side, which leads down to the beachfront restaurant and the soft white-sand beach.

Ao Chao Lok Lum

$$$$-$$$ Chaloklum Bay T077-374147-8, www.chaloklumbay.com. Attractive beachfront bungalows on stilts with a/c and hot water or fan. There are also a couple of large, attractive beach houses for groups or families.

$$$-$ Malibu Beach Resort, after Wantana Resort, T077-374057, www.malibubeachbungalows.com. Simple, well-maintained and clean bamboo huts with attached bathrooms. Further back are a/c bungalows which are large but rather dark inside. The bathrooms are also spacious with bathtub. Plenty of hammocks hanging from the trees. Beach BBQ.

$$$-$ Fantasea Bungalows, 113/1 Moo 7, T08-9443 0785 (mob), www.fantasea-resort-phangan.info. Distinctive and well-kept A-frame wooden bungalows, some right on the beach, with TVs and hot water. All have interior bathroom and mosquito net. Good deal for the location.

$$ Buritara Resort (formerly Niramon Villas), next to Fantasea Bungalows, T077-374115, www.buritararesort.com. Large concrete bungalows on stilts, some with sea views. Comfortably furnished with a/c, minibar, cable TV and hot water. The beach is a short walk away over a rather precarious wooden suspension bridge. Friendly management. Swimming pool.

$$-$ Wattana Resort, T077-374022, www.wattanaresort.info. Spacious, restful bungalow resort run by a family. The larger, modern ones have balconies on 2 sides with hammocks and mosquito screens. The cheaper rooms are large, but basic, with mosquito nets.

Hat Salat and Ao Mae Hat

$$$$ Green Papaya Resort, T077-349280, www.greenpapayaresort.com. 18 luxury wooden cottages and rooms with stylish interiors set in a lush garden around a beachfront pool.

$$$$-$$$ Salad Beach Resort, T077-349149, www.phangan-saladbeachresort.com. Bungalows and 2-storey rooms with fan or a/c, TV and hot water set around a lovely pool. There's a pool table and jacuzzi too.

$$$ Salad Hut, 61/3 Moo 8, T077-349 246, www.saladhut.com. A smaller cluster of attractive bungalows including 4 family rooms. The bungalows facing the beach have nice big rooms with carved balconies complete with a day-bed and 2 hammocks. There's a restaurant, snorkelling and boat trips. Friendly management.

$$$-$ Wang Sai Resort, Ao Mae Hat, T077-374238. In a beautiful setting behind a stream close to the sandbar, the attractive bungalows, some perched on boulders, are clean and well maintained, although few have sea views. It is quiet and secluded but the sea is not so clear. Snorkelling equipment for hire, book exchange and volleyball net. Restaurant serves cheap Thai and Western food.

$ My Way Bungalows, T077-349267. Bamboo fan bungalows with thatched roofs and hammocks. Electricity stops at 2300. Clean, with bathroom attached. The restaurant serves good, cheap Thai cuisine.

$ Island View Cabana, Ao Mae Hat, T077-374172. One of the oldest places on the island, set in a wide part of the beach where a sandbar stretches out to Koh Ma which provides good snorkelling. Simple huts, some have attached shower rooms with Western toilets. The restaurant serves good, cheap food, pool table. This is a popular, well-organized place.

West coast *p89, map p86*
Ao Hat Yao

$$$$-$$ Long Bay, T077-349057, www.long-bay.com. A classy option with swish, modern a/c rooms and some cheaper fan options all with relative luxuries such as dressing tables and wardrobes, set around a large swimming pool by the sea.

$$$-$ High Life Resort, Moo 8, T077-349114, www.highlifebungalow.com. Various rooms from fan to a/c with jacuzzi and TV. There's a swimming pool and the beach is a 5 min walk away. Attracts a young crowd, but the expensive rooms are overpriced.

$$$-$ Sandy Bay, 54/1 Moo 8, T077-349119, www.sandybaybungalows.com. A good selection of smart spacious a/c and traditional fan bungalows on the beach. All are kept clean and have large verandas with hammocks or varnished wood furniture. This is a popular place with tables and chairs on the sand and the best restaurant on the beach which mainly serves cheap Thai food. Kayaking and island trips offered. Movies shown. **Haad Yao Divers** attached. Recommended.

Ao Chaophao

$$$$-$$$ Sunset Cove, Sea & Forest Boutique Resort, 78/11 Moo 8, T077-349211, www.thaisunsetcove.com. All cottages have a/c and are furnished to a very high standard, with comfy duvets on the beds and open bathrooms. The sea-view cottages have a separate lounge area and wooden bathtubs. Swimming pool and beachfront restaurant.

$$$-$$ Seaflower, T077-349090, www.seaflowerbungalows.com. Prices vary with distance from the beach. Run by a Canadian-Thai couple, well-laid out wooden bungalows, with high peaked thatched roofs set in a mature, shady garden. Camping expeditions, snorkelling (equipment is free for guests), fishing, cliff diving and caving trips, as well as overnight boat trips to Ang Thong National Park available. Restaurant has an interesting menu. Recommended.

$$-$ Jungle Huts, T077-349088, www.junglehutresort.com. Offers 2 rows of large and airy huts made of board, timber and thatch with attached shower rooms ranging

from the cheapest with just fans to those with a/c. Hammocks on the large verandas. Restaurant specializes in cocktails, plus Thai and Western dishes. Motorbike rental.

$ Haad Chaophao Resort. Bungalows set in pleasant garden. All have verandas, attached shower rooms and mosquito nets. Restaurant with backpacker staples.

$ West Coast Bungalow, Moo 8 Had Chaophao, T08-7898 4220 (mob). Breezy, light and spacious bungalows on a steep rise above the sea. Coffee- and tea-making facilities in the rooms. Both a/c and fan available.

Ao Sri Thanu

$$$-$$ Chills Bay Resort, T08-9036 7128 (mob), www.chillsresort.com. 9 stylish bungalows with fan or a/c on the beach facing the sunset. The more expensive have high-raftered ceilings with living rooms and loft bedrooms. Rock swimming pool.

$$$-$ Nice Sea Resort, Sritanu Village, T077-349177, www.niceasearesort.resort. phanganbungalows.com. From the road cross a rickety wooden bridge. Bamboo fan bungalows, some with hot water. Basic but clean. There is also a large brick bungalow with a/c and TV.

$$-$ Laem Son, T077-349032, www. phangan.info/laemson. Family-run bungalows close to a pine plantation and set back a bit off the beach. There's a volleyball net and beach bar. There are no rocks and the sea is sandy underfoot. It's one of the nicest places on this stretch and is popular.

$ Nantakarn Bungalow, follow the rough dirt track next to Shanti Guesthouse, T077-445986. Humble wooden bungalows spread out on the sand. Very quiet. Beach is beautiful but not suitable for swimming, meaning there's little else to do but claim a hammock and enjoy the serenity.

$ Seaview Rainbow, Moo 8, T077-349084. Little log cabins next to the beach with bathrooms inside, mosquito screen and balcony. Restaurant.

Ao Hin Kong and Ao Nai Wok

$$$-$ Bounty Bungalows, Ao Plaay Laem, T077-349105. Offers 15 clean and attractive board huts with tiled shower rooms and fans run by friendly staff. Snorkelling gear available. There's also a restaurant, and lovely granite boulders in front.

$$ Shambala, 69/10 Moo 4 Nai Wok, T077-239620, www.shambala-phangan. com. Opened in 2010, these stylish and comfortable wooden bungalows spread from the sand all the way up the cliff towards the road, so each has spectacular views over Plaay Laem. Each bungalow has a small terrace with hammock and comfortable beds. Recommended.

$$-$ Cookies, Ao Plaay Laem, T077-377499, cookies_bungalow@hotmail.com. 30 attractive bamboo bungalows, set in a green garden with a small splash pool. Some have shared bathroom, some have a/c and DVD players. The restaurant has a raised platform and the beach is secluded and attractive. Run by the friendly Aom and An. The watersports club offers windsurfing, kayaking and laser boats. Recommended.

$$-$ Phangan Bungalows, Aow Nai Wog, T077-377191. Different size wood and bamboo huts at various prices. Raised on stilts with generous balconies these bungalows are popular with people staying long term. Very peaceful.

$ Bee House Bungalow, Wok Tum Bay, T08-1719 0679, panit_38@hotmail.com. 5 nice wooden bungalows spaced apart in a huge garden. They're across the road from the beach, but the water's muddy and not good for swimming. Bigger bungalows have kitchen, living room and big balcony with hammock. Can also rent by the month if you plan on staying longer.

❼ Restaurants

Many visitors eat at their bungalows and some serve excellent, cheap seafood. Prices are fairly standard though it's worth checking to avoid a shock at the end of your stay. There are also increasing numbers of restaurants in virtually every village. Word-of-mouth recommendations are the best guide; new ones open all the time. See each area for details.

Thong Sala and around *p86, map p86*
$$ Big Mango, T077-377300. Thai fusion and barbecue in attractive, plant-strewn indoor and outdoor dining areas. Specialities include alligator and ostrich.

$$ Pizza Chiara, on the town's main road, T077-377626. Open 1200-2300. Authentic pasta and pizza (it is run by an Italian). Spaghetti carbonara is delicious.

$$ Yellow Café, T08-6281 1735. A popular stop, painted yellow and looking out to the pier. Menu includes full English breakfasts and baked potatoes, though a recent change of owner has seen the quality drop.

$ Khao Kloop Kapi, next to Mr Kim's tour service. Hidden behind a wall of greenery, this Thai restaurant's specialty is also its namesake – khao kloop kapi (rice mixed with shrimp paste, herbs and pork). Also serves up generous portions of other Thai favourites at reasonable prices.

$ Phantip Food Market, just before the 7/11 on the main road to the pier. Reasonable examples of Thai street food.

Ban Tai
$$ Fishermen's Restaurant & Bar Ban Tai (near the pier), T08-4454 7240 (mob). Idyllic spot for a memorable seafood supper. The lucky few get to dine in a moored longtail boat. Recommended.

Hat Rin *p87, map p86*
$$ Bamboozle, Hat Rin West, T08-5471 4211 (mob). Open 1300-late. This is run by an Englishman and his Thai wife. Serves Mexican food. There's covered seating or a little garden with tables and umbrellas and a row of terracotta lamps marking the boundaries of the restaurant.

$$ Lazy House, on the road to Hat Rin West. Offering full English breakfast and movies all day. Wooden and cosy, it's popular with expats. Also has a little brother across the street, aptly named 2 Lazy, though ironically, it has a slightly less chilled-out vibe.

$$ Lucky Crab, T077-375124. The original seafood place in Hat Rin, on the main road between east and west. Full of 'unlucky' crabs, since its popularity and extensive menu means they're eaten at a rate of knots. It is usually packed every night but often under-staffed, leading to excruciatingly inefficient service. Punters eat at long tables in a party atmosphere. The soups and salads are also excellent.

$$ Nic's Restaurant & Bar, Moo 5, T08-0041 8023, heike.heike_64@web.de. 1700-2230. A stylish restaurant/bar/lounge, serving delicious, but very reasonably priced, tapas, pasta, pizza and Thai food. Chill-out areas and big screen showing major sporting events. Recommended.

$$ Outback Bar and Restaurant, T077-375126. Big TV screens make this a popular place with the sporting crowd. Big cushions and comfy seating add to its pull. Its full-monty breakfast is mighty fine.

$$ The Rock, run by **Paradise Bungalows**. The Rock has unbeatable views of the beach, and dishes out exquisite seafood, an unusual range of bar snacks including the ever-popular garlic bread and salads, imported organic coffee, super cocktails and higher quality wine than you'll find anywhere else. Relaxing music makes for a welcome break from the booming tunes elsewhere. Recommended.

$ Nira's Bakery, 74/10 Moo 1 (between Chicken Corner and 7-11), T08-6595 0636 (mob), www.phanganholidaybaking.com. Open 24 hrs. A bakery selling a gorgeous range of cakes, pastries, brownies and bread. The spinach and feta pastries and spinach muffins are recommended. The nextdoor café (0800-2400) does great coffee, spirulina shakes and breakfasts. Watch TV out the back or sit roadside at wooden picnic tables.

$ Om Ganesh, at Hat Rin pier, T077-375123. An old favourite for Indian food, offers delicious traditional tandoori, curries and thalis. Also the Himalayan Art Gallery next door with art for sale.

East coast *p88, map p86*
$$ Dolphin Bar & Restaurant, see Where to stay, page 93. Breakfast and lunch, tapas served in the evenings. Excellent range of international food served at various seating areas from raised platforms to cabanas hidden in the jungle. The ingredients are of the highest quality and the food here is amongst the best on the island. The cocktails are worth a try too. Highly Recomended.

$$ Su's Bakery, Thong Nai Pan Yai, 1st shop on the left as you enter the village, www-su-cafe-andhouseforrent.com. Fantastic thin-base pizzas are definitely worth the walk from the beach to the village. Very popular with regulars. Fresh coffees, brownies and banana cake are also a big hit. Recommended.

$ Luna Lounge, 8/25 Moo. 5 Ao Thong Nai Pan Noi, T08-3136 8130 (mob). Choice spot for global cuisine, from mango quesadillas to Greek salads to straight-up Thai and cheesecakes. A warmly lit bar-restaurant-lounge hybrid with a loyal following and cool vibe. They also whip up cocktails.

$ Memory, Thong Nai Pan Yai, opposite **Nu Bar**. Serves some of the best Thai food on the beach. Very friendly owner, Nat.

North coast *p89, map p86*
$$-$ Sheesha, Chao Lok Lum, T077-374161, www.sheesha-bar.com. A funky addition to the north coast catering for this craze that has seized Phangan and Koh Tao. International food, cocktails, dancefloor, sundeck and private outdoor booths for sucking on fruity tobacco flavours.

West coast *p89, map p86*
$$-$ Angels Bay, Ao Hin Kong. T08-4326 7031, www.angelsbay.fr.gd. Open 1700-

late. Phillipe and his team produce some magical French and Italian dishes in an equally magical setting. Wood-fired pizza oven. Recommended,

$ Lake Hut, Sri Thanu, T08-1743 0062. Open 1000-2000. A chilled-out little bar/restaurant on the lagoon. But despite the reasonable food, the real attraction to this place is the rope swing and inflatable obstacle courses that have been set up around the lake. Has a nice wooden deck built over the water from which to watch the drunken aerial acrobatics on show.

🍷 Bars and clubs

Hat Rin *p87, map p86*
At full moon, every shop, bar and restaurant turns itself into a bar selling plastic buckets stuffed with spirits and mixers. The 3 best and loudest clubs on Hat Rin Beach East are **Vinyl Club**, **Zoom Bar** and the **Drop in Club**, www.dropinclub.com, which play upbeat dance music and not just on full moon nights.

Backyard Club, on Hat Rin West. Infamous for its Full Moon after-parties which start at 1100 with the best of the DJs.

Cactus Club, a little further down the beach with a great bar right on the beach, plays a more melodic set than most with hip hop, R'n'B and a bit of rock.

Esco Bar, fabulous position on some rocks overlooking the sea at Hat Rin West between the **Siam Healing Centre** and the **Phangan Buri Resort**. Open 1200-2400. Reggae seems the order of the day at this great little wooden bar.

Nargile House, close to the **Drop in Bar** on Hat Rin East. Open until late. Smoking the sheesha at tables costs ฿300 at this roadside bar. Alcohol also available.

East coast *p88, map p86*
In Thong Nai Pan Noi there's the notoriously hip **Flip Flop Pharmacy**, on the beach, then along the road there's the low-level wooden **Jungle Bar**, the more rocking

Rasta Baby, the Mexican bar and restaurant **Que Pasa** and the **Hideaway Bar**, decorated in bunting.

West coast *p89, map p86*
Amsterdam Bar, Ao Plaay Laem, T077-238447, www.amstardambar.com. From 1200. This hilltop bar gets going in the late afternoon when it puts on probably the best sunset party on the island. Sells drinks and a few naughty goodies, too.

The Eagle, Ao Hat Yao, T04-8397143. A good option for a bit of house.

Jam Bar, Moo 6 Hin Kong Beach rd, www.thejamphangan.com. A gathering point for local and international musicians, with live jam sessions on the beach every Sat night, and spontaneous ones most other nights. BYO instrument or feel free to grab one from the bar.

The Pirate's Bar, Ao Chaophao, accessed through the **Seatanu Bungalows**. Hosts the moon set party, 3 days before full moon. The bar in the shape of a ship is set in the tiniest of coves accessed by a woodenbridge that winds around boulders.

🎭 Entertainment

Hat Rin *p87, map p86*
Cabaret
Cabaret is sometimes held at **Coral Bungalows** on Hat Rin West. See flyers for details.

Muay Thai (Thai boxing)
3 stadiums in Thong Sala, 1 in Had Rin and 1 on Tong Nai Pan Noi. Look out for flyers or listen out for the incessantly annoying megaphone announcements for fight days. Expect to pay around ฿500.

🛍 Shopping

Hat Rin *p87, map p86*
Fashion
Shops selling leather goods, funky fashions and books abound in Hat Rin. **JD Exotic**

sells swish shirts for men and **Napo-po** sells stylish boho fashions, accessories and photographs. **Fusion** offers funkier, contemporary fashions.

Furniture
Beautiful World, T077-238935, www.beauti fulworldthailand.com, on the road to Thong Sala, sells stylish contemporary and antique furniture and interior accessories.

⊙ What to do

Koh Phangan *p84, map p86*
Diving
For the trained diver, the west coast offers the best diving with hard coral reefs at depths up to about 20 m. There are also some islets which offer small walls, soft coral and filter corals. Dive trips are also available to further sites such as **Koh Wao Yai** in the north of the Ang Thong Marine National Park or **Hin Bai** (Sail Rock). Here the dives are deeper.
Chaloklum Diving, 25/29-30 Moo 7, Chao Lok Lum Village, T077-374025, www.chaloklum-diving.com. One of the longest-standing operations on the island with an excellent reputation. Small group policy guarantees personal attention.
Crystal Dive, Hat Rin T077-375535, www.crystaldive.com. This booking branch of the respected dive resort in Koh Tao is run by the good folk at the **Backpackers Information Centre**.
Lotus Diving, Ao Chao Lok Lum, T077-374097, www.lotusdiving.com. Offers PADI courses and dive trips.
Phangan Divers, based in Hat Rin, near the pier on the west side, Ao Hat Yao, Ao Thong Nai Pan and Koh Ma, T077-375117, www.phangandivers.com.
Tropical Dive Club, Thong Nai Pan Noi, T077-445081, www.tropicaldiveclub.com.
H2O Scuba, Ao Thong Nai Pan Noi, T08-1186 1616 (mob), www.h2oscubaschool.com.

Fishing and sailing
Rin Beach Tours, T08-1979 5939 (mob). Day or night fishing on Thai boats.

Gym and Muay Thai (Thai boxing)
Jungle Gym, Hat Rin, T077-375115, www.jungle gym.co.th. Thai boxing courses as well as aerobics, yoga and other training and courses.
Muay Thai Boxing Training, Tong Sala, T08-6953 8253 (mob). Run by a Thai boxing champion there are 2-hr introductoryclasses or 1-month courses available.

Snorkelling
Coral is to be found off most beaches, except for those on the east coast. Particularly good are those in **Mae Hat** where corals are just a few metres below the surface.

Tour operators and travel agents
Numerous operators run trips around the island to several beaches and waterfalls and the price includes food and drink on the tour.
Backpackers Information Centre, Hat Rin, T077-375535, www.backpackersthailand. com. An invaluable source of information and the only TAT-registered independent travel agent on the island. Run by Thai-British couple Rashi and Bambi who are experts on accommodation, tickets, health and safety. The agency also organizes lifeguard and full moon volunteer services on Hat Rin beach.
Phangan Adventure, Ao Chao Lok Lum, T077-374142, www.phanganadventure. com. Boat trips, snorkelling, fishing trips, wake-boarding, kayaking trips and rental, and mountain-bike tours and rental.
Reggae Magic Boat Trip, Reggae Magic Bar, Hat Rin East, T08-1606 8159 (mob). Long-tailed boat trips to the highlights of the island with post-trip party and dinner.
Thong Sala Centre, 44/13 Thong Sala Pier, T077-238984, jamareei@hotmail.com. Run

by twin sisters for the last 25 years. Can organize boat, train, plane tickets and offer sound travel advice. Trustworthy.

Paintball
Paintball Warfare T077-377300, paintball warfare@hotmail.com. A huge paintball battlefield in Thong Sala, open daily 1000-1800, ฿300 for a full day.

Therapies
Agama Yoga School, Ananda Resort, 16/3 Moo 6 Ao Hin Kong (Hin Kong Bay), T08-9233 0217 (mob), www.agamayoga.com. The place to fine tune your chakra, offering esoteric yoga workshops, retreats and training.

Chakra, Hat Rin, off the main drag leading up from the pier, T077-375401, www.chakrayoga.com. Open until 2400. Run by a real master, Yan, and his English wife Ella. Whether you're looking for simple relaxation, or you've a specific complaint that needs working on, the staff here dish out any number of good traditional body, face and foot Thai massages, reiki, reflexology and acupressure treatments. For those looking to learn the art themselves, they also run certificated courses: traditional Thai massage (30 hrs), reiki, levels 1-4; oil massage (30 hrs), foot and head massage (15 hrs), and massage therapy course – similar to acupuncture, but with thumbs instead of needles (30 hrs).

Monte Vista Retreat Centre, 162/1 Nai Wok Beach, T08-9212 9188 (mob), www.montevistathailand.com. This recent addition to the island's holistic vacation scene has won rave reviews. Daily yoga and meditation, cleansing and fasting courses, in-house training for reiki, palm and psychic readings, herbal facials and several types of massage. Basic accommodation also available.

The Sanctuary, Hat Yuan, T08-1271 3614 (mob), www.thesanctuarythailand.com. See Hat Thien, Where to stay, page 93.

Wat Pho Herbal Sauna, close to Ban Tai beach on the southwest coast. This traditional herbal sauna is run on donations and uses traditional methods and ingredients.

The Yoga Retreat, Hat Salad, T077-374310, www.yogaretreat-kohphangan.com. A family business run by qualified instructors offering courses in yoga, pilates, Alexander technique and chakra healing in the peaceful jungle.

⊖ Transport

Koh Phangan p84, map p86
Boat
Boats to **Hat Rin** run from both Thong Sala and Ban Khai. Long-tailed boats take passengers from Hat Rin, Ao Thong Nai Pan, Ao Hat Yao and Ao Hat Kuat to Thong Sala and Ban Khai piers for somewhat inflated prices. Most boats use the pier at Thong Sala, although a ferry, the *Haad Rin Queen*, T077-375113, returns from Hat Rin direct to Big Buddha pier on **Koh Samui** at 0930, 1140, 1430 and 1730, 50 mins, ฿200.

From **Thong Sala** there are departures from to Koh Samui with Songserm, T077-377704, to Nathon pier at 0700 and 1230, ฿200; with Lomprayah, T077-238411, www.lomprayah.com, to Mae Nam beach at 1100 and 1600, and to Nathon at 0715 and 1200, ฿300; with Seatran, T077-238679, to Big Buddha pier at 1100 and 1630, ฿250, and with Speed Boat Line to Bophut at 0600, 0930, 1300 and 1530, 20 mins.

To **Koh Tao** with Seatran, 0830, 1400, 1½ hrs, ฿450; Lomprayah, 0830, 1300, 1 hr 20 mins, ฿450; Songserm, 1230, ฿350.

To **Surat Thani** from with Songserm, 1230, ฿400; Lomprayah, 0715, 1200, ฿550; Raja Ferry, 0700, 1100, 1300, 1700, 2½ hrs, ฿310; prices include the bus ticket to bus and train stations. The night boat leaves Koh Phangan for **Surat Thani** at 2200 (although times can vary, so it's worth checking in good time), 6 hrs, ฿400.

To **Chumphon** with **Lomprayah** at 0830, 3 hrs 15 mins, and 1230, 3 hrs 40 mins, ฿1000.

Motorcycle hire
Available in Thong Sala and from the more popular beaches. Some guesthouses also hire out motorbikes, from ฿150 per day for manual, or ฿200 for automatic (If you plan to ride from Thong Sala to Hat Rin, a manual bike is recommended safely to negotiate the steep hills that lie between them.)

Train
The **State Railways of Thailand** runs a train/ bus/ferry service between Koh Phangan and **Bangkok**'s Hualamphong Station.

❶ Directory

Koh Phangan *p84, map p86*
Medical Services Koh Phangan Hospital, about 2.5 km north of Thong Sala, offers 24-hr emergency services. Facilities are better in Samui or Bangkok. **Bandon International Hospital**, in Hat Rin, T077-375471, is a 24-hr private clinic with English-speaking staff. **Police** about 2 km north of Thong Sala, T077-377114; **Tourist Police**, T077-421281. **Post office** Hat Rin, close to pier, Mon-Fri 0830-1640, Sat 0900-1200.

Koh Tao

Koh Tao, the smallest of the three famous islands in the Gulf of Thailand, is a big dive and snorkelling centre with plenty of shallow coral beds and tropical fish. The waters – especially in the south and east – are stunning, a marbling of turquoise blue, sapphire, emerald and seaweed green. For non-divers this small island offers a surprisingly high number of exceptionally well-designed, independent upmarket resorts, with the added bonus of quiet beach life by day and fairly sophisticated nightlife due to the underwater preferences of the majority of visitors. The name Koh Tao, translated as 'turtle island', relates to the shape of the island.

Arriving on Koh Tao

Getting there

Several companies operate regular express boats from Chumphon, Surat Thani, Koh Samui and Koh Phangan; there's also a slow night ferry direct from Surat Thani. Songserm, www.songserm-expressboat.com, sells a combination ticket from Bangkok to Koh Tao for ฿700. The bus service leaves Bangkok at 1800 and arrives in Chumphon at 0200; passengers then sleep on the office floor before catching the 0700 boat to Koh Tao. The return journey to Bangkok leaves Chumphon at 2030. The rail connection from Bangkok to Koh Tao leaves Bangkok at 2250 and arrives in Chumphon at 0552 (theoretically); ticket price depends on class.

Getting around

There is just one surfaced road on Koh Tao, which runs from the north end of Sai Ri to Chalok Ban Kao, passing through Ban Mae Hat. Motorbike taxis and pickups are the main form of local transport. These can be found just north of the dock next to the exchange booth. They operate from dawn to 2300; rates tend to double after dark. Motorbikes, jeeps and bicycles are available for hire. Long-tailed boats can be chartered to reach more remote beaches and coves, either by the trip, hour or day. ▸▸ *See Transport, page 115, for further information.*

Getting around

There is just one surfaced road on Koh Tao, which runs from the north end of Sai Ri to Chalok Ban Kao, passing through Ban Mae Hat. Motorbike taxis and pickups are the main form of local transport. These can be found just north of the dock next to the exchange booth. They operate from dawn to 2300; rates tend to double after dark. Motorbikes, jeeps and bicycles are available for hire. Long-tailed boats can be chartered to reach more remote beaches and coves, either by the trip, hour or day. ▸▸ *See Transport, page 115, for further information.*

Tourist information

The **TAT** office on Koh Samui, see page 58, is responsible for Koh Tao as there is no office on the island. The website, www.kohtao.com, provides lots of information, or see the free quarterly *Koh Tao Info* magazine, www.kohtaoinfo.tv.

Koh Tao

1 km
1 mile

Sleeping
Aow Leuk 2 **7**
Beach Side Resort **1**
Bohemia Resort **8**
Casa del Sol **9**
Charm Churee Villa & Spa **2**

Diamond Resort **5**
New Heaven **7**
Pahnun View Bungalows **6**
Siam Cookies **3**
View Rock Resort **4**

Avoid bringing any plastic bottles or tin cans to the island as these are difficult to dispose of. Some environmentalists advise people to drink cans rather than bottles of beer as few businesses find it economically viable to recycle bottles and simply dump them. In addition, due to reduced rainfall in recent years, water is now a great problem on the island, and much of it is imported from the mainland. Visitors should use it sparingly.

Background

The accessibility of interesting marine life at depths available to beginners, the fairly gentle currents and the relatively low costs all contribute to making Koh Tao a particularly good place to learn to dive. The presence of giant manta rays and whale sharks (plankton feeders which can reach 6 m) means that more experienced divers will also find something of interest here. With these attractions in its favour, Koh Tao's reputation as a good, low-cost dive centre has grown rapidly, and in the space of just 10 years the island has made the transition from backwater to mainstream destination. See Diving, page 114. Improved transport links with the mainland have also made the island more accessible to the short-stay tourist, and so it is no surprise that the former economic mainstay of coconuts has now been eclipsed by the still-expanding tourist trade. Already, the number of rooms for tourists outnumbers the Thai residents on the island. Sensibly, though, as on Koh Samui, there are height restrictions on new buildings and this, in conjunction with the poor infrastructure, means the 'palm tree horizon' has not yet been blotted by multi-storey monstrosities. However, there do seem to be a worrying number of tall hotels being built. While most people come here for the swimming, snorkelling and diving – as well as beach life – the fact that most paths are not vehicle-friendly makes the island walker-friendly and there are some good trails to explore. Land-based wildlife includes monitor lizards, fruit bats and various non-venomous snakes. If planning to go on walks it is worth purchasing V Honsombud's *Guide Map of Koh Phangan & Koh Tao*.

Around the island → *For listings, see pages 107-116.*

Ban Mae Hat and the west coast

The harbour is at the island's main village of Ban Mae Hat. On both sides of the harbour there are small beaches with a few resorts. These areas have easy access to the town. There are numerous shops from fashion boutiques to bookstores and supermarkets and some of the best restaurants as well as a burgeoning nightlife, post office, money exchanges, dive shops, tour operators, transport and foodstalls.

To the north of Ban Mae Hat on the west coast, is the white-sand curved beach of **Hat Sai Ri**. Stretching to around 2 km, it is the longest beach on the island, the sweep of sand is only interrupted by the occasional large boulder. It has the widest range of accommodation, and many restaurants, shops, dive centres and bars. Although it is a bustling beach with some great bars, the debris – plastic bottles, rotting wood and the like – left by the retreating tide is really unsightly.

North coast

The little cove of **Ao Mamuang** is only accessible by boat so it remains quiet and unfrequented. It is a great place for solitude and there is some good snorkelling.

Off the northwest coast of Koh Tao is **Koh Nang Yuan**. Once a detention centre for political prisoners, this privately owned island consists of three peaks and three connecting sandbars, making it a mini-archipelago. It's surrounded by crystal-clear water and some wonderful coral. **Lomprayah** runs boats to the island at 1030, 1500 and 1800, returning at 0830, 1330 and 1630.

East coast

Ao Hin Wong is a peaceful bay with fantastic views but no beach. However, you can swim off the rocks and boulders and there is some great snorkelling – turtles have been spotted here. The accommodation consists of simple huts tumbling down the steep hillsides.

South of Ao Hin Wong, the bay of **Ao Mao** has just one resort and some great snorkelling, particularly at the **Laem Thian** pinnacle. It is among the more remote and secluded places to stay on Koh Tao.

Continuing south, the bay of **Ao Ta Not** is served by a poor road but vehicles brave the conditions to ferry guests. This is one of the more remote bays and it has a good beach. Although it is not as pretty as Hin Wong, it is wider, has boulders, and more facilities, more expensive accommodation, restaurants, watersports and scuba-diving.

Lang Khaai Bay is littered with dozens of boulders which are reached from a steep slope. The bay is good for snorkelling but there is only a tiny slither of beach.

The beach at **Ao Leuk** shelves more steeply than most of the others around Koh Tao and so is good for swimming and has some of the best snorkelling on the island. This is a quiet beach in spite of visiting groups.

South coast

Next to Ao Chalok Ban Kao, **Ao Thian Ok**, also known as Shark Bay, is a beautiful, privately owned bay with the **Jamahkiri Spa and Resort** set on one hillside. The sea is a stunning mix of blues and greens while the attractive beach is lined with a strip of coconut palms. The bay is known for the black-tip reef sharks that congregate here.

The area of **Taa Toh** 'lagoon' is on the south coast and consists of three beaches, the largest of which is **Hat Taa Toh Yai**. There is good snorkelling on the far side of the lagoon from Hat Taa Toh Yai with reef sharks and more. There is easy access from here to Chalok Ban Kao.

Ao Chalok Ban Kao is a gently shelving beach, enclosed within a horseshoe bay on the south coast capped with weirdly shaped giant boulders. It has a good range of accommodation, restaurants and nightlife. This large bay also has the highest concentration of diving resorts.

Hat Sai Nuan is a quiet, isolated bay, only accessible by long-tailed boat or by a pleasant 30-minute walk around the hilly headland. There are just a handful of places to stay and a relaxed atmosphere. It is arguably the best spot on the island.

Koh Tao listings

For hotel and restaurant price codes and other relevant information, see pages 10-14.

🛏 Where to stay

The densest areas of accommodation are **Hat Sai Ri** and **Ao Chalok Ban Kao**. These offer restaurants, bars and easy access to the dive schools. If you are looking for a greater sense of remoteness, the other bays are more secluded. This has largely been due to the poor roads which makes them difficult to reach without a trek or taxi boat.

Despite the rapid rate of bungalow construction it remains difficult for non-divers to find empty, cheap accommodation unassisted during the high season. If you don't want to risk having to hike around in search of free rooms, the simplest option is to follow a tout from the pier. You can always move out the following day, but book the next place in advance.

Alternatively, make your way straight to one of the more remote bays where places are often less booked out. If diving, you should head straight for the dive shops where they will find you a place to stay in affiliated accommodation – often at a subsidized rate on the days when you are diving.

The other unusual point about accommodation in Koh Tao is the early checkout times. These reflect the need to free up rooms for those arriving on the early boats from the mainland. Most guesthouses have restaurants attached but guests have sometimes been evicted from their bungalows if they have not been spending enough in the restaurant so it is worth enquiring if there is a minimum expenditure before checking in.

Ban Mae Hat and the west coast *p105, map p104*

Ban Mae Hat

$$$$ Charm Churee Villa and Spa, Jansom Bay, T08-1346 5657, www. charmchureevilla.com. The island's most stylishly upmarket resort, in an exquisite cove, just south of Mae Hat. Bungalows on stilts are perched on the hillside, amongst coconut trees, with wonderful sea views from the balconies. Seafood restaurant, beach bar and spa. Tranquillity guaranteed. Recommended.

$$$$ Sensi Paradise, T077-456244, www.sensiparadise.com. A great range of rooms. At the top of the price range the buildings are sensitively designed wooden affairs with traditional Thai architectural features and are incredibly romantic. The garden is also richly planted and the small bay behind the resort is truly idyllic. The pretty beach in front is tiny with several boulders.

$$$$-$$ Koh Tao Royal Resort, T077-456156, kohtaoroyal@hotmail.com. Smart, well-maintained wood and bamboo bungalows. Cheaper rooms climb the hill behind the beach. Lively restaurant in a great location. It has a reasonable secluded beach.

$$$ Beach Club, T077-456222, www. kohtaobeachclub.com. Attractive, airy rooms with high bamboo-lined ceilings, some with a/c. Discounts for divers available.

$$$ Beach Side Resort, 24/5 Baan Mae Haad, T077-456565, www.kohtaobeach sideresort.com. Immaculate, newly built, large concrete and teak bungalows with hot water showers can either be a/c or fan. There are 2 rooms right on the beach, for the others it's a 30-sec walk past the restaurant. Friendly owners. Discount for stays of 3 days or more.

$$$-$$ Crystal Dive Resort, just left of the pier on the beach, T077-456106, www.crystal dive.com. One of the longest-standing dive centres on the island and awarded the prestigious PADI Gold Palm 5 star IDC Resort qualification for its excellent facilities. A range of rooms and bungalows are available with good rates for divers. Pool, restaurant, bar with large screen movies shown, yoga school attached.

Hat Sai Ri

$$$$ Casa del Sol, at the northern end of the beach, T08-5655 6523, www.kohtao casas.com. 5 luxury villas, all decked out in elegant, minimalist style and covering 160-300 sq m. All but the cheapest have a private pool.

$$$$ Koh Tao Cabana, T077-456505, www.kohtaocabana.com. 33 villas built into the headland at the northern end of the beach including 10 attractively designed white circular villas – which have a Mediterranean feel – climbing up the hillside. Bathrooms are open-air and built into rock faces. There are pleasant gardens with attractive wooden sun loungers.

$$$$-$$$ Koh Tao Coral Grand Resort, 15/4 Moo 1, T077-456432, www.kohtaocoral.com. Large, pastel pink and yellow cabins with wooden floors, TVs, fridges, coffee-making facilities and shower rooms dot the landscape of this quiet resort popular with couples and families. The pool is close to the beach with sun loungers and the restaurant is on the beach. The sea is beautiful at this northern end of the beach. Dive centre attached, www.coralgrand divers.com. Recommended.

$$$$-$$$ Thipwimarn Resort, T077-456409, www.thipwimarnresort.com. Beyond the northern end of the beach on the northwest headland, this beautiful resort has 11 bungalows perched on the rocks. Its infinity pool enjoys spectacular views. The deservedly popular restaurant overlooks Sai Ri Bay and the sea.

$$$$-$$ Seashell Resort, T077-456299, www.seashell-kohtao.com. Attractive wood and bamboo huts with spacious verandas in well-manicured grounds. Some a/c rooms and family bungalows available. Divers get cheaper rates. Massage available and courses in massage, too. PADI dive centre attached, T077-456300, seashelldivers@ hotmail.com.

$$$$-$ Ban's Diving Resort, T077-456061, www.bansdivingresortkohtao.com. This resort offers everything from gorgeous a/c luxury rooms with silk furnishings and large balconies to plain fan rooms around the pool reserved for divers. Partial views of the sea. As well as diving, wake-boarding, waterskiing and kayaking is offered, ฿200 per hr. Recommended.

$$$$-$ Bow Thong Beach, T077-456351, www.bowthongresort.com. Offers 30 well-spaced white-board bungalows with an attractive restaurant (0500-1900), private and quieter than most. Pleasant and good value.

$$$-$$ Tommy's Dive Resort, T077-456039. Attractive large a/c rooms with spacious bathrooms in well-furnished concrete bungalows close to the beach, or smaller rooms above the office with or without a/c. All rooms are clean and roomy. Homely family bungalows are also available.

$$$-$ AC Resort, T077-456197, www.acresortkohtao.com. Well-maintained bungalows ina pleasing resort on the 'wrong' side of the road with mosquito screens on the windows and nets over the beds. Tiled shower rooms, fan and verandas. The resort has a nice pool. **Phoenix Divers**, www.phoenix-divers.com,is attached. Divers using the school get cheaper accommodation.

$$$-$ AC Two Resort, T077-456195. On the landward side of the road, this small, older resort has large rooms with small bath rooms, fan and veranda. They are a little dark but set in an appealing ramshackle garden. The excellent Thai food restaurant overlooks the sea and holds popular parties. There is also a supermarket.

$$$-$ DD Hut Bungalows, Moo 2, T077-456077, deedee_hut@hotmail.com. All the bungalows have bathrooms, which makes the cheapest ones a good deal. A/c rooms are also available. Relaxed atmosphere. Property leads down to the sea, but there isn't a beach here. Restaurant.

$$$-$ Sairee Cottage, T077-456126, www.saireecottagediving.com. A well-established resort with the more expensive rooms on the beach in a grassy compound, with the remainder across the road. It is both relaxed and friendly. The restaurant here serves reasonably priced food and cocktails.

$$$-$ Sai Ree Huts, T077-456000, www.saireehutresort.com. There are bamboo weave and timber bungalows with hammocks right up to higher end luxury rooms. A pool has been added in recent years and the restaurant has had a makeover, but the overall vibe remains relaxed.

$$$-$ SB Cabana, opposite Scuba Junction, T077-456005. Typical wooden bungalows in an excellent location very near to the beach. Some fan, some a/c, all with bathroom. Managed by a cantankerous old woman.

$$-$ Blue Wind Bakery and Resort, T077-456116, bluewind_wa@yahoo.com. A small, friendly and attractive place with excellent value fan and a/c rooms and a charming beach restaurant. Pretty wood bungalows nestled in a beautiful mature garden. Their bakery serves pastries, pasta and ice cream. Daily yoga classes. Recommended.

$$-$ In Touch Resort, 1/1 Moo 1, T077-456 514, www.intouchresort.com. Funky resort with an equally cool beachfront restaurant. Brightly coloured individual huts have lots of character. Arranged in a garden opposite the beach, the fan option are the best designed. The cheapest huts are wooden bungalows with open-air bathrooms. Recommended.

$$-$ Queen Resort, T077-456002, moo_mmm@hotmail.com. Rooms with fan, a/c and rooms with shared bathroom available. Some blocks look right out over the sea. ฿20 to use the shower for non-guests. Friendly management.

$$-$ View Cliff, T077-456353, www.kohtaoviewcliff.com. A mixture of concrete, wood and bamboo huts mostly with twin beds, some a/c, all clean.

$ Koh Tao Backpackers Hostel, in Silver Sands Resort, central Sairee Beach. T077-601828, www.kohtaobackpackers.com. Very basic 8-bed dorm accommodation, but its cheap price and central location make it the best option for the budget conscious. They also have a deal with Davy Jones Locker Diving, which allows guests to use the pool and bar area.

$ Sun Lord, T077-456139. Only accessible along an unconvincing track through the jungle on the northwest headland of the island, north of Sai Ri Beach with fantastic views. The cheapest rooms, made of bamboo and without showers, are perched precariously on huge granite boulders. Beneath them there is good coral, perfect for snorkelling.

North coast p105, map p104

$$$$-$$ Nangyuan Island Dive Resort, Koh Nang Yuan, T077-456088, www.nang yuan.com. The only bungalow complex on this beautiful trio of islands has a/c rooms. PADI dive courses and diving trips arranged. Facilities and atmosphere are excellent but it's a little overpriced. Environmental awareness is encouraged. Guests receive a free transfer to Koh Samui.

$$$-$$ Mango Bay Grand Resort, Ao Mamuang, T077-456097, www.kohtao mangobay.com. 15 bungalows, various prices, on stilts overlooking the bay in this secluded spot. This bay is popular for snorkelling.

Ao Hin Wong

$$$-$ View Rock Resort, T077-456548.
Popular with Germans, this isolated resort
clings to a steep hill as it tumbles to the
rocky shore. The more expensive of the14
rooms have a/c and 2 beds, while the
cheapest have shared toilets. Taxi boats
from Ban Mae Hat cost ฿50, one way.

$$-$ Hin Wong Bungalows, T077-
456006. The newer wooden huts with
verandas overlooking the sea are pretty.
Plenty of windows to let in the sea breeze,
reasonably priced restaurant, snorkelling
equipment and canoes for hire. Discounts
available after 3 nights. Electricity available
1800-0600. Mol, the friendly owner, used
to have a gallery in town and can paint
to order.

Ao Ta Not

$$$-$ Tanote Family Bay Dive Resort,
T077-456757. At the northern end of the
bay, spread out amid the rocks, this resort
offers cheap, dark fan rooms or more
expensive brighter rooms with balconies.
All have tables and chairs. No special rates
for divers, www.calypso-diving-kohtao.
de. Taxi to main island pier twice a day.
Restaurant open 0700-2200.

$$-$ Diamond Resort, 40/7 Aow Tanote,
T077-456591. The cheaper rooms are
excellent value; they have cold water
showers and are fan only but are very
comfortable and spacious with plenty
of windows. Homely feel. Next to a very
quiet beach. Restaurant, with others within
walking distance. Recommended.

$$-$ Poseidon, T077-456735, poseidontao.
atspace.com. Cheaper rooms are small,
stuffy and dark but with balconies and
some are set right back from the beach. It's
a small set up with only 14 bungalows and
a restaurant with free Wi-Fi, see Restaurants,
page 113. A taxi leaves the resort daily at
1300 for the island pier.

$ Mountain Reef Resort, T077-456697/9,
T08-1956 2916 (mob). A family-run resort

at the southern end of the bay. Guests are
taken out fishing for their dinner. Larger
rooms are more expensive; go for the ones
overlooking the beach, which get great
sunrise views. There's a daily taxi to the
island pier. Friendly and welcoming staff.

Lang Khaai Bay

$$ Moondance Magic View Bungalow,
T08-9909 0083, www.moondancemagic
viewkohtao.com. 14 thatched timber
cottages completely built in to the granite
boulders and steep coastal landscape
around them. It's set high up, which means
the 'magic' views come at the expense of a
beach, but it's almost a worthwhile sacrifice.

$ Pahnun View Bungalows, Aow Lang
Khaay, T077-456541, pahnun_kohtao@
hotmail.com. Bamboo huts on the cliff-side
with fan, mosquito net and bathroom.
Painted light blue inside, making them
bright and cool. Sweeping views from the
balcony and restaurant. There's no beach.

$ Snorkelling Point Resort, next to
Pahnun View, T077-456264. Wooden
bungalows with impressive views of the
bay. Super comfy beds and a hammock on
the balcony. 24-hr electricity. Restaurant.
Owner speaks a very good level of English.

Ao Leuk

There are only a handful of establishments
on this charming beach and all are small
and simple.

$$-$ Aow Leuk 2 Bungalows, 34/4 Moo 3,
T077-456779, www.aowleuk2.com. A
friendly family-run resort with 5 big
bungalows built up on stilts above the
rocks. Rooms are fairly basic but clean and
comfortable, and the panoramic windows
offer magical views. Prices fluctuate wildly
depending on the season. Also has a
decent restaurant.

$$-$ Nice Moon Bungalows, T077-
456737, nicemoon43@hotmail.com.
About 200 m south of the beach on cliffs
overlooking the bay. Free snorkelling
equipment, friendly and informative.

Restaurant serves delicious Thai food. Recommended.

South coast *p106, map p104*
Ao Thian Ok
$$$$ Jamahkiri Spa & Resort, T077-456400, www.jamahkiri.com. A well-designed and exceptionally private resort which incorporates large boulders into the fabric of the buildings. The handful of boutique rooms with their exquisite interiors, floor to ceiling windows and wide balconies all sit on concrete stilts looking out to sea. Private sun decks lead straight into Shark Bay. The restaurant enjoys an incredible view over the bay. The spa's fresh aloe vera wraps are recommended for sunburn. Free pickup for the resort, restaurant and spa. There's car, kayak and snorkel hire. See also Therapies, page 114.
$$$$-$$ New Heaven, next to OK II, T077-456462, www.newheavenkohtao.com. Very nicely furnished dark teak bungalows with tropical-looking bathrooms. Restaurant has sweeping views of the bay. The newer, more expensive bungalows have a/c. From this cliff-side setting, the sea, which is good for snorkelling, is a short walk away.
$$ Bohemia Resort, T08-7906 5619, www.bohemia resort.com. Run by a friendly Swiss and Italian couple who speak 6 languages between them, this intimate resort is a true labour of love. About 10 mins' walk from the beach, the 4 Thai-style cottages each have a mini fridge, electric kettle, fan and mosquito net. Bathrooms are half open air. Stunning views. Recommended, particularly for the environmentally conscious.
$$ OK II Bungalows, 44/1 Aow Taa Choa, T077-456506, www.kohtaook2bungalow.com. Wooden fan bungalows nestled on the cliff leading down to the water's edge. The ones at the front command an interrupted view of the sea. No beach.
$$-$ Rocky Resort, T077-456035. It's all about the stunning location in this beautiful bay. Bungalows, though a little

weathered, are built around the boulders and many have balconies over the sea with tables and chairs. Basic, but well spaced out and friendly with reasonably priced food.

Ao Chalok Ban Kao
$$$$-$$ View Point Resort, T077-456444, www.kohtaoviewpoint.com. Lofty resort that has recently gone upmarket. The large wood, concrete and thatch cottages in Balinese style are clean, attractive and quiet, with gorgeous views. Much more expensive and luxurious villas have infinity pools, cute little pavilions and unobstructed sea views. The restaurant perches high on stilts over the ocean. Fairly secluded. Recommended.
$$-$ Freedom Beach Resort & Taatoh Resort, T077-456192, www.freedombeach resort.info. A mix of 50 wooden and concrete bungalows with a broad range of price options available, but you get what you pay for. Very friendly staff. Rooms furthest from the restaurant have the best view.
$ Sunshine 2, T077-456154. Offers 62 attractive blue-roofed wooden bungalows lined with bamboo weave with tiled bath-rooms. Set a little back from the beach in nicely manicured gardens. The more expensive ones have a/c. Friendly restaurant.

Hat Sai Nuan
$$$-$ Sai Thong Resort and Spa, T077-456868. It's well worth venturing off the beaten track to reach this rather special and secluded spot. Accommodation ranges from cheap hillside huts with shared bathrooms to slightly overpriced but romantic beachfront bungalows. The simple outdoor spa has a distinctly bohemian appeal, set among jungle and offering relaxation treatments in a small saltwater pool. Relaxed restaurant with cushions, hammocks, a garden and small private beach. Recommended.
$$$-$ Siam Cookies, T077-456301. Attractive bamboo huts. The cheaper

rooms share clean and well-maintained shower rooms.

$ Tao Thong Villa, T077-456078. On the headland so seaviews on both sides. Large variety of simple wood and bamboo huts with large verandas, well placed to make the most of sea breezes. Excellent location. Cheapest rooms have shared bathroom.

🍴 Restaurants

Ban Mae Hat and the west coast *p105, map p104*

Ban Mae Hat
$$ Café del Sol, 9/9 Moo 2, Mae Hat, T077-456 578, www.cafedelsol.ws. Great place for breakfast. It also serves sandwiches, bruschetta and coffee, and for dinner the French/Italian chef prepares salmon or steak and other international cuisine.
$$ El Gringo, Pier Rd, T077-456323. Open 0800-2300. The full Mexican works with fajitas, nachos, steaks and burgers served on tables overlooking the main road. Also make their own ice cream and serve a decent if not huge selection of imported beer and wine. Takeaways and deliveries possible.
$$ Farango Pizzeria, Pier Rd, T077-456205. Open 1200-1500, 1800-2200. Italian restaurant which serves excellent wood-fired pizzas and salads. Has a delivery and takeaway service.
$ Pranee's Kitchen, Mae Hat Sq. 0800-late. More authentic Thai food than the Koh Tao norm, served in an open-sided hardwood sala with cushion or table seating.

Hat Sai Ri
$$$ Thipwimarn Restaurant, on the northwest headland, T077-456409, www.thipwimarnresort.com. 0700-2200. This has become one of the more popular spots for fashionable dining due to the stunning views over Sai Ri bay and excellent Thai food and seafood. Free pickup.
$$ Morava Restaurant and Lounge Bar, T077-456270, T08-2806 3749 (mob), www.moravarestaurant.com. A delightful mix of Western and Japanese cuisine in a stylish, upmarket setting. Also produces a mean Sun night roast.
$$ Noori India, on the hill between Mae Had and Sai Ri, T08-7892 9970 (mob), nooriindia.com. This thatched restaurant serves up a magnificent array of delicious dishes including vegetarian specials and great lunch deals. Delivery available.
$$ White Elephant, main road, Sai Ri Village, T08-9292 8249 (mob). A sweet restaurant in a little garden with a pond serving up delicious seafood and succulent duck dishes.
$$-$ Blue Wind Bakery, towards the northern end of the beach, T077-456116. Specializes in breads and desserts and serves reasonable sandwiches. Also offers fresh pasta including speciality fillings.
$$-$ Intouch Restaurant and Bar, at the southern end of the beach, T077-456514. Breakfasts (including porridge), burgers, sandwiches, soups, salads and noodles form part of a vast menu at this place which has decking on the beach. Relax in a hammock, play pool or eat looking over the sea.
$$-$ Suthep Restaurant, centre of the beach. Thai food, lasagne, fish cakes, fish pie, burgers, great mashed potato, toad in the hole and Marmite sandwiches. The Bailey's cheesecake is an indulgence. Cushion seating. Popular with long-term residents. Good value. Stops serving at 2200.
$ Coffee Boat, on the main road just before the main drag down to the beach in Sai Ri village, T077-456178. A cheap and cheerful authentic Thai diner and bakery. Ample proportions of tasty, hot Thai food. Cakes made to order.
$ The Snack Shack, next to Lotus Bar, T08-5478 8753. Open 1800-0200. The quintessential late-night pit-stop serves up all the greasy favourites, including burgers, kebabs and fries. Delivery available.
$ Zanzibar, T077-456452. An African-themed slice of urban bohemia serving up

good quality coffee and an extensive range of sandwich options with imported meats and cheeses, as well as some sweet treats.

East coast *p106, map p104*
Ao Ta Not
$$ Poseidon, T077-456735. Open 0730-2200. A popular restaurant serving fried fish, a good range of vegetarian dishes and unusual milk-shakes – including cookie vanilla flavour and prune lassies.

South coast *p106, map p104*
Ao Chalok Ban Kao
$$ New Heaven, 44 Moo 3, a decent climb to the top of the hill, T077-456462, www.newheavenkohtao.com. Evenings only. A bit pricey but good food and fantastic views over the gorgeous Thian Og Bay.
$$ Sunshine Divers Resort, T077-456597, www.sunshine-diveresort.com. Has a BBQ evening buffet every night with baked potatoes, garlic bread, calamari, kebabs, salad and some rice dishes.
$$ Taraporn Bar & Restaurant, across the slatted walkway at the west of the beach. Seating on hammocks, cushions and mats on the floor. The restaurant itself is on stilts above the sea. A great venue.
$$-$ Viewpoint Restaurant, beyond the Bubble Dive Resort at the eastern end of the beach, T077-456777, www.kohtaoviewpoint.com. Open 0700-2200. Wide menu of Thai and some Western food that is filling and tasty served in this laid-back restaurant. Also perched above the sea it enjoys great views of the horseshoe-shaped Chalok Ban Kao Bay.

🔾 Bars and clubs

Koh Tao, once a quiet neighbour of Koh Phangan, is now well provided with night spots. The party tends to rotate to different bars throughout the week, so the best way to discover what's happening is to look out for flyers and ads in shop windows, or simply ask one of the dive instructors.

Ban Mae Hat and the west coast *p105, map p104*
Ban Mae Hat
Dragon Bar, Pier Rd. 1800-0200. Wooden tables spill onto the street from this Bruce Lee-inspired bar playing different music every night: indie, 1980s, hip hop, jazz and alternative rock.
Safety Stop Pub, Mae Hat Sq, close to the pier. Popular with tourists and locals, with a late night disco on Sat nights and sports coverage throughout the week.
Whitening, on the road to the Sensi Paradise Resort. The staple diver's after-hours spot with a pleasant bar on the beach and decent menu. Fri night parties.

Hat Sai Ri
Choppers, Sai Ri Village, T077-456641. Open 0800-late. A popular large, Western-style pub which shows sport. It pastes timetables for all events outside the pub. Friendly staff.
FIZZ Beach Lounge (formerly Dry Bar). A popular place amongst the trees on the beach, decked out with green bean bags, fairy lights and candles in the sand. Perfect place to watch the sunset with a beer or cocktail in hand.
Lotus Beach Bar, www.tonylotusbar.com. The buckets never stop flowing, loud tunes blare until the early hours and flame throwers perform until the fires completely die out. Fancy dress parties are popular.
Pure, south Sai Ri beach, www.project-32.com/pure. The hippest place in town, stylishly scattered with big red bean bags. Open every night until 0200 but watch out for the popular party nights.

South coast *p106, map p104*
Ao Chalok Ban Kao
Babaloo, excellent bar set in the rocks and decorated with sculptures, open from sunset until the early hours.

⚙ What to do

Koh Tao p103, map p104
Diving
Diving is popular year round here. It is said to be the cheapest place in Thailand to learn to dive, and the shallow waters and plenty of underwater life, make it an easy and interesting place to do so. There's a **recompression chamber** in Ban Mae Hat (Badalveda, opposite the main petrol station on the island, north up the main road and turn right, T077-456 661 (main office), T08-1081 9777 (24-hr emergency number), www.sssnetwork.com.

Dive schools have an arrangement where they charge roughly the same for an **Open Water** course (฿9000). Fixed prices also apply to other courses: ฿8500 for **Advanced**, and ฿9500 for rescue. What varies are the sizes of the groups and the additional perks such as a free dive or free/subsidized accommodation. A discover scuba dive is around ฿3000, and a fun-dive for qualified divers is around ฿1800, although the more dives you do the cheaper each dive becomes. All schools accept credit cards. If you are considering diving but want to watch the divers in action before making the investment, many of the dive schools are prepared to take you out to dive sites with their groups. You only pay for the snorkelling equipment.

Asia Divers, Ban Mae Hat, T077-456054, www.asia-divers.com.

Ban's, Hat Sai Ri, T077-456466, www.amazingkohtao.com.

Big Blue, 17/18 Moo 1, Hat Sa Ri, T077-456415, www.bigbluediving.com. Fully-fledged dive resort.

Big Bubble, Chalok Ban Kao, T077-456669, www.tauchen-diving.de.

Buddha View Dive Resort, Chalok Ban Kao, T077-456074, www.buddhaview-diving.com.

Calypso Diving, Ao Ta Not, T077-456745, eugentao@yahoo.de.

Crystal Dive Resort, Ban Mae Hat and Sai Ri, T077-456107, www.crystaldive.com.

Easy Divers, Ban Mae Hat, T077-456010, www.thaidive.com.

Kho Tao Divers, Hat Sai Ri, T08-6069 9244 (mob), kohtaodivers@hotmail.com.

Planet Scuba, Ban Mae Hat, T077-456110, www.planet-scuba.net.

Scuba Junction, Sai Ri Beach, T077-456164, www.scuba-junction.com.

Sunshine Divers, Chalok Ban Kao, T077-456597, www.sunshine-diveresort.com.

Muay Thai (Thai boxing)
Sai Ri Stadium, near Asia Divers. ฿500. Look out for flyers for dates.

Snorkelling kayaking and surfing
Many of the guesthouses hire out their own equipment, but this can be of low quality and dirty. The most reliable gear is that hired from the dive shops. You generally pay ฿50 for the mask and snorkel and a further ฿50 for fins. Boats around the island cost around ฿500 per person for a day trip with stops for snorkelling.

Kayak hire is available from hotels and guesthouses, including **Ban's Diving Resort**, see page 108.

Therapies
Jamahkiri Spa & Resort, Ao Thian Ok, T077-456400, www.jamahkiri.com. 1000-2200. Free pickups available. Indulge in one of the reasonably priced packages available at this spa in grounds overlooking the sea. The aloe vera body wrap is the signature experience and produces quite a strange sensation. There's a steam sauna and facials and a variety of massages are available. After your massage have a drink overlooking the sea. Recommended.

Tour operators
A long-tailed boat trip around the island starts from about ฿1500 for up to 4 people. **Good Time Adventures**, T08-7275 3604, www.gtadventures.com. These self-confessed adrenaline junkies lay on

Travel warning: the Malaysian border

This guide does not cover the provinces of Narathiwat, Songkhla, Pattani and Yala, which extend to the Malaysian border. At the beginning of 2007, due to the ongoing political situation in Southern Thailand, the UK Foreign and Commonwealth Office (www.fco.gov.uk) and the US State Department (www.state.gov) both issued travel warnings advising visitors NOT to travel to, or through, these provinces. These warnings are still in place as this book goes to press.

Travellers should also be reminded that when such warnings are issued, if you chose to ignore them, insurance companies may withdraw their cover. This situation and warnings are also subject to change and visitors should check the present situation before they make plans to travel.

rock-climbing, abseiling, cliff jumping, wakeboarding, scuba, even bi-monthly pub crawl excursions.

⊖ Transport

Koh Tao *p103, map p104*
Bicycle hire
Mountain bikes are available for hire from guesthouses and travel agencies.

Boat
There are boats of various speeds and sizes connecting Koh Tao with Chumphon (see page 48) and Surat Thani, via Koh Samui and Koh Phangan.

To **Chumphon**, there are departures with **Lomprayah**, T077-456176 (office hours 0830-1900), at 1015 and 1425, 2 hrs, ฿600; with **Songserm**, T077-456274, at 1430, 3 hrs, ฿450; with **Seatran**, T077-456907, at 1000 and 1600, 2hrs, ฿550. **Ko Jaroen**, T08-1797 0276 (mob) runs the nightboat at 2200, 5 hrs.

To **Koh Samui**, **Lomprayah** is the most comfortable, with a/c, TV and shortest journey time, though it's also the most expensive; it has departures at 0930, 1500, 1½ hrs, ฿600. The alternatives are **Songserm**, T077-456274, at 1000, 2 hrs 45 mins, ฿500, or **Seatran**, T077-456907, at 0930 and 1500, 1½ hrs, ฿550.

To **Koh Phangan** with **Lomprayah**, at 0930 and 1500, 1 hr, ฿450; with **Songserm**,

T077-456274, at 1000, 1½ hrs, ฿400; with **Seatran**, at 0930 and 1500, 1 hr, ฿400.

To **Surat Thani** with **Songserm**, at 1000, 6½ hrs, ฿600; with **Lomprayah**, at 2100 (night service), 8½ hrs, ฿700; with **Seatran**, at 0930 and 1500, ฿550, free transfer from Bang Ruk pier to Nathon on Samui for boats to Surat Thani.

To **Hua Hin** with **Lomprayah**, at 1015 and 1425, ฿1000.

To **Bangkok** with **Lomprayah**, with boat and VIP bus, at 1015 and 1445, ฿1000.

Motorbike hire
Unless you are an experienced dirt bike rider, this is not really an advisable form of transport, as reaching any of the isolated bays involves going along narrow, twisting, bumpy, severely potholed tracks.
Lederhosenbikes, Ban Mae Hat, T08-1752 8994 (mob), www.cycling-koh-tao.com. German owner rents scooters for ฿150-200 per day, and motorbikes from ฿400.

Taxi
Taxis and motorbike taxis wait at the end of Mae Hat pier. Sharing taxis makes sense as the cost is per journey, not per person. From Mae Hat to Ao Ta Not costs ฿200-300 with a minimum of 4 in the car. To Sai Ri or Chalok, ฿150-200.

❶ Directory

Koh Tao *p103, map p104*

Medical services Badalaveda Diving
Medicine Centre, Sai Ri, T077-456664; Koh
Tao Physician Clinic, Sai Ri T077-456037,
T081-7375444, 0800-1900; Koh Tao Health
Centre, Mae Hat, T077-456007. **Post office**
Thongnual Rd, Mae Hat, straight up from
the pier and turn left, Mon-Fri 0830-1630.
Telephone Facilities are easily available on
Sai Ri Beach, Ao Chalok Ban Kao and
Ban Mae Hat.

Nakhon Si Thammarat and around

Nakhon Si Thammarat ('the Glorious city of the Dead') or Nagara Sri Dhammaraja ('the city of the Sacred Dharma Kings') has masqueraded under many different aliases: Marco Polo referred to it as Lo-Kag, the Portuguese called it Ligor – thought to have been its original name – while to the Chinese it was Tung Ma-ling. Today, it is the second biggest city in the south and most people know it simply as Nakhon or Nakhon Si.

It is not a very popular tourist destination and it has a rather unsavoury reputation as one of the centres of mafia activity in Thailand, but otherwise it is friendly and manageable with a wide range of hotels, some excellent restaurants, a good museum and a fine monastery in Wat Phra Mahathat. It is also famed for its shadow puppetry.

Around Nakhon are the quiet beaches of Khanom and Nai Phlao. The Khao Luang and Khao Nan national parks offer waterfalls, caves, whitewater rafting and homestays.

Arriving in Nakhon Si Thammarat
Getting there Nakhon is a provincial capital and therefore well connected. There is an airport north of town with daily flights to Bangkok (with Nok Air and Air Asia). Nakhon also lies on the main north–south railway line linking Bangkok with southern Thailand. The station is within easy walking distance of the town centre on Yommarat Road. However, only two southbound trains go into Nakhon itself; most stop instead at the junction of Khao Chum Thong, 30 km west of Nakhon, from where you must take a bus or taxi into town. The main bus station (for non air-conditioned connections) is 1 km out of town over the bridge on Karom Road, west of the mosque. It has connections with Bangkok and most destinations in the south. There are also minibus and shared taxi services to many destinations in the south. ▶ *See Transport, page 127, for further information.*

Getting around The centre is comparatively compact and navigable on foot. But for sights on the edge of town – like Wat Phra Mahathat – it is necessary to catch a public *songthaew*, *saamlor* or motorcycle taxi. The *songthaew* is the cheapest option, a trip across town costs ฿10. The old pedal *saamlor* is still in evidence though it is gradually being pushed out by the noisier and more frightening motorcycle taxi, of which there seem to be hundreds.

Tourist information TAT ⓘ *Sanam Na Muang, Rachdamnern Rd, T075-346515-6, www.tat. or.th/south2 (Thai only), daily 0830-1630*, is situated in an old, attractive club building. The staff here produce a helpful pamphlet and hand-out sheets of information on latest bus and taxi prices. It is a useful first stop.

Background
Nakhon is surrounded by rich agricultural land and has been a rice exporter for centuries. The city has links with both the Dvaravati and Srivijayan empires. Buddhist monks from Nakhon are thought to have propagated religion throughout the country perhaps even influencing the development of Buddhism in Sukhothai, Thailand's former great kingdom.

Nakhon was at its most powerful and important during King Thammasokarat's reign in the 13th century, when it was busily trading with south India and Ceylon. But as Sukhothai and then Ayutthaya grew in influence, the city went into a gradual decline. During the 17th century, King Narai's principal concubine banished the bright young poet Si Phrat to Nakhon. Here he continued to compose risqué rhymes about the women of the governor's court. His youthful impertinence lost him his head.

Nakhon used to have the dubious honour of being regarded as one of the crime capitals of Thailand – a position it had held, apparently, since the 13th century. Locals maintain that the city has now cleaned up its act and Nakhon is probably best known today for its prawn farms and nielloware industry. The shop where the industry started some 50 years ago still stands on Sitama Road and production techniques are demonstrated on Si Thammasok I Road. Elsewhere, other than in a few handicraft shops on Tha Chang Road, nielloware is an elusive commodity, although the National Museum has some examples on display. The art and craft and performance of shadow puppetry is also being kept alive in Nakhon, see page 127.

Nakhon Si Thammarat

Wat Phra Mahathat

ⓘ *T075-345172, cloisters are open daily 0800-1630.*

A 2-km-long wall formerly enclosed the old city and its wats – only a couple of fragments of this remain (the most impressive section is opposite the town jail on Rachdamnern Road). Wat Phra Mahathat, 2 km south of town on Rachdamnern Road, is the oldest temple in town and the biggest in South Thailand – as well as being one of the region's most important. The wat dates from AD 757 and was originally a Srivijayan Mahayana Buddhist shrine. The 77-m high stupa, *Phra Boromathat* – a copy of the Mahathupa in Ceylon – was built early in the 13th century to hold relics of the Buddha from Ceylon. The wat underwent extensive restoration in the Ayutthayan period and endured further alterations in 1990. The *chedi*'s square base, its voluptuous body and towering spire are all Ceylonese-inspired. Below the spire is a small square platform decorated with bas-reliefs in gold of monks circumambulating (*pradaksina*) the monument. The spire itself is said to be topped with 962 kg of gold, while the base is surrounded by small stupas. The covered cloisters at its base contain many beautiful, recently restored Buddha images all in the image of subduing Mara. The base is dotted with attractive elephant heads. Also here is **Vihara Bodhi Langka** ⓘ *0800-1600, entry by donation,* a jumbled treasure trove of a museum. It contains a large collection of archaeological artefacts, donated jewellery, bodhi trees, Buddhas and a collection of

Where to stay 🛏
Grand Park **1**
Ligor City **7**
Nakhon Garden Inn **3**
Thai **4**
Thai Lee **5**
Thaksin **6**
Twin Lotus **2**

Restaurants 🍴
A&A **1**
Hao Coffee Shop **3**

Krour Nakorn **3**

Bars & clubs 🍸
60 Bar **2**

Minibuses 🚐
Minivan to Hat Yai **5**
Minivan to Surat Thani & Khanom **4**
Share taxi terminal to Airport, Trang & Songkhla **2**
To Phuket **3**

Terrorism in the deep south

Along with Narathiwat, Songkhla, Pattani and Yala, Satun province was a hotbed for Islamic insurgents during the 1970s and 1980s until a government amnesty saw 20,000 fighters handing in their arms in 1987. Then, in December 2001, it all began again with hit-and-run attacks on police, military outposts, schools and commercial sites.

The Australian government, following the Bali bombings, warned its citizens to exercise particular vigilance in Satun province and overland travel to the Malaysian border. The UK Foreign Office advises against all but essential travel to the four southern provinces. Among the risks are kidnapping from resorts and piracy in the Straits of Malacca.

Much of the violence has been blamed on Thaksin Shinawatra's hair-brained attempts to stamp out the separatist movement by rounding up suspected militants (but on the basis of unsound intelligence), thus creating a wave of resentment in the region. The military leaders who deposed the oligarch-turned-politician in late 2006 made overtures to the separatists, apologising for Thaksin's policies, with mixed success.

Much of the tension in Satun province and throughout the deep south can be traced back to the late 1890s when these provinces – once part of Muslim and animist Malaysia – were Siamised, their names translated to Thai and the people reclassified as Malay-Thais. Satun was formerly called Setol. But the south also claims that, because it is not fully Thai, it is punished with low funding and poor schools and has become a dumping ground for corrupt and inept military and government officials. Certainly, banditry is rife throughout the southern provinces.

The Bahasa-speaking inhabitants certainly see themselves as more Malaysian than Thai and this is evident in the excellent cuisine, which is not as hot as Thai food but is spicier with quieter, more layered curries and a subtler sweetness. And the restaurant owners may often tell you that the ingredients are all Malaysian.

The far south also has spectacular national parks, including Tarutao with its marine life and awe-inspiring scenery.

---

sixth- to 13th-century Dvaravati sculpture – some of the latter are particularly fine. The mural at the bottom of the stairs tells the story of the early life of the Buddha, while the doorway at the top is decorated with figures of Vishnu and Phrom dating from the Sukhothai period.

Phra Viharn Luang

The nearby Phra Viharn Luang (to the left of the main entrance to the stupa) is an impressive building, with an intricately painted and decorated ceiling, dating from the 18th century. The best time to visit the monastery is in October during the Tenth Lunar Month Festival when Wat Mahathat becomes a hive of activity. Foodstalls, travelling cinemas, shadow-puppet masters, the local mafia, businessmen in their Mercedes, monks and handicraft sellers all set up shop, making the wat endlessly interesting.

Puppet workshop and museum

ⓘ 110/18 Si Thammasok, Soi 3, T075-346394, daily 0830-1700, 20-min performance, ฿100 for 2; 3 or more ฿50 each.

Not far from Wat Mahathat is the puppet workshop of Nakhon's most famous *nang thalung* master – Khun Suchart Subsin. His workshop is signposted off the main road near the Chinese temple (hard to miss). As well as giving shows (see Entertainment, page 126) and selling examples of his work starting at ฿200 or so for a simple elephant, the compound itself is interesting and peaceful with craftsmen hammering out puppets under thatched awnings and dozens of buffalo skulls hung everywhere. There is also a small museum exhibiting puppet characters from as far back as the 18th century.

Saan Chao Mae Thap Thim Chinese Pagoda
① *It's a 2-km hike out to the monastery; blue songthaews constantly ply the road to the monastery and back (฿6).*
Returning to the main road, this Chinese pagoda offers a respite from Theravada Buddhist Thailand. Magnificent dragons claw their way up the pillars and inside, wafted by incense, are various Chinese gods, Bodhisattvas and demons.

Nakhon Si Thammarat National Museum
① *Rachdamnern Rd, about 700 m beyond Wat Mahathat, Wed-Sun 0830-1630, ฿30. The museum is a 2-km walk from most of the hotels; catch one of the numerous blue songthaews running along Rachdamnern Rd and ask for 'Pipitipan Nakhon Si Thammarat' (฿6).*
The Nakhon branch of the National Museum is one of the town's most worthwhile sights. The impressive collection includes many interesting Indian-influenced pieces as well as rare pieces from the Dvaravati and later Ayutthaya periods. Some exhibits are labelled in English. The section on art in South Thailand explains and charts the development of the unusual local Phra Phutthasihing (or Buddha Sihing) style of Buddha image, which was popular locally in the 16th century. Also in this section is the oldest Vishnu statue in Southeast Asian art (holding a conch shell on his hip), which dates from the fifth century. The museum has sections on folk arts and crafts and local everyday implements. To the right of the entrance hall, in the prehistory section, stand two large Dongson bronze kettle drums – two of only 12 found in the country. The one decorated with four ornamental frogs is the biggest ever found in Thailand.

Chapel of Phra Buddha Sihing
The Chapel of Phra Buddha Sihing, sandwiched between two large provincial office buildings just before Rachdamnern Road splits in two, may contain one of Thailand's most important Buddha images. During the 13th century an image, magically created, was shipped to Thailand from Ceylon (hence the name – Sihing for the Sinhalese people). The Nakhon statue, like the other two images that claim to be the Phra Buddha Sihing (one in Bangkok and one in Chiang Mai, northern Thailand), is not Ceylonese in style at all; it conforms with the Thai style of the peninsula.

Wat Wang Tawan Tok
Back in the centre of town is Wat Wang Tawan Tok, across Rachdamnern Road from the bookshop. It has, at the far side of its sprawling compound, a southern Thai-style wooden house built between 1888 and 1901. Originally the house (which is really three houses in one) was constructed without nails – it has since been poorly repaired using them. The door panels, window frames and gables, all rather weather-beaten now, were once intricately carved but it is still infinitely more appealing than the concrete shophouses going up all over Thailand.

Hindu temples
There are two 13th- to 14th-century Hindu temples in the city, along Rachdamnern Road. **Hor Phra Isuan**, next to the Semamuang Temple, houses an image of Siva, the destroyer. Opposite is **Hor Phra Narai** which once contained images of Vishnu, now in the city museum.

Morning market
A worthwhile early-morning walk is west across the bridge along Karom Road to the morning market (about 1 km), which sells fresh food. This gets going early and is feverish with activity from around 0630.

Thai Traditional Medicine Centre
① Take a local bus, ฿8.
On the outskirts of the city, after Wat Mahathat is the small **Wat Sa-la Mechai**. While the temple is fairly ordinary, at one end of the temple grounds is a recently established centre for traditional medicine, including massage. If you want a traditional massage, it costs about ฿100 per hour – you pay before you begin. You can also take a course in massage, paying by the hour, and learn more about traditional herbal medicine (there is a small garden of medicinal plants at the front).

Around Nakhon → *For listings, see pages 124-127.*

Khanom and Nai Phlao beaches
① Regular buses from Nakhon (฿20), a/c micro buses (฿60) leave from Wat Kit Rd and also from Surat Thani. The beaches are about 8 km off the main road; turn at the Km 80 marker.
Eighty kilometres north of Nakhon, near Khanom district, there are some secluded stretches of shoreline: Khanom beach (2 km from town), Nai Phlao beach to the south, and a couple of other bays are opening up to development. This area is predominantly visited by Thai tourists. Newer operations seem to be targeting Western tourists who are beginning to look towards the mainland in this area for reasonably priced peace and quiet, and convenience they have failed to find on Samui. There are better beaches in Thailand but you're likely to have most of what you find to yourself – particularly if you come mid-week. Khanom beach is a long run of coconut-grove fringed sand that slopes steeply into the sea. Development is picking up here but it still has a remote feeling. Khanom town is a very lively rough and ready fishing port. There are few facilities aimed at *farang* in this town meaning that it offers a genuine slice of Thai rural life to the more adventurous traveller. Nai Phlao beach offers a much shorter run of beach and has a greater concentration of resorts. That's not saying much though as it still feels like a relatively untouched spot, despite the best efforts of the new development at the **Chada Racha Resort** to introduce an unhealthy dose of concrete to the coastline.

Khao Luang National Park
① To get to Karom Waterfall take a bus to Lan Saka (then walk 3 km to falls) or charter a minibus direct. To get to Phrom Lok Waterfall take a minibus from Nakhon then hire a motorbike taxi for the last very pleasant 8 km. The villagers at Khiriwong village can organize trips up Khao Luang mountain but do not speak English. See What to do for further options, homestays and guides. Songthaews leave Nakhon for Khiriwong every 15 mins or so (฿15).
The Khao Luang National Park is named after Khao Luang, a peak of 1835 m – the highest in the south – which lies less than 10 km west of Nakhon. Within the boundaries of the

mountainous, 570-sq-km national park are three waterfalls. **Karom Waterfall** lies 30 km from Nakhon, off Route 4015, and has a great location with views over the lowlands. Also here are cool forest trails and fast-flowing streams. The park is said to support small populations of tiger, leopard and elephant, although many naturalists believe they are on the verge of extinction here. **Phrom Lok Waterfall** is about 25 km from Nakhon, off Route 4132. However, the most spectacular of the waterfalls is **Krung Ching** – 'waterfall of a hundred thousand raindrops' – 70 km out of town, and a 4-km walk from the park's accommodation. The 1835-m climb up **Khao Luang** starts from Khiriwong village, 23 km from Nakhon, off Route 4015. The mountain is part of the Nakhon Si Thammarat range, running from Koh Samui south through Surat Thani to Satun. The scenic village, surrounded by forest, was partially destroyed by mudslides in 1988 – an event which led to the introduction of a nationwide logging ban at the beginning of 1989. The climb takes three days and is very steep in parts, with over 60° slopes. If you plan to do this walk on your own, there is no accommodation so it is necessary to carry your own equipment and food. See also Where to stay, page 125.

Khao Wang Thong Cave
① *Charter a songthaew for around ฿800 per day. The entrance is past the cave keeper's house, 15 mins' walk uphill from the village.*
One of the less-publicized sights in the Nakhon area is Khao Wang Thong Cave. The cave is on the south side of the middle peak of three limestone mountains near Ban Khao Wang Thong in Khanom district. It lies 100 km north of Nakhon, 11 km off Route 4142. Villagers and a group of Nakhon conservationists saved the cave from a dolomite mining company in 1990. A few tight squeezes and a short ladder climb are rewarded by some of Thailand's most spectacular cave formations. Its four spacious chambers – one of which has been dubbed 'the throne hall' – are decorated with gleaming white curtain stalactites. It is presently maintained by groups of local villagers and plans are afoot to install a lighting system. Until then, it is advisable that you bring your own torch (flashlight).

Khao Nan National Park
① *Take the main route up to Khanom beyond Ta Sala and turn left down the road from where there are signposts to the park.*
Just north of Khao Luang National Park is the new Khao Nan National Park. At 1430 m, Khao Nan Yai is not as high as Khao Luang, but is still tall enough to support cloud forest on its summit. The national park has a beautiful waterfall near its entrance, lush forests, waterfalls and caves. One cave, **Tham Hong**, has a waterfall inside it and is well worth visiting, and fairly easily accessible but you'll need a torch. Treks to the top of Khao Nan Yai taking three to four days are organized by the Forestry Department staff. You should call the Forestry Department in Bangkok at least a couple of days in advance to arrange a guide. The treks go to the top of Khao Nan where you can camp out in cloud forest. Temperatures at the top are always cool and there is a wide variety of ferns and mosses in the understorey of the forest. Khao Nan and Khao Luang are also known for *pa pra* – a deciduous tree which loses its leaves during the dry season (February to April) with the leaves first changing colour to a brilliant red.

Nakhon Si Thammarat and around listings

For hotel and restaurant price codes and other relevant information, see pages 10-14.

◉ Where to stay

Nakhon *p117, map p119*
At the top level of accommodation, Nakhon has a couple of options, and the middle range now has a few hotels worthy of a mention, but for the rest, there is little to choose between them.

$$$$-$$ Ligor City Hotel, 1488 Sri-Prach Rd Tawang, centre of town, T075-312555, www.ligorcityhotel.com. Clean, comfortable rooms decorated in traditional Thai textiles and teak wood. Friendly staff. Rooms near the stairs can pick up Wi-Fi coverage. A worthy rival to the Twin Lotus.

$$$$-$$ Twin Lotus Hotel, 97/8 Hatankarnhukwag Rd, outskirts of town, T075-323777, www.twinlotushotel. com. Nearly 400 a/c rooms, with TV and minibars, and a good-sized swimming pool and fitness centre, plus the usual services expected of a top-end hotel. The reasonable tariff includes a good buffet-style breakfast. A well-run and well-maintained hotel.

$$$-$$ Grand Park Hotel, 1204/79 Pak Nakhon Rd, T075-317666, www.grandpark nakhon.com. Opposite the **Nakhon Garden Inn**, this is a bit of a block architecturally and doesn't really live up to its grand name, but it has adequate rooms and is centrally located with lots of parking. A/c, hot water, bathtubs, TV, minibar. One of the better hotels in this category.

$$-$ Thaksin Hotel, 1584/23 Si Prat Rd. T075-342790, www.thaksinhotel. com. Comfortable, good-value rooms, with cable TV, en suite and a/c. Decent location, friendly and some English spoken. Recommended.

$ Nakhon Garden Inn, 1/4 Pak Nakhon Rd, T075-344831. A surprising amount

of charm for a budget hotel in a Thai provincial city, and a nice escape from the usual concrete box options: red brick motel-style accommodation set around a lush courtyard oasis within walking distance of the city centre. Rooms are a little quirky, but comfortable enough for the price. Free Wi-Fi. Recommended.

$ Thai Hotel, 1375 Rachdamnern Rd, T075-341509. Some a/c in newer rooms away from the noise of the street with beds large enough to sleep 4. Restaurant and internet access too.

$ Thai Lee, 1130 Rachdamnern Rd, T075-356948. Large, bright, clean rooms with fan and attached bathroom (Western toilet), best-value accommodation in the lower end of the market.

Khanom and Nai Phlao beaches *p122*
$$$$-$$$ Racha Kiri (formerly Chada Racha Resort), Nai Phlao Beach 99, T075-300245, www.rachakiri.com. A luxury resort on a rocky outcrop at the far end of the beach, this seems a little out of place in the otherwise undeveloped area. The rooms and villas are very comfortable, though, and most have good views. There's no beach, but it has a nice pool that overlooks the ocean. The restaurant food is quite expensive.

$$$-$$ Khanom Golden Beach Hotel, 59/3 Moo 4, Ban Na Dan, T075-326690, www.khanomgoldenbeach.com. Hotel block with pool, snooker room, children's room, tour desk, restaurant and rental of windsurf boards, sailing dinghies and bicycles. Friendly and professional staff. Rooms are rather characterless but clean and comfortable. The larger more expensive suites are very spacious and well equipped.

$$$-$$ Khanom Maroc Resort & Spa, 91 Moo 8 Khanom, T075-300323, www.khanommaroc.com. Rooms in this

Moroccan-themed resort each have a TV, fridge, private bathroom and balcony. All are located in a central block, designed to resemble a Moroccan palace whose architecture can best be described as 'unusual'. It's quirky, but a bit tacky, and it's disappointing that the same effort wasn't put into the rooms, which are clean and comfortable but rather uninspired.

$$$-$$ Supar Royal Beach Hotel, 51/4 Moo 8, Hat Nai Phlao, T075-300300, www.suparroyal.com. Hotel block under same management as the **Supar Villa**. Clean rooms, horribly dated pink tiled floors, generally very characterless and could use some maintenance, but at least every room has a sea view.

$$ Alongot Resort, Khanom beach, T075-529119. The promising exterior of these bungalows is ruined by very drab interiors. The location is great – right in the middle of Khanom beaches' long sweep. They sell a decent array of food as well. Friendly.

$$-$ Nai Phlao Bay Resort, 51/3 Ban Nai Phlao, T075-529039. Large resort with a/c rooms, restaurant and impersonal service. Average bungalows set back from the beach – nice tree-lined lawn. Quite pricey for what it is.

$ Sri Khanom Hotel, 77 Tambon Rd, T075-529259. Only hotel in Khanom town. No English is spoken at this friendly, family-run hotel. Some rooms are worn and grim – go for the ones on the upper floors for more air and light. No hot water though all rooms are en suite. Aimed at Thai businessmen.

Tumble SaoPao

$$$-$$ Ekman Garden Resort, 39/2 Moo 5 Tumble SaoPao, T075-367566, www.ekmangarden.com. About half way between Nakhon and Khanom, this resort, run by extremely friendly Thai and Swedish owners, Ann and Stefan, is designed for those with relaxation in mind. It's about 2 km to the ocean, which may deter some, but the real draw is the stunning flower garden and man-made lakes where you can catch your own dinner. Rooms are very private and homely, though the furniture is a little dated. Also has a pool, putting green and restaurant.

Khao Luang National Park *p122*
The **$$** bungalows at the park office of the **Karom Waterfall** sleep up to 10 people. Camping is possible if you have your own gear. The 2nd park office at **Krung Ching Waterfall**, T075-309644-5, has 2 guest-houses **$$$$-$$** and a campsite. For homestay, see What to do, page 127.

🍴 Restaurants

Nakhon *p117, map p119*
Prawns are Nakhon's speciality and farms abound in the area. Good seafood (including saltwater prawns) is available at reasonable prices in most of the town's restaurants. Roadside stalls sometimes sell a Nakhon speciality: small prawns in their shells, deep fried in a spicy batter and served as a sort of prawn pattie. The **Bovorn Bazaar**, in the centre of town off Rachdamnern Rd, is a good place to start in any hunt for food. It has restaurants, a bakery, a bar and a coffee shop.

$$ A & A Restaurant, T075-311047. Open 0700-2200. A/c restaurant just down the road from the **Nakorn Garden Inn** and marked with flags boasting fresh coffee. Serves Thai-style toasted bread with jam, marmalade, condensed milk and sugar, excellent coffee, and very tasty Thai food. It also does Western breakfasts for a very reasonable price. Try the pork rib noodle soup and the fried minced chicken noodles. The brownies and sticky cakes, puddings and jellies are delicious. There's a menu in English.

$$-$ 99 Rock Bar and Grill, Bovorn Bazaar, Rachdamnern Rd, T075-317999, jarrock@rocketmail.com. Open 1600-2300. A Western-style bar with cold beer and a menu including pasta, pizzas, baked potatoes and grilled chicken. One of the few places to drink after 2100, it sometimes has live music.

$ Hao Coffee Shop, Bovorn Bazaar, off Rachdamnern Rd. It is charmingly decorated with antiques and assorted oddities and is like a museum piece with glass display cabinets everywhere. Recommended.

$ Krour Nakorn, at the back of Bovorn Bazaar off Rachdamnern Rd next to the massive trunk of an Indian rubber tree. Pleasant eating spot, with open verandas, art work, wicker chairs and a reasonable line in seafood and other spicy dishes. You get given an entire tray of herbs and vegetables to go with your meal. Recommended.

$ 60 Bar, 130/1 Ratchadamnoen Rd, next to Walailat University. 1800-0100. A popular local watering hole, where you can sit back over some light snacks and a cold beer, listen to some live music, and put your Thai language skills to the test until the early hours of the morning.

Bakeries

Ligo, Rachdamnern Rd and Bovorn Bazaar. A good selection of pastries and doughnuts.

Sinocha (sign only in Thai), down the narrow alleyway by the **Thai Hotel**. Perhaps even better than **Ligos**, it sells Danish pastries, doughnuts, more sickly concoctions, as well as a good range of dim sum. Recommended.

Foodstalls

Nam Cha Rim Tang is a stall in the Bovorn Bazaar, which sets up early evening and produces exceedingly good banana rotis. Lining Rachdamnern Rd, along the wall of the playing fields, there are countless stalls selling *som tam*, a chilli-hot papaya salad from Thailand's northeastern region usually served with grilled chicken (*kai yaang*).

Khanom and Nai Phlao beaches *p122*
There are lots of foodstalls in Khanom town on Tambon Rd. On the beaches the only

food is provided by the hotels, resorts and bungalows operators.

🎭 Entertainment

Nakhon *p117, map p119*
Shadow plays
Most of the plays relate tales from the **Ramakien** and the *Jataka* tales. Narrators sing in ear-piercing falsetto accompanied by a band comprising *tab* (drums), *pi* (flute), *mong* (bass gong), *saw* (fiddle) and *ching* (miniature cymbals). There are 2 sizes of puppets. *Nang yai* (large puppets) which may be 2 m tall, and *nang lek* (small puppets). Shows and demonstrations of how the puppets are made can be seen at the workshop of **Suchart Subsin**, 110/18 Si Thammasok Soi 3 (take the road opposite Wat Phra Mahathat, turn left – at the top of the *soi* Suchart Subsin's house is signposted – and walk 50 m). This group has undertaken several royal performances.

✳️ Festivals

Nakhon *p117, map p119*
Feb Hae Pha Khun That A 3-day event when homage is paid to locally enshrined relics of the Buddha.
Sep-Oct Tenth Lunar Month Festival (movable) A 10-day celebration, the climax of which is the colourful procession down Rachdamnern Rd to Wat Phra Mahathat.

🛍️ Shopping

Nakhon *p117, map p119*
Nakhon is the centre of the south Thai handicrafts industry. Nielloware, *yan liphao* basketry (woven from strands of vine), shadow puppets, Thai silk brocades and *pak yok* weaving are specialities.

Handicrafts
Shops on Tha Chang Rd, notably the **Thai Handicraft Centre** (in the lime green

wooden house on the far side of the road behind the tourist office), **Nabin House** and **Manat Shop**. With the exception of the **Thai Handicraft Centre**, silverware predominates.

Shadow puppets
From the craftsmen at **Suchart Subsin's House**, Si Thammasok Rd, Soi 3 (see Entertainment, above) and stalls around Wat Phra Mahathat.

⚙ What to do

Khao Luang National Park *p122*
Tours in the province can be also organized through companies in Nakhon Sri Thammarat or at the park office.
Khiriwong Agro Tourism Promotion Center, Moo 5, Tambon Kam Lon, Amphoe Lan Saka (near the park office), T075-309010, T08-1229 0829 (mob). Tours to Krung Ching Waterfall, including whitewater rafting. Organizes homestays and guides.

⊖ Transport

Nakhon *p117, map p119*
Air
Nok Air, www.nokair.com, T026-272000, and Air Asia, www.airasia.com, T02-515 9999, both fly from Nakhon SI Thammarat Airport, T075-369540, to Bangkok daily.

Bus
Most people pick up a bus as it works its way through town. There are overnight connections with **Bangkok**'s Southern bus terminal, 12 hrs, ฿454, or ฿900 for VIP bus. Regular non a/c and a/c bus services connect Nakhon with **Krabi**, 3 hrs, ฿100-160; **Surat Thani**, 2½-3 hrs, ฿80; **Hat Yai**, 3 hrs, ฿90; **Phuket**, 8 hrs, from ฿240; **Trang**, 2 hrs, ฿80; **Songkhla**, 3 hrs, ฿85; and other southern towns.

A number of minibus services also operate to destinations in the south including **Hat Yai**, ฿90; **Phuket**, ฿500; **Krabi**, ฿120; **Trang** ฿80, and **Surat Thani**, ฿110. They tend to be marginally quicker and slightly more expensive than a/c coaches. See the town map for their departure points but check beforehand, as these seem to change from time to time.

Songthaew
The terminal is on Yom-marat Rd. Prices are fixed and listed on a board at the terminal. Most large centres in the south are served from here, including **Hat Yai**, **Phuket**, **Krabi**, **Trang**, **Surat Thani**, **Phattalung** and **Songkhla**.

Train
Overnight connections with **Bangkok**.

Contents

Footnotes

Useful words and phrases

Thai is a tonal language with five tones: mid tone (no mark), high tone (´), low tone (`), falling tone (ˆ), and rising tone (ˇ). Tones are used to distinguish between words which are otherwise the same. For example, 'see' pronounced with a low tone means 'four'; with a rising tone, it means 'colour'. Thai is not written in Roman script but using an alphabet derived from Khmer. The Romanization given below is only intended to help in pronouncing Thai words. There is no accepted method of Romanization and some of the sounds in Thai cannot be accurately reproduced using Roman script.

Polite particles
At the end of sentences males use the polite particle **krúp**, and females, **kâ** or **ká**.

Learning Thai
The list of words and phrases below is only very rudimentary. For anyone serious about learning Thai it is best to buy a dedicated Thai language text book or to enrol on a Thai course. Recommended among the various 'teach yourself Thai' books is Somsong Buasai and David Smyth's *Thai in a Week,* Hodder & Stoughton: London (1990). A useful mini-dictionary is the Hugo *Thai phrase book* (1990). For those interested in learning to read and write Thai, the best 'teach yourself' course is the *Linguaphone* course.

General words and phrases

Yes/no	chái/mâi chái, or krúp (kâ)/mâi krúp (kâ)
Thank you/no thank you	kòrp-kOOn/mâi ao kòrp-kOOn
Hello, good morning, goodbye	sa-wùt dee krúp(kâ)
What is your name? My name is ...	Koon chêu a-rai krúp (kâ)? Pom chêu ...
Excuse me, sorry!	kor-tôht krúp(kâ)
Can/do you speak English?	KOON pôot pah-sah ung-grìt
a little, a bit	nít-nòy
Where's the ...?	yòo têe-nai ...?
How much is ...?	tâo-rài ...?
Pardon?	a-rai ná?
I don't understand	pom (chún) mâi kao jái
How are you?	Mâi sa-bai
Not very well	sa-bai dee mái?

At hotels

What is the charge each night?	kâh hôrng wun la tâo-rài?
Is the room air conditioned?	hôrng dtìt air reu bplào?
Can I see the room first please?	kor doo hôrng gòrn dâi mái?
Does the room have hot water?	hôrng mii náhm rórn mái?
Does the room have a bathroom?	hôrng mii hôrng náhm mái?
Can I have the bill please?	kor bin nòy dâi mái?

Travelling

Where is the train station?	*sa-tahn-nee rót fai yòo têe-nai?*
Where is the bus station?	*sa-tahn-nee rót may yòo têe-nai?*
How much to go to ...?	*bpai ... tâo-rài?*
That's expensive	*pairng bpai nòy*
What time does the bus/ train leave for ...?	*rót may/rót fai bpai ...òrk gèe mohng?*
Is it far?	*glai mái?*
Turn left/turn right	*lée-o sái / lée-o kwah*
Go straight on	*ler-ee bpai èek*
It's straight ahead	*yòo dtrong nâh*

At restaurants

Can I see a menu?	*kor doo may-noo nòy?*
Can I have ...?/ I would like ...?	*Kor ...*
Is it very (hot) spicy?	*pèt mâhk mái?*
I am hungry	*pom (chún) hew*
Breakfast	*ah-hahn cháo*
Lunch	*ah-hahn glanhq wun*

Time and days

in the morning	*dtorn cháo*	Monday	*wun jun*
in the afternoon	*dtorn bài*	Tuesday	*wun ung-kahn*
in the evening	*dtorn yen*	Wednesday	*wun pÓOt*
today	*wun née*	Thursday	*wun pá-réu-hùt*
tomorrow	*prÓOng née*	Friday	*wun sÒOk*
yesterday	*mêu-a wahn née*	Saturday	*wun sao*
		Sunday	*wun ah-tít*

Numbers

1	*nèung*	20	*yêe-sìp*
2	*sorng*	21	*yêe-sìp-et*
3	*sahm*	22	*yêe-sìp-sorng... etc*
4	*sèe*	30	*sahm-sìp*
5	*hâa*	100	*(nèung) róy*
6	*hòk*	101	*(nèung) róy-nèung*
7	*jèt*	150	*(nèung) róy-hâh-sìp*
8	*bpàirt*	200	*sorng róy ... etc*
9	*gâo*	1000	*(nèung) pun*
10	*sìp*	10,000	*mèun*
11	*sìp-et*	100,000	*sairn*
12	*sìp-sorng ... etc*	1,000,000	*láhn*

Basic vocabulary

airport	*a-nahm bin*	beach	*hàht*
bank	*ta-nah-kahn*	beautiful	*oo-ay*
bathroom	*hôrng náhm*	big	*yài*

boat	*reu-a*	medicine	*yah*
bus	*ót may*	open	*bpèrt*
bus station	*sa-tah-nee rót may*	police	*dtum-ròo-ut*
buy	*séu*	police station	*sa-tah-nee,*
chemist	*ráhn kai yah*		*dtum-ròo-ut*
clean	*sa-àht*	post office	*bprai-sa-nee*
closed	*bpìt*	restaurant	*ráhn ah-hahn*
cold	*yen*	road	*thanon*
day	*wun*	room	*hôrng*
delicious	*a-ròy*	shop	*ráhn*
dirty	*sòk-ga-bpròk*	sick (ill)	*mâi sa-bai*
doctor	*mor*	silk	*mai*
eat	*gin (kâo)*	small	*lék*
embassy	*sa-tahn tôot*	stop	*yÒOt*
excellent	*yêe-um*	taxi	*táirk-sêe*
expensive	*pairng*	that	*nún*
food	*ah-hahn*	this	*nèe*
fruit	*pon-la-mái*	ticket	*dtoo-a*
hospital	*rohng pa-yah-bahn*	toilet	*hôrng náhm*
hot (temp)	*rórn*	town	*meu-ung*
hot (spicy)	*pèt*	train station	*sa-tah-nee rót fai*
hotel	*róhng rairm*	very	*mâhk*
island	*gòr*	water	*náhm*
market	*dta-làht*	what	*a-rai*

Glossary

A

Amitabha the Buddha of the Past(see Avalokitsvara)

Amulet protective medallion

Arhat a person who has perfected himself; images of former monks are sometimes carved into arhat

Avadana Buddhist narrative, telling of the deeds of saintly souls

Avalokitsvara also known as Amitabha and Lokeshvara, the name literally means 'World Lord'; he is the compassionate male Bodhisattva, the saviour of Mahayana Buddhism, and represents the central force of creation in the universe; usually portrayed with a lotus and water flask

B

Bai sema boundary stones marking consecrated ground around a Buddhist bot

Ban village; shortened from muban

Baray man-made lake or reservoir

Bhikku Buddhist monk

Bodhi the tree under which the Buddha achieved enlightenment (*Ficus religiosa*)

Bodhisattva a future Buddha. In Mahayana Buddhism, someone who has attained enlightenment, but who postpones nirvana to help others reach it.

Bor Kor Sor (BKS) Government bus terminal

Bot Buddhist ordination hall, of rectangular plan, identifiable by the boundary stones placed around it; an abbreviation of ubosoth

Brahma the Creator, one of the gods of the Hindu trinity, usually represented with four faces, and often mounted on a hamsa

Brahmin a Hindu priest

Bun to make merit

C

Caryatid elephants, often used as buttressing decorations

Celadon pottery ware with blue/green to grey glaze

Chakri the current royal dynasty in Thailand. They have reigned since 1782

Chao title for Lao and Thai kings

Chat honorific umbrella or royal multi- tiered parasol

Chedi from the Sanskrit *cetiya* (Pali, *caitya*), meaning memorial. Usually a religious monument (often bell-shaped), containing relics of the Buddha or other holy remains. Used interchangeably with stupa

Chofa 'sky tassel' on the roof of wat buildings

D

Deva a Hindu-derived male god

Devata a Hindu-derived goddess

Dharma the Buddhist law

Dvarapala guardian figure, usually placed at the entrance to a temple

G

Ganesh elephant-headed son of Siva

Garuda mythical divine bird, with predatory beak and claws, and human body; the king of birds, enemy of naga and mount of Vishnu

Gautama the historic Buddha

Geomancy the art of divination by lines and figures

Gopura crowned or covered gate, entrance to a religious area

H

Hamsa sacred goose, Brahma's mount; in Buddhism represents the flight of the doctrine

Hang yaaw long-tailed boat, used on canals

Harmika box-like part of a Burmese stupa that often acts as a reliquary casket

Hinayana 'Lesser Vehicle', major Buddhist sect in Southeast Asia, usually termed Theravada Buddhism

Hong swan

Hor kong a pavilion built on stilts, where the monastery drum is kept

Hor takang bell tower

Hor tray/trai library where manuscripts are stored in a Thai monastery

Hti 'umbrella' surmounting Burmese temples, often encrusted with jewels

I

Indra the Vedic god of the heavens, weather and war

J

Jataka(s) the birth stories of the Buddha; they normally number 547, although an additional three were added in Burma for reasons of symmetry in mural painting and sculpture. The last 10 are the most important

K

Kala (makara) literally 'death' or 'black'; a demon ordered to consume itself, often sculpted with grinning face and bulging eyes over entranceway to act as a door guardian; also known as kirtamukha

Kathin/krathin a one-month period during the eighth lunar month, when lay people present new robes and other gifts to monks

Ketumula flame-like motif above the Buddha head

Khao mountain

Kinaree half-human, half-bird, usually depicted as a heavenly musician

Krating wild bull, most commonly seen on bottles of *Red Bull* (Krating Daeng) drink

Krishna incarnation of Vishnu

Kuti living quarters of Buddhist monks in a monastery complex

L

Laem cape (as in bay)

Lakhon traditional Thai classical music

Lak muang city pillar

Linga phallic symbol and one of the forms of Siva. Embedded in a pedestal, shaped to allow drainage of lustral water poured over it; the linga typically has a succession of cross sections: from square at the base, through octagonal, to round. These symbolize, in order, the trinity of Brahma, Vishnu and Siva

Lintel a load-bearing stone spanning a doorway; often heavily carved

M

Mahabharata a Hindu epic text, written about 2000 years ago

Mahayana 'Greater Vehicle', Buddhist sect

Maitreya the future Buddha

Makara a mythological aquatic reptile, somewhat like a crocodile and sometimes with an elephant's trunk; often found along with the *kala* framing doorways

Mandala a focus for meditation; a representation of the cosmos

Mara personification of evil and tempter of the Buddha

Matmii Northeastern Thai cotton ikat

Meru sacred or cosmic mountain at the centre of the world in Hindu-Buddhist cosmology; home of the gods

Mondop from the sanskrit, *mandapa*. A cube-shaped building, often topped with a cone-like structure, used to contain an object of worship like a footprint of the Buddha

Muban village, usually shortened to ban

Mudra symbolic gesture of the hands of the Buddha

N

Naga benevolent mythical water serpent, enemy of Garuda

Naga makara fusion of naga and makara

Nalagiri the elephant let loose to attack the Buddha, who calmed him

Namtok waterfall

Nandi/nandin bull, mount of Siva

Nang thalung shadow play/puppets

Nikhom resettlement village

Nirvana release from the cycle of suffering in Buddhist belief; 'enlightenment'

P

Pa kama Lao men's all-purpose cloth, usually woven with checked pattern

paddy/padi unhulled rice

Pali sacred language of Theravada Buddhism

Parvati consort of Siva

Pha sin tubular bit of cloth, similar to sarong

Phi spirit

Phnom/phanom Khmer for hill/mountain

Phra sinh see pha sin

Pradaksina pilgrims' clockwise circumambulation of holy structure

Prah sacred

Prang form of stupa built in Khmer style, shaped like a corncob

Prasada stepped pyramid (see prasat)

Prasat residence of a king or of the gods (sanctuary tower), from the Indian prasada

Q

Quan Am Chinese goddess of mercy

R

Rai unit of measurement, 1 ha = 6.25 rai

Rama incarnation of Vishnu, hero of the Indian epic, the *Ramayana*

Ramakien Thai version of the *Ramayana*

Ramayana Hindu romantic epic, known as *Ramakien* in Thailand

S

Saamlor three-wheeled bicycle taxi

Sakyamuni the historic Buddha

Sal the Indian sal tree (*Shorea robusta*), under which the historic Buddha was born

Sala open pavilion

Sangha the Buddhist order of monks

Sawankhalok type of ceramic

Singha mythical guardian lion

Siva the Destroyer, one of the three gods of the Hindu trinity

Sofa see dok sofa

Songthaew 'two rows': pick-up truck with benches along either side

Sravasti the miracle at Sravasti, the Buddha subdues the heretics in front of a mango tree

Stele inscribed stone panel

Stucco plaster, often heavily moulded

Stupa chedi

T

Talaat market

Tambon a commune of villages

Tam bun see bun

Tavatimsa heaven of the 33 gods, at the summit of Mount Meru

Tazaungs small pavilions, found within Burmese temple complexes

Tham cave

Thanon street in Thai

That shrine housing Buddhist relics, an edifice commemorating the Buddha's life or the funerary temple for royalty

Thein Burmese ordination hall

Theravada 'Way of the Elders'; major Buddhist sect, also known as Hinayana Buddhism ('Lesser Vehicle')

Traiphum the three worlds of Buddhist cosmology – heaven, hell and earth

Trimurti Hindu trinity of gods: Brahma, the Creator, Vishnu the Preserver, Siva the Destroyer

Tripitaka Theravada Buddhism's Pali canon

U

Ubosoth see bot

Urna the dot or curl on the Buddha's forehead

Usnisa the Buddha's top knot or 'wisdom bump',

V

Vahana a mythical beast, upon which a deva or god rides

Viharn an assembly hall in a Buddhist monastery; may hold Buddha images

Vishnu the Protector, one of the gods of the Hindu trinity

W

Wai Thai greeting, with hands held together at chin height as if in prayer

Wat Buddhist 'monastery'

Z

Zayat prayer pavilion found in Burmese temple complexes

Zedi Burmese term for a stupa

Food glossary

a-haan food
ba-mii egg noodles
bia beer
chaa tea
check bin/bill cheque
chorn spoon
gaeng curry
gaeng chud soup
jaan plate
kaafae (ron) coffee (hot)
kaew glass
kai chicken
kap klaem snacks to be eaten when drinking
khaaw/khao rice
khaaw niaw sticky rice
khaaw tom rice gruel
khai egg
khai dao fried egg
khanom sweet, dessert or cake
khanom cake cake
khanom pang bread
khanom pang ping toast
khing ginger
khuan scramble
khuat bottle
kin to eat

kleua salt
krueng kieng side dishes
kung crab
kwaytio noodle soup, white noodles
laap pa raw fish crushed into a paste, marinated in lemon juice and mixed with chopped mint, chilli and rice grains
laap sin raw meat dish, see above
lao liquor
man root vegetable
man farang potatoes
manaaw lemon
mekong a Thai whisky
mit knife
muu pork
nam chaa tea
nam kheng ice
nam kuat bottled water
nam manaaw soda lime soda
nam plaa fish sauce
nam plaa prik fish sauce with chilli
nam plaaw plain water

nam som orange juice
nam taan sugar
nam tom boiled water
nom milk
nua meat (usually beef)
phak vegetables
phat to stir fry
phet hot (chilli)
phon lamai fruit
pla fish
priaw sour
priaw waan sweet and sour
prik hot chilli
raan a-haan restaurant
ratnaa in gravy
rawn hot (temperature)
sa-te satay
sorm fork
talaat market
thao mai luai morning glory
thua nut/bean
tom to boil
tort to deep fry
waan sweet
yam salad
yen cold

Thai dishes

It is impossible to provide a comprehensive list of Thai dishes. However (and at the risk of offending connoisseurs by omitting their favourites), popular dishes include:

Soups (gaeng chud)
Kaeng juut bean curd and vegetable soup, non-spicy

Khaaw tom rice soup with egg and pork (a breakfast dish) or chicken, fish or prawn. It is said that it can cure fevers and other illnesses. Probably best for a hangover.

Kwaytio Chinese noodle soup served with a variety of additional ingredients, often available from roadside stalls and from smaller restaurants – mostly served up until lunchtime.

Tom ka kai chicken in coconut milk with laos (loas, or ka, is an exotic spice)

Tom yam kung hot and sour prawn soup spiced with lemon grass, coriander and chillies

Rice-based dishes
Single-dish meals served at roadside stalls and in many restaurants (especially cheaper ones).

Khaaw gaeng curry and rice

Khaaw man kai rice with chicken

Khaaw mu daeng rice with red pork

Khaaw naa pet rice with duck

Khaaw phat kai/mu/kung fried rice with chicken/pork/prawn

Noodle-based dishes
Ba-mii haeng wheat noodles served with pork and vegetables

Khaaw soi a form of *Kwaytio* with egg noodles in a curry broth

Kwaytio haeng wide noodles served with pork and vegetables

Mee krop Thai crisp-fried noodles

Phak sii-u noodles fried with egg, vegetables and meat/prawns

Phat thai Thai fried noodles

Curries (gaeng)
Gaeng khiaw waan kai/nua/phet/pla green chicken/beef/duck/fish curry (the colour is due to the large number of whole green chillies pounded to make the paste that forms the base of this very hot curry)

Gaeng mussaman Muslim beef curry served with potatoes

Gaeng phanaeng chicken/beef curry

Gaeng phet kai/nua hot chicken/ beef curry

Gaeng plaa duk catfish curry

Meat dishes
Kai/mu/nua phat kapow fried meat with basil and chillies

Kai/nua phat prik fried chicken/beef with chillies

Kai tort Thai fried chicken

Kai tua chicken in peanut sauce

Kai yang garlic chicken

Laap chopped (once raw, now frequently cooked) meat with herbs and spices

Mu waan sweet pork

Nua priaw waan sweet and sour beef

Priao wan sweet and sour pork with vegetables

Seafood
Haw mok steamed fish curry

Luuk ciin fishballs

Plaa nerng steamed fish

Plaa pao grilled fish

Plaa priaw waan whole fried fish with ginger sauce

Plaa too tort Thai fried fish

Thotman plaa fried curried fish cakes

Salads (yam)
Som tam green papaya salad with tomatoes, chillies, garlic, chopped dried shrimps and lemon (can be extremely hot)

Yam nua Thai beef salad

Vegetables
Phak phat ruam mit mixed fried vegetables

Sweets (kanom)
Kanom mo kaeng baked custard squares
Khaaw niaw mamuang sticky rice and mango (a seasonal favourite)
Khaaw niaw sankhayaa sticky rice and custard
Kluay buat chee bananas in coconut milk
Kluay tort Thai fried bananas
Leenchee loi mek chilled lychees in custard

Fruits
Chomphu rose apple
Khanun jackfruit. Jan-Jun
Kluay banana. Year round
Lamyai longan; thin brown shell with translucent fruit similar to lychee. Jun-Aug

Lamut sapodilla
Linchi lychee. Apr-Jun
Majeung star apple
Makham wan tamarind. Dec-Feb
Malakho papaya. Year round
Mamuang mango. Mar-Jun
Manaaw lime. Year round
Mang khud mangosteen. Apr-Sep
Maprao coconut. Year round
Ngo rambutan. May-Sep
Noi na custard (or sugar) apple. Jun-Sep
Sapparot pineapple. Apr-Jun, Dec-Jan
Som orange. Year round
Som o pomelo. Aug-Nov
Taeng mo watermelon. Oct-Mar
Thurian durian. May-Aug

Notes

Index → *Entries in bold refer to maps.*

Titles available in the Footprint *Focus* range

Latin America	UK RRP	US RRP
Bahia & Salvador	£7.99	$11.95
Brazilian Amazon	£7.99	$11.95
Brazilian Pantanal	£6.99	$9.95
Buenos Aires & Pampas	£7.99	$11.95
Cartagena & Caribbean Coast	£7.99	$11.95
Costa Rica	£8.99	$12.95
Cuzco, La Paz & Lake Titicaca	£8.99	$12.95
El Salvador	£5.99	$8.95
Guadalajara & Pacific Coast	£6.99	$9.95
Guatemala	£8.99	$12.95
Guyana, Guyane & Suriname	£5.99	$8.95
Havana	£6.99	$9.95
Honduras	£7.99	$11.95
Nicaragua	£7.99	$11.95
Northeast Argentina & Uruguay	£8.99	$12.95
Paraguay	£5.99	$8.95
Quito & Galápagos Islands	£7.99	$11.95
Recife & Northeast Brazil	£7.99	$11.95
Rio de Janeiro	£8.99	$12.95
São Paulo	£5.99	$8.95
Uruguay	£6.99	$9.95
Venezuela	£8.99	$12.95
Yucatán Peninsula	£6.99	$9.95

Asia	UK RRP	US RRP
Angkor Wat	£5.99	$8.95
Bali & Lombok	£8.99	$12.95
Chennai & Tamil Nadu	£8.99	$12.95
Chiang Mai & Northern Thailand	£7.99	$11.95
Goa	£6.99	$9.95
Gulf of Thailand	£8.99	$12.95
Hanoi & Northern Vietnam	£8.99	$12.95
Ho Chi Minh City & Mekong Delta	£7.99	$11.95
Java	£7.99	$11.95
Kerala	£7.99	$11.95
Kolkata & West Bengal	£5.99	$8.95
Mumbai & Gujarat	£8.99	$12.95

Africa & Middle East	UK RRP	US RRP
Beirut	£6.99	$9.95
Cairo & Nile Delta	£8.99	$12.95
Damascus	£5.99	$8.95
Durban & KwaZulu Natal	£8.99	$12.95
Fès & Northern Morocco	£8.99	$12.95
Jerusalem	£8.99	$12.95
Johannesburg & Kruger National Park	£7.99	$11.95
Kenya's Beaches	£8.99	$12.95
Kilimanjaro & Northern Tanzania	£8.99	$12.95
Luxor to Aswan	£8.99	$12.95
Nairobi & Rift Valley	£7.99	$11.95
Red Sea & Sinai	£7.99	$11.95
Zanzibar & Pemba	£7.99	$11.95

Europe	UK RRP	US RRP
Bilbao & Basque Region	£6.99	$9.95
Brittany West Coast	£7.99	$11.95
Cádiz & Costa de la Luz	£6.99	$9.95
Granada & Sierra Nevada	£6.99	$9.95
Languedoc: Carcassonne to Montpellier	£7.99	$11.95
Málaga	£5.99	$8.95
Marseille & Western Provence	£7.99	$11.95
Orkney & Shetland Islands	£5.99	$8.95
Santander & Picos de Europa	£7.99	$11.95
Sardinia: Alghero & the North	£7.99	$11.95
Sardinia: Cagliari & the South	£7.99	$11.95
Seville	£5.99	$8.95
Sicily: Palermo & the Northwest	£7.99	$11.95
Sicily: Catania & the Southeast	£7.99	$11.95
Siena & Southern Tuscany	£7.99	$11.95
Sorrento, Capri & Amalfi Coast	£6.99	$9.95
Skye & Outer Hebrides	£6.99	$9.95
Verona & Lake Garda	£7.99	$11.95

North America	UK RRP	US RRP
Vancouver & Rockies	£8.99	$12.95

Australasia	UK RRP	US RRP
Brisbane & Queensland	£8.99	$12.95
Perth	£7.99	$11.95

For the latest books, e-books and a wealth of travel information, visit us at:
www.footprinttravelguides.com.

Join us on facebook for the latest travel news, product releases, offers and amazing competitions:
www.facebook.com/footprintbooks.